Music in the Air

ALSO BY RALPH J. GLEASON

Jam Session: An Anthology of Jazz (1958)

The Jefferson Airplane and the San Francisco Sound (1969)

Celebrating the Duke: And Louis, Bessie, Billie, Bird, Carmen, Miles, Dizzy and Other Heroes (1975, 1990 reprint)

Music
in the Air

■

The Selected Writings
of Ralph J. Gleason

■

EDITED BY
TOBY GLEASON

Foreword by Jann Wenner
Introduction by Paul Scanlon

Yale
UNIVERSITY PRESS
NEW HAVEN AND LONDON

Yale University Press books may be purchased in quantity for educational, business, or promotional use. For information, please e-mail sales.press@yale.edu (U.S. office) or sales@yaleup.co.uk (U.K. office).

Designed by Sonia Shannon
Set in Electra type by Integrated Publishing Solutions, Grand Rapids, Michigan.
Printed in the United States of America.

Library of Congress Control Number: 2015956594
ISBN 978-0-300-21216-7 (cloth : alk. paper)

A catalogue record for this book is available from the British Library.

This paper meets the requirements of ANSI/NISO Z39.48-1992 (Permanence of Paper).

10 9 8 7 6 5 4 3 2 1

To my father, to my mother, and to my wife, Vera

Contents

■

FOLK, ROCK, AND POP

COMEDY

POLITICS AND CULTURE

Foreword

I WAS A STUDENT AT UC Berkeley when I started reading Ralph Gleason's column "On the Town" in the *San Francisco Chronicle*. It was the only place I knew to find a certain social, cultural, and political mix that was coming to define my world.

He understood rock and roll and became a singular voice that stood out among other music and jazz writers. He got the Beatles and Bob Dylan and what was making them so special to a generation. The Free Speech Movement, the first of numerous student uprisings in the sixties, had overwhelmed the Berkeley campus. He was the only journalist in the Bay Area who gave the FSM a fair shake.

I started writing a column for the *Daily Californian* that was, of course, an homage to Ralph. I went to concerts. I wrote about rock and roll music. My efforts were filtered through a matrix of drugs and youth, and his through wisdom and perspective. We both loved the music. Ralph was 48 then, and the "knock" on him was that he couldn't decide if he was three 16-year-olds or four 12-year-olds.

We first met at one of the early hippie rock dance concerts, "A Tribute to Dr. Strange," at Longshoremen's Hall near Fisherman's Wharf in San Francisco. Amidst the echoing, ricocheting music and the oozing and wildly flickering colors of the light show, Ralph was leaning casually against a wall, wearing his signature trench coat, placidly taking it all in. I introduced myself and he said, "I know exactly who you are!" Turned out he was reading *my* column.

We started meeting at and then going together to dance concerts and other events, constantly talking, teaching, learning along the way. He took me to jazz clubs in North Beach, tried to get me to dig his favorite music. He took me into his home on Ashby Avenue, in Berkeley, where I met and would get to know his wife, Jean, and his kids, Toby, Bridget, and Stacy. The foyer, his study, the living room, and even the kitchen were what seemed to be a flowing wave of floor to ceiling shelves packed with books and records. In the middle of it all, Ralph loved to hold forth, pipe in hand, in his big leather easy chair. I became a family member.

He was friend and counselor to a great many people, and very much enjoyed helping them out: musicians—be they rock, jazz, or folk—writers, poets, members of the FSM, various cats including the dance promoters who created the local rock concert scene—The Family Dog, Chet Helms, Bill Graham, and the newbie managers of upcoming groups like the Grateful Dead, Big Brother and Janis Joplin, the Jefferson Airplane, and one very specific comedian, Lenny Bruce. I was the only journalist.

Ralph and I talked often about what we could do together, and the discussions kept coming back to the idea of starting a rock and roll magazine.

We decided to go forward. We fooled around with various names, mostly in the style of psychedelic rock bands. Ralph suggested we take the name from the title of his 1967 essay in the *American Scholar:* "Like A Rolling Stone." Done.

Ralph gave me two thousand dollars and a bound set of *Jazz Quarterly*, his previous attempt at magazine publishing back in his New York days. "I tried this once," he said, "see if you can do better."

It was a blind jump off a small cliff. I had no idea how long it would last. There was no business plan, no strategy. Ralph directed me to music industry people he knew. They agreed to buy advertising, and little bits of money began to trickle in, just enough to keep us afloat. He brought in writers he knew, most notably Jonathan Cott, who has been with us since Issue One.

Ralph was our *éminence grise*. He gave us credibility as well as contacts. At his insistence, I sent the first two issues to legendary producer Jerry Wexler, who responded, writing in the margins of the cover note: "First issue strong. Second one weak. Giant, Ralph Gleason, ever." Jerry became one of our first subscribers.

Ralph's column, "Perspectives," appeared in just about every issue, and was our principal editorial voice (of course, I had my own column as well). He covered a lot of territory, from politics to music to popular culture. He also showed early on that he wasn't timid about challenging readers' expectations.

Ralph constantly tried to impose his rigorously high journalistic standards on us (and was often frustrated). Putting out *RS* in the early years was usually a study in lightly controlled deadline frenzy; stuff would fall through the cracks. On the occasion of our third anniversary, his column, "What We Are & What We Ain't," put the whole situation in, well, perspective.

"It is a peculiar publication in many ways. It is quite possible that there have been issues of *RS* in which as much as 75 percent of the printed material was not seen by the editor until after the issue was off the press. I remember once early in 1970 when a two page story appeared which *nobody* would admit to having seen before it was printed!

"*Rolling Stone* is far from perfect, too far to suit me. But nevertheless, even those who hate it or scorn it, read it. They have to. *Rolling Stone* is hip to something *The New York Times* does not know. I think now and then of what it must be like to live in, say, Paducah or Winnetka or Wappinger's Falls and get *RS* every two weeks. A letter from home? You bet! Just to know you are not alone when all around you say you are, is the kind of pleasure poets write of."

Two attributes of his column were consistent. When arguing about politics or society in general, he always sought, and secured, a position of high moral ground. When writing about music, he returned again and again to the power it conveyed, noting that an entire generation was finding its prophets in strange places, in dance halls and on the jukebox. Here's how he ended that 1967 essay from which *Rolling Stone* got its name:

"Hail hail rock n' roll," as Chuck Berry sings. "Deliver me from the days of old!"
I think he's about to be granted his wish.

Jann Wenner

Introduction

■

I HAD BEEN WORKING AT *Rolling Stone* for exactly one week when Fantasy Records threw a serious bash in December 1970, to promote a new album by Creedence Clearwater Revival. Music writers from across the country flew to Berkeley to partake of food and drink at Cosmo's Factory, the band's clubhouse and rehearsal space, followed by a brief concert. Early on, I sought out Ralph J. Gleason, *Rolling Stone's* co-founder three years earlier, who was now working at Fantasy as—in his own words—a "minister without portfolio," while continuing to write for and advise the magazine. I wanted to introduce myself, and was more than a little anxious.

I'd been reading his music column in the *San Francisco Chronicle* since my teenage days, and by college I had become a serious jazz buff and collector. Ralph's column informed me about my favorite music, as did his show, *Jazz Casual*, on San Francisco's public television station, KQED. But by the early sixties he had started writing about rock music. I specifically remember a column praising the Four Seasons. It surprised me, but I would shortly learn that he was taking rock quite seriously. I was impressed.

I walked up to Ralph and we shook hands. He was perfunctory and seemed distracted. He rattled off some boilerplate Journalism 1.0. Our conversation lasted maybe 90 seconds. I was put off. Hell, I had almost three years' daily newspaper experience!

Before long, Jann Wenner appointed me to edit Ralph's column, "Perspectives." That went off pretty much without a hitch; his copy was always on time and the length was consistent. He remained a cool and distant voice on the phone, there in Berkeley. In the years I knew him, I think he crossed the Bay to San Francisco twice, three times tops.

The great Louis Armstrong died in the summer of 1971. Ralph wrote a long, thoughtful tribute to his old friend ("God Bless Louis Armstrong," *Rolling Stone*, August 5, 1971), and sent if forth. It was quite good but needed some work. I employed a technique practiced by the page one editor at the *Wall Street Journal*: a list of questions—some of them challenges—to various items in the manuscript, point by point.

I walked into Ralph's Berkeley office and handed him my queries. He was incredulous. Nobody had ever given him a list of particulars like that, ever. We argued. We shouted. I cajoled, he resisted. But a couple of hours later we were both warily satisfied with the results. The article would eventually win an ASCAP-Deems Taylor award. More important, we became fast friends. In the course of our wrangling, I had earned his respect.

If there is a through line in this collection of Ralph Gleason's writings, it rests pretty much on the work of artists such as John Coltrane, Miles Davis, Bob Dylan, and Lenny Bruce. Each, in his own way, found it necessary to break the boundaries of his craft in order to go forward. Ralph was justifiably proud of his liner notes for *The Real Lenny Bruce* (Fantasy, March 1975), actually a thoughtfully critical biography of the comedian: "Since the first night when I saw Lenny Bruce at Ann's 440, it has been one of the aims of my life to turn the entire world on to his humor. In the first place because I found him so devastatingly funny . . . but also because I found the vision implicit in his work so very useful as a tool with which to examine this insane society in which we live."

A few pages later, he nails it: "Jerry Lewis was astounded that Lenny turned down an offer of $10,000, when he was out of work, to write comedy material for him. Lenny could not do that. He had passed the point where he could write for others. . . . In the end, Lenny had also passed the point where he was interested in doing set pieces, no matter how much he might change them from performance to performance. Like Miles Davis and the other modern jazz musicians who had stopped playing songs in order to create totally everything they did, Lenny just wanted to stand up and improvise."

I prefer to think of "Like a Rolling Stone," which appeared in the

American Scholar in 1967, as Ralph's manifesto. And I love his auda-
cious introduction, presented here slightly abridged:

> "Forms and rhythm in music are never changed without pro-
> ducing changes in the most important political forms and ways."
> Plato said that.
> "For the reality of politics, we must go to the poets, not the
> politicians."
> Norman O. Brown said that.
> "For the reality of what's happening today in America, we must
> go to rock 'n roll, to popular music."
> I said that.

An ambitious essay that defined the youth culture of the mid-sixties
from a variety of perspectives, it was, in many ways, Ralph's template for
his idea of *Rolling Stone*, the magazine, the jumping off point for his
meditations on Bob Dylan, the Jefferson Airplane, the San Francisco
Sound, on youth activism in the sixties and seventies. And who else
would quote Nietzsche and Chuck Berry on the same page?

This book contains many wonderful pieces on jazz greats such as
Billie Holiday, Carmen McRae, and Vince Guaraldi as well as the San
Francisco club scenes of that era and, of course, the Monterey Jazz
Festival (Ralph was a co-founder, a fact he chose not to mention). And
he vividly covered the next San Francisco scene, including "The Times
They Are A Changin'" for *Ramparts* magazine in 1965 and "The Flower
Children" for the *Encyclopedia Britannica Yearbook* in 1968. Not to
mention countless columns for the *San Francisco Chronicle* and *Rolling Stone*. At the *Chronicle*, he covered the dance concerts, the people
that promoted them, and the conflicts they encountered with the city
Establishment like a beat reporter with a taste for sociology. And he
stayed about a light year ahead of his city room counterparts, who were
still trying to understand "hippies."

His columns for *Rolling Stone* drew attention from another quarter.
He was delighted to find himself in 1974 on the White House Enemies
List, one of many amazing artifacts of the Nixon presidency. He had a
rubber hand stamp made announcing his membership, and he used

it constantly on his personal correspondence. Ralph liked to muse on how he wound up in such exceptional company. His columns on the Nixon administration in this volume offer some clues.

Reading over these pages, I was struck by something obvious that I had forgotten. So many of the people he wrote about—musicians, entertainers, writers, and artists—were also, in reality, his friends. Over the time I knew him, Ralph showed me wonderful correspondence to and from Louis Armstrong, Duke Ellington, Miles Davis, and Dizzy Gillespie. Lenny Bruce had a habit of sending outrageous postcards from whatever city he was playing.

And because Ralph and I were friends, I got to meet people who enriched my own life: music industry legends such as John Hammond and Orrin Keepnews, writers Nat Hentoff, Studs Terkel, and Joseph Heller, and two wonderful guys from KQED, Bob Zagone and Ed Azlant.

There's a photograph by Jim Marshall of John Lennon and Ralph relaxing backstage at Candlestick Park following what would be the Beatles' last public concert. When I first met Ralph about five years later, he had clearly aged at least ten. He seldom spoke of his severe diabetes. But there was one time I remember well: After a stupefying board meeting at Fantasy, he told me how he longed for a shot of verboten whiskey. We'd lunch four times a year, usually at Spenger's Fish Grotto in Berkeley, or Ruthie's, a great soul food place in Oakland. He could partake only of dry toast and tea, but he got a kick out of watching me eat and drink with glee.

My favorite image of Ralph is on a *Jazz Casual* DVD, televised some years before I met him. The John Coltrane Quartet is performing "Afro Blue," and 'Trane has just launched a fiery soprano sax solo. Seated on a stool next to McCoy Tyner's piano, pipe in hand, Ralph is grinning furiously and shaking his head at the wonder of it all.

Paul Scanlon

JAZZ AND BLUES

Jazz

Black Art/American Art

▪

J AZZ: We don't know where it was born (although the first authenticated appearance of the word "jazz" in print was in the San Francisco Call, March 6, 1913) and we certainly don't know the first players, those forgotten men who started it all. Legend has it that the first jazz musician was Buddy Bolden, a New Orleans trumpet player before the days of phonograph recording, who went mad and died in a Louisiana insane asylum in the '30s.

We don't really know, despite the legend, that New Orleans was even its true birthplace. What we do know is that this music has spread throughout the world in the twentieth century; that American jazz musicians are treated as major artists everywhere but at home; and we know that in an era in American history when our official government representatives abroad are stoned and picketed, when even presidential visits to friendly countries are cancelled, the American jazz musician is welcomed everywhere.

Everyone has seen—or seen pictures of—the legend YANKEE GO HOME scrawled on some wall. It crops up all over the world. Yet no one has reported ever seeing a similar legend reading YANKEE JAZZMAN GO HOME, and jazz always means America.

Jazz had to wait for a Frenchman, Hugues Panassié, and a Belgian, Robert Goffin, for the first books about itself. Louis Armstrong, who was the sensation of London in 1932 in his first appearance at the Palladium there, who played before royalty in England and Italy, was the guest of honor at a special reception at the Palace of Fine Arts in Brussels, played for the League of Nations Delegates in Geneva, went back home to New Orleans after his European triumph. Following a huge street parade and reunions with childhood friends, Armstrong and his band were to play in the Suburban Gardens and to broadcast from there, one of the first black bands to do so. As the white announcer began to introduce Armstrong, he suddenly turned away and said, "I haven't got the heart to introduce that nigger!" Louis knew he was home.

Jazz was born in New Orleans. Ferdinand La Menthe "Jelly Roll" Morton, the late composer and pianist, told us in his Library of Congress recordings of his reminiscences of the early jazz days. Morton's version squared with the legend, even enhanced it, lending the touch of first person authenticity to rumor. But we really don't know. It is demonstrable, of course, that many of the first jazz players were from the New Orleans area. Of all the jazz musicians listed in the first edition of the *Encyclopedia of Jazz* who were old enough to have been playing when Louis Armstrong first began to hear them, an overwhelming majority were from the New Orleans or Southern Louisiana region.

And of course the functional use of jazz music in New Orleans was certainly a larger part of that city's ghetto life than in any other form—though such jazzmen as Willie "The Lion" Smith place hearing what they remember as jazz music close to the turn of the century in New York.

A revisionist school of jazz historians in recent years has dedicated itself to destroying the theory of the origin of jazz in New Orleans. But acceptance of that position almost makes it mandatory to accept a giant conspiracy on the part of all the musicians and fans and early writers who have all agreed in crediting New Orleans as the source.

THE STORYVILLE STORY:

The legend goes even further than naming the city. It says that jazz was born in Storyville, the red light district of New Orleans, child of the fancy brothel and musical accompaniment to sporting house entertainment of the turn of the century's walk on the wild side. Again, we know there certainly was jazz in the New Orleans Storyville district before World War I. Survivors of the era have eloquently testified to that, as well as to its use in street parades and funeral processions. Increasingly, though, musicians tend to believe jazz was born in the church where the African heritage flourished. Whether or not this is fruit of a desire to rid jazz of its raffish associations is open to question. But there seems to be reason to accept Duke Ellington's observation made to the California Arts Commission several years ago, that while there was jazz in Storyville's brothels, the musicians "didn't learn it there."

BLACK, WHEREVER IT STARTED:

We never will know precisely and it really doesn't matter any more where jazz came from. It is obvious today, no matter what its origin, that jazz is an art, that it is the creation of black musicians and it is a music completely original to the United States of America. Its first creators were black. Its most important innovative players, the delineators of all its styles and the greatest of its solo performers right down to last night's session in the concert hall or on the night club stage, have all been black men. White musicians have played jazz—Bix Beiderbecke, Benny Goodman, Jack Teagarden to name three—but as Archie Shepp, the controversial black playwright and tenor saxophonist has remarked, "they are very few." It is even possible to speculate that all the white jazz musicians could be eliminated from the history of the music without significantly altering its development.

So take New Orleans at the end of the Nineteenth and the beginning of the Twentieth century, with its heritage of French and Spanish culture, and Caribbean mixtures of Africa, France and Spain thrown in, and you have the multi-racial cultural melting pot that spawned a music. Curiously, Mobile, Alabama, founded by a brother of the Sieur de Bienville who founded New Orleans, and seeded with the same cultural traditions and racial mixtures, did not produce the early jazz men. History shows us that New Orleans did.

The city was a harbor, a river city. The river was the roadway to the North. The black men went North and took that music with them, to Memphis (where W. C. Handy wrote down the first blues) and on to Chicago where King Oliver and Louis Armstrong made their records and reputations.

THE UNORIGINAL DIXIELAND BAND:

The first white Americans who picked up on jazz music took it out to the world at large. They were the Original Dixieland Jazz Band, a group of New Orleans youths who heard the music in the black ghetto and began to play it. They had been preceded in New York—then as now the show business capital of the country—by the black originals—Freddie Keppard and "That Creole Band"—but it was the white players who made the front pages with jazz, and made the first hit jazz recordings and brought jazz world-wide attention, albeit as a novelty craze. Curiously, World War I had sent some jazz to France with James Reese Europe's "Hellfighters," the band of the 369th Infantry, which had played concerts in the final days of the war throughout France. In the first years following the war to end all wars, Sam Wooding's orchestra, among others, toured Europe with the Chocolate Kiddies revue, and even performed in Russia. The trumpeter Tommy Ladnier was with this band; so was Sidney Bechet, the virtuoso clarinetist and soprano saxophonist. Somehow, however, these early bands, while they were successful, missed. It was the Original Dixieland Jazz Band that made the big impression and began the pattern of white musicians becoming huge successes by playing music originated by black men who remained in relative obscurity.

History lends itself eagerly to "what if." The question haunts us about jazz. "What if" Keppard and his Creole Band, by all accounts a marvelously inventive group, had recorded when they had the chance—before Victor recorded the Original Dixieland Jazz Band—would they have been the ones? "What if" Jim Europe had not been stabbed to death in Boston in a backstage brawl after his return from France? In the event Europe died at 40, and Keppard did not record—fearful, the legend says, that his music would be stolen if it were to be permanently available on records. What Keppard feared has been the story, literally and symbolically, over the years of jazz in America.

EUROPE LISTENED FIRST:

Freddie Keppard, who battled King Joe Oliver for the jazz crown in New Orleans after the reign of Buddy Bolden, knew his city's music was something special. So did the young composer and critic Ernest Ansermet (later to become world famous as a symphonic conductor with the Orchestra de Suisse Romande) when he heard New Orleans jazz. Ansermet encountered jazz in the person of Sidney Bechet who, despite his skill on the clarinet and soprano saxophone, did not read music but played it all by ear. Bechet, who died in the mid-Fifties in France after becoming something of a national celebrity there as an American expatriate, played a concert in Europe with the Southern Syncopated Orchestra in 1919 and Ansermet wrote of Bechet's solos:

"They gave the idea of a style and their form was gripping, abrupt, harsh with a brusque and pitiless ending like that of Bach's second Brandenburg Concerto . . . what a moving thing it is to meet the very black, fat boy . . . who can say nothing of his art save that he follows his 'own way' and when one thinks that this 'own way' is perhaps the highway the whole world will swing along tomorrow."

UP OUT OF NEW ORLEANS:

So the music crept out of New Orleans. The street parades and the funeral marches had much pageantry and ritual: "We'd play the slow marches on the way to the graveyard, dead marches like 'Flee As The Bird,' and on the way back we'd play 'Didn't He Ramble . . . he was a good man 'till the butcher cut him down . . .'" Kid Ory, the trombonist, recalled years later. It became part of the New Orleans mystique. Sporting house piano players and bordello bands from Storyville moved, without a break in rhythm, to the prohibition underworld of Chicago and other Northern cities. En route they played briefly on the Strekfus Mississippi River steamship lines. Musicians still talk of the night Emmitt Hardy, a white cornetist of the mid-west, sat in with Louis Armstrong on a Strekfus riverboat. Bix Beiderbecke, the hero of Dorothy Baker's "Young Man With A Horn," sat at the feet of Armstrong when the boats came to Bix's home town of Davenport, Iowa. But the first great spurt of jazz into the consciousness of America and the world was through the Original Dixieland Jazz Band. These players became international figures, as vaudeville novelties to be sure, but also as phonograph recording artists for Victor.

While they were headlining in New York and London, the black entertainment circuit spawned hundreds, perhaps thousands of singers, musicians and composers, lost now in the fog of time. Many played out their entire careers before black audiences. Others broke through into the white world to make known their names there. They made their livings from a string of night clubs, dance halls and tent show stands throughout the South and in the Northern city ghettos. Sometimes they were recorded, but always for what were called "race" records, a term used to designate records produced for the black audience—"the race"—and sold exclusively in the black neighborhoods.

UNKNOWN TO THE WHITE WORLD:

Gertrude "Ma" Rainey, who toured that circuit for years with her show, The Rabbit's Foot Minstrels, had such musicians as the tenor saxophone stylist Coleman Hawkins working for her. "Ma" Rainey was the teacher of Bessie Smith but she was absolutely unknown in the white entertainment world. A singer of amazing power and capable of evoking deep, almost mystical emotion, she survives on a few records, in a few photographs and in the memories of jazz musicians.

Bessie Smith, "Ma" Rainey's protégé, became the most successful of all the blues singers. She was known as the Empress of the Blues and, unlike Trixie Smith, Maggie Jones, Victoria Spivey, Mamie Smith and "Ma" Rainey, who were her peers, Bessie broke through into the aboveground world of music. Her active career lasted on into the late Thirties. She recorded a marvelous series of discs for Columbia, one of that company's most profitable items during the Depression. Many are still available on Columbia albums of jazz classics.

ONE SUNDAY NIGHT:

By the time she was the top selling blues artist on records and one of the leading black vaudeville performers, Bessie Smith began to be noticed by white society. Carl Van Vechten photographed her. Members of the New York literary set, as part of their interest in the Black Renaissance, talked about her. She even sang one Sunday night at the 52nd Street nightclub, The Famous Door, during the late Thirties and was mentioned in the *New Yorker's* Talk of the Town.

She made her last recordings on that New York trip, then went back to the road again and to her fatal automobile accident in her native Tennessee. Bessie died after that accident, bleeding to death when a white hospital would not admit her.

Ethel Waters, long before she starred on Broadway and in films, made records as a blues singer and toured the black vaudeville circuit, Theater Owners Booking Association.

Though New Orleans has become glamorous in memory, the diaspora of prostitutes and musicians from Storyville during World War I caused by an Armed Forces drive to clean up the city, was not the sentimental event Hollywood made it in the film "New Orleans." It did add force to the drive to break out that motivated the most talented New Orleans musicians. They went North seeking what James Baldwin was later to call "the gimmick" in order to escape.

TO THE COAST, TO CHICAGO:

Jelly Roll and Papa Mutt Carey, originator of the growl trumpet style went to the West Coast. Kid Ory, who wrote "Muskrat Ramble" and "Savoy Blues," went to Chicago along with Johnny and Baby Dodds, the clarinet and drum playing brothers. Johnny St. Cyr, the banjoist, and Bud Scott, who stopped playing piano after he heard Jelly Roll and took up guitar. Sugar Johnny, Punch Miller and Henry "Red" Allen, the trumpeters, Jimmy Noone, the clarinet player who inspired Goodman, Barney Bigard, who joined Duke Ellington for a decade as featured clarinetist after working with Oliver and Morton, Minor and "Ram" Hall, the two brothers who played drums. George "Pops" Foster, who made the string bass into a solo instrument. Zue Robertson and Honoré Dutrey, the trombonists. Tommy Ladnier and Sidney Bechet . . . the list is long. It gleams with talent.

HORN IN A PAPER BAG:

Bechet, Armstrong, Oliver and Jelly Roll Morton were the first quartet of New Orleans musicians to establish themselves in the North. Of them, only Armstrong survived. Louis not only had the talent to last but he emerged at the right time. Oliver brought him up from New Orleans and Louis arrived with his cornet in a paper bag, frightened of the big city and terrified that he could not succeed there. But he met Joe Glaser, who ran the Sunset Café, and who became Armstrong's manager, guiding his career all the way to the top of the entertainment world, forming one of the biggest of all artists' booking agencies along the way. Oliver continued after Louis left him, but his recording career faded out and he lapsed into obscurity, eventually dying in the late Thirties after spending his last years eking out a meager living as a porter in a dance hall.

Bechet, demonstrably as much a virtuoso soloist as Armstrong—after all, he was recognized by the European critics before Louis—gave up entirely at one point in the Thirties and became a tailor after a brief period in the pit band at Billy Rose's Diamond Horseshoe in New York. Bechet returned to jazz later, then went to France and in the Fifties became a celebrity there, even making the cover of Life shortly before he died.

Morton, like Oliver an organizer and a composer, saw his recording career, like Oliver's, shrivel up and disappear. He died in obscurity in California in the early Forties after contributing to some of jazz' greatest legends. For instance, there was Morton in the Thirties, telling everyone who would listen that he, not Paul Whiteman, was the King of Jazz and that he, Jelly Roll, had actually invented it, in fact. His claims seemed extravagant. They still do. But there was a substance in them as he showed when he turned on the radio and picked up the Benny Goodman orchestra playing one of its first hits, Morton's own composition, "King Porter Stomp!" Morton turned from the radio to announce disgustedly, "Chicago style! New Orleans style! Hell! It's all Jelly Roll style!"

LOOKING BACKWARD:

Looking back now on what went on in the early days of jazz with the expanded vision of hindsight, it all begins to take shape.

In an America coming of age at the turn of the century and seeking its identity as a world power, European music was the standard of culture; it was "classical" and "good." Anything American, therefore, must be somehow less valuable, especially anything which came from the black citizens who, only so recently as to be within the memory of a majority of the adult population, had been slaves.

So the music of the black artists—jazz music—was not to be respected. To be enjoyed, certainly, to be used in the settings of night life and underworld, prostitution, gambling and vice. "UNSPEAKABLE JAZZ MUST GO," the headline in the *Ladies' Home Journal* said in December, 1921. Jazz was "jungle music." Even the line in the hit song, "Birth of the Blues," so implied with "the wail of a downhearted frail . . ."

But the white man was invariably drawn to the music of the American black man. White Americans found the world represented by black music to be exciting and fascinating and valuable. They found it to be honest, poignant and more dimensional than their own world. Even in slave times, it seemed, slaves appeared to have more fun, when they had fun, than their masters.

CROSSING THE COLOR LINE:

So increasingly the strange process of crossing the color line in reverse began, with whites imitating black speech, dress, style, and music. When Louis Armstrong left King Oliver to go out on his own in Chicago, one of his first white friends was the Jewish clarinet player Milton Mezzrow, who declared officially that he was more at home with black friends and musicians than with anybody else. Once, when he was arrested, Mezzrow even put "Negro" in the space marked "RACE" on his prison registration card.

The strength of the artistic drive of these musicians is quite remarkable, looking back now. American popular song, as it developed, was a wildly Freudian wish-dream fantasy world, so thoroughly euphemistic that it seemed determined to have no connection with reality. The black musicians took that music and, despite all opposition, made it real. It wasn't only Louis Armstrong singing and playing "I'm Confessin'," or "Song of the Islands," or "Stardust," it was the classically trained pianist Fats Waller doing, "I'm Gonna Sit Right Down And Write Myself A Letter" and Duke Ellington performing "In The Shade of the Old Apple Tree."

What does the ordinary American, even today, think of when you say "jazz" to him? He thinks of Louis Armstrong on the Ed Sullivan TV show rolling his eyes and making jokes about Man-Tan or he sees, on the late night show, the cannibal costumes in some faded film reflecting the Hollywood stereotype of the black man as a savage.

THEY SANG IT LIKE IT WAS:

He doesn't think of Louis Armstrong singing "Coal Cart Blues," which is a pure folk song written out of Louis' own experience as a juvenile in New Orleans at the Andrews Coal Company, hauling hard coal at fifteen cents a load, making about 75 cents a day. "Coal Cart Blues" is not only a poignant personal story but a remarkable vehicle for Armstrong's trumpet improvisations.

On late night TV he certainly doesn't see "The Louis Armstrong Story." He sees films made of the lives of Benny Goodman, the Dorsey Brothers and Glenn Miller and, good musicians as they were and good as their bands were, they had less relationship to the truth of jazz during their time than the fiction in the average slick magazine has to the American novel. It's just that it was possible, given the social attitudes in this society, to make the Goodman, the Dorsey and the Miller stories in Hollywood but to have made "The Fats Waller Story" or "The Louis Armstrong Story" would have meant facing up to what America was all about.

Even if he sees Armstrong on a late show, it will be in one of his vaudeville roles in a Bing Crosby picture. The pattern was repeated again and again through jazz history. In Chicago, white jazz men literally copied King Oliver's numbers and issued them as their own. Benny Goodman's career was helped by original compositions (however well he played them) that were written by Edgar Sampson and Chick Webb, black musicians who played in Webb's band at Harlem's Savoy Ballroom and who produced "Stompin' At The Savoy." Jelly Roll Morton, who wrote "King Porter Stomp," and Fletcher Henderson (who had led one of the first swing bands, but could not be accepted for the radio show which launched Goodman) and whose arrangements were the core of the Goodman band's repertoire. Later, when Goodman's band went into a decline in popularity, it took on new vitality with the compositions of the Kansas City black musicians Count Basie and Jimmy Rushing.

THE SWING ERA:

Goodman was not alone in this in the Swing Era. Tommy Dorsey made one of his first commercial hits with a song called "Marie," in which the singer, Jack Leonard, sang the lyric while the band, acting as a chorus, sang off-beat riffs in answer to him. It had to be played five, six, ten times a night at the original Dorsey engagement at the Commodore Hotel's Palm Room in New York. It was so successful it started a whole series of ballads treated in a similar fashion, and these were also Dorsey hits. The thousands of white collegians who flocked to hear Tommy Dorsey do "Marie" never knew it was an original arrangement, note for note, by Doc Wheeler's Sunset Royal Serenaders Orchestra. Dorsey played opposite the Sunset Royal group at a Philadelphia theater, heard the arrangement, liked it and made a trade—eight Dorsey arrangements for a hit. Doc Wheeler and the Royal Sunset Serenaders were black.

The Swing Era of Goodman, Dorsey, Miller, et al., came about fifteen years after the first novelty explosion of jazz. It made the big band adaptation of jazz into the most popular music in America. The success of the leading white bands was so great (Goodman and Dorsey actually became millionaires) that even the black bands became what for them were financial successes. Yet Count Basie, whose concept for big band jazz is the prototype swing band, was actually paid less than the standard musician's union scale for recording sessions and the American Federation of Musicians had to force a readjustment.

Even Glenn Miller's huge success was in part founded on the contributions of black musicians. His big hit, "In The Mood" was written and arranged by Joe Garland, the tenor saxophone player in Louis Armstrong's big band of the time. "Tuxedo Junction" was a number Miller picked up from Erskine Hawkins, a black bandleader who never really made the big time but played at New York dance halls. Dorsey, too, altered his band's style in the late Forties by hiring Sy Oliver away from Jimmy Lunceford's band. The Harry James debt to Count Basie was demonstrated over and over again through the years. Even Woody Herman was part of the syndrome. His first big hit was "Caledonia," which he first heard done by the man who wrote it, Louis Jordan, who led small bands on the black vaudeville circuit.

BILLIE AND THE BLUES:

By the beginning of the Fifties, jazz was rather well established as a part of American culture. Books, articles, lectures, and a multitude of recordings contributed. But the image jazz had with the average American again was less than pretty. When the ordinary person thought of jazz, the immediate connotation was narcotics and dissipation. The tortured career of Billie Holiday, the gifted blues and ballad singer whose disc of "Strange Fruit" was one of the first pure uncompromising jazz performances to become even a minor hit in the phonograph record field, made continual headlines. Arrested for narcotics, institutionalized in Louisville's rehabilitation center, "Lady Day," as all the jazz musicians called her, confirmed the stereotypes not only by her actions but in her autobiography, "Lady Sings The Blues." Charlie Parker, the alto saxophonist from Kansas City, and one of the originators of the modern jazz style called bebop, was another admitted narcotics addict. Outstanding creators from DeQuincy to Baudelaire to Maugham have used drugs, and have been considered victims, rather than having their art judged for their weaknesses. But jazz is a short word, adaptable to newspaper headlines. Whenever anybody owning a musical instrument was arrested, he was called a "jazz" musician.

Billie Holiday was the bridge between the blues singers of the Bessie Smith generation (Bessie and Louis were her inspirations) and today's popular music. She influenced so many singers herself that one could truly call her the main influence of an entire generation.

THREE AFTER THE WAR:

Billie Holiday was one of the top trinity of jazz artists of the post World War II years, along with Lester Young, the wispy tenor saxophonist, model of the central character in Clellan Homes' "The Horn," who died alone in a New York hotel room after setting the style that made others famous, and Charlie Parker, found dead under mysterious circumstances, an admitted teen age junkie who devised a style that is heard today in almost every television sound track, just as Lester Young's tenor style is heard in the big bands on all the late night TV talk shows.

Early in 1969, a jazz/rock band named Blood, Sweat & Tears released an album that became the best selling album in the country. On it was a long alto saxophone solo so like Parker as to sound like his ghost.

Parker and Dizzy Gillespie, and the moody and opaque pianist Thelonious Monk, developed the modern jazz style by extending to the furthest limits all the things that could be done with the standard ballad form and the standard, European, popular music harmonies. Parker was called "Bird," the famous jazz night club Birdland was named after him. When he died, Lenny Tristano, one of the few original white jazz pianists, said sadly that all the players who soloed in that club every night ought to have paid Parker royalties, they borrowed so much from him.

AN ORIGINAL JAZZ LITERATURE:

After Parker and Monk, younger players such as Charles Mingus and Miles Davis began to create their own literature, no longer content to improvise, however brilliantly, on the scores of others, as had the bebop era jazzmen even when they made an intellectual game out of creating new compositions from the chords of old. Davis and Mingus created a body of emotion-packed recordings utilizing the blues form and original structures and becoming international stars. Davis even evolved, after the white jazz pianist Dave Brubeck opened the door, into a college concert favorite and was one of the few black players to become wealthy.

In the Sixties, jazz has assumed a militant tone, reflecting new attitudes of the black people. No longer is there an attempt to structure jazz in the framework of European music. The new jazz creators, startlingly brilliant musicians such as Cecil Taylor, the pianist and composer, Archie Shepp, Ornette Coleman, John Coltrane and Sun Ra, have by and large abandoned even the traditional restrictions of chord structure and tonality. Instead they now play what they call "free form," completely extemporaneous improvised music.

Unusual it certainly is. But it is no less effective at its best than the classical Louis Armstrong solo on "Song of the Islands" or Coleman Hawkins's "Body and Soul" or Dizzy Gillespie and Charlie Parker on "Groovin' High" (their improvisation on the chords and melody of the old ballad, "Whispering"). Yet again even today the music suffers from an inability of the white community to accept it unless it is watered down.

John Coltrane is a hero to the young black Americans, almost as widely known as Malcolm X. One of the first of the jazz musicians to abandon the traditional methods of improvising and to work towards the new "free form" style, he has been accused of "playing hate." I once had a long discussion about this with a highly intelligent man, an executive in a large corporation dealing with the news, who was convinced that Coltrane's music was "a music of hate." What he really meant was that Coltrane's music was far different from that of Armstrong and Basie. The melodies were not familiar and the sounds were sometimes harsh by his standards. Even more, the titles of the compositions and the totality of the music's sound had a non-European, non-American cast to it. In a word, it made him uncomfortable not only because of how it sounded but because other kinds of non-verbal communication went with it—Eastern beaded headpieces and the black "natural" hair style.

The truth is that John Coltrane's music was openly and obviously a music of love. His most famous composition, "A Love Supreme," was a tone poem to his God and he defined that God, both in the music itself and in the accompanying poem, as a God of love.

Art precedes social change as well as mirroring the society from which it comes and the turbulence and strident tone that accompanies some of the black struggle for true freedom is found in modern jazz. But that is a part of life and as such is as valid as any of the other aspects of the music.

BLUES IS A FEELING:

"Jazz is America's classical music," a rock 'n' roll musician remarked recently. If that is true, then the blues is the folk music of jazz, full brothers though they may be. Like jazz, blues emerged anonymously in the ante-bellum South and was not, despite another legend, invented by W.C. Handy. Handy wrote down what he heard, but somebody else before him started it.

The blues is a feeling and a form. It is singular and plural at will. It is the story of a man and his troubles in life, his personal story. The great blues singers of the Twenties and the early Thirties bred the jazz men but they also bred a line of itinerant musicians who sang and played only the blues.

Huddie Ledbetter, "Leadbelly," was one of the first to become known to the white world, was a pardoned murderer who sang the blues and work songs of the chain gangs in the night clubs of New York and wrote two songs which were hits long after he died in the early Forties. They were "Rock Island Line," which the British singer Lonnie Donegan later made into a hit, and "Goodnight Irene," which was earlier put into the nation's jukeboxes by the Weavers, the prototype folk singing group. It is interesting to note, again, how Leadbelly's songs were unpalatable in the original but not in the toned-down white versions. Similarly, Duke Ellington's own recorded versions of his songs were never played on one of the biggest independent radio stations in the country in the Fifties because they were "too noisy." Black, even then, automatically equated with "loud" and "raucous." The "jungle music" syndrome again.

Big Bill Broonzy, another powerful and creative blues singer and guitarist, made a series of records in the Thirties that became part of the inspiration for today's young musicians of the pop world. Although he traveled to Europe after World War II, Big Bill shared the common fate of many black artists: he died in poverty. One of the leading folk musicologists of America once praised a Western university when it had Carl Sandburg on the campus. Big Bill got on a university campus, too, shortly before he died. But he got there the hard way, sweeping the floors as a janitor.

Sam "Lightning" Hopkins, who was the link between the folk/blues of the Thirties and the rhythm and blues of today's black community, was resurrected in the autumn of his life by young blues fans. He has been touring folk music clubs and appearing in concerts in recent years. Howlin' Wolf (Chester Burnett), another blues singer of seminal importance, made a startling appearance before white America when the Rolling Stones insisted on bringing him onstage for a TV show during one of their tours, his first American television appearance. Howlin' Wolf, like many other black musicians, was better known to British youth than he was in white America.

Ray Charles, the blind pianist and singer, was one of the heroes of black America before the white community's radio stations would play his music, but Charles' career, unlike those of Leadbelly and Big Bill, came at a time when black radio stations had emerged and could bring his music to the masses. Eventually, he became, like James Brown and Otis Redding, one of the top show business figures.

Nevertheless, his early career, and the period many consider his most original and productive, was spent playing on what Lou Rawls, another singer, has immortalized as "the chitlin' circuit," the small bars and dance halls that dot the ghettos.

Muddy Waters is relatively famous today, though almost never seen on television, due to the upsurge of interest in blues in the past two years resulting from its advocacy by British pop musicians and their American followers. As McKinley Morganfield, he made Library of Congress folk music discs from a prison farm over twenty years ago. Many of his blues songs have been revised and recorded under other names as the compositions of other people. B. B. King, known as the "King of the Blues," and the originator of the electric guitar style heard today in thousands of white rock bands, made his first American television appearance on National Educational Television as late as 1968.

Today Europe, which has been so kind to black musicians through the years since Jim Europe and others first played there, treats the blues singers and instrumentalists like Muddy Waters, Howlin' Wolf, Chuck Berry, John Lee Hooker and Willie Mae "Big Mama" Thornton as artists of the first rank and they regularly appear in concert halls there.

THE DUKE:

Two other jazz groups deserve special mention for they are not only great artists but unique even within this unique art form. They are Duke Ellington and his orchestra and the Modern Jazz Quartet.

Ellington celebrated his 70th birthday in 1969 at a special White House dinner at which President Nixon presented him with a Presidential Medal of Honor. This came so late in life, after such a long struggle that Ellington is a remarkable man not to be bitter.

One of the most prolific writers of popular melodies as well as a composer of major stature, Ellington has utilized his songwriting and his nightclub careers to subsidize his "traveling workshop," his orchestra, for over thirty years. Despite his recognition in Europe, Ellington has had to remain on the road, working steadily all of his life with no leisure to compose. His masterpieces have been written on buses and trains, in hotel rooms, or in backstage waits at night clubs. For over three decades he has contributed a series of compositions unparalleled in American music for their eloquence, depth of emotion and lasting qualities. In 1965 he brought back his early composition, "New World A-Comin'," for his Sacred Concert series and audiences found it refreshingly appropriate to the mood of the day. In 1969 he began to perform again his "Tone Parallel to Harlem," another early composition, which had renewed relevance to today's urban problems.

AT THE QUEEN'S COMMAND:

America has long neglected Duke Ellington. London had an apartment house named for him in the Thirties. He has played command performances for the Queen. Oddly, his autumnal recognition does not come as a serious composer, though Ellington himself said, "there has never been a serious musician who was as serious about his music as a serious jazz musician," a comment that said it all for all jazz men for all time. He was invited to write but once for a symphonic group, the NBC Symphony of the Air, and he composed "Night Creatures." But Ellington would have enhanced the musical reputation of any American orchestra had its prime interest been in other than traditional European music.

Ellington is beyond style and fads. His success as an entertainer has enabled him to give us some of America's most profound musical expression, whether in his songs or in his longer works.

THE MODERN JAZZ QUARTET:

The Modern Jazz Quartet was formed in the early Fifties by four graduates of the Dizzy Gillespie big band: pianist and musical director John Lewis, bassist Percy Heath, drummer Kenny Clarke and vibraphonist

Milt Jackson. They set out to train themselves to do two things: to improvise as a free swinging jazz group with full virtuosity while making it appear effortless through practice, and to perfect a musical unit for the compositions of Lewis.

Both projects were fulfilled. The Modern Jazz Quartet ranks as the supremely polished small jazz unit today. Its performance of film scores by Lewis, longer works by him, and an extensive library of jazz numbers, has put the Modern Jazz Quartet, like the Ellington organization, in a class by itself. Completely abandoning any attempts to entertain, the Modern Jazz Quartet insisted on its music being heard and judged on its own standards alone. Time has proven its own assessment of its merit to be correct.

IT STANDS FOR FREEDOM:

Jazz still seeks its own from white America. *The Times* of London, in a survey of America, "The American Imagination," noted that "The white man's idea of the Negro, often operating below the level of consciousness, stands for freedom. That is what drew the flappers of the Twenties to the world of Harlem Negroes and jazz. This is what draws the young and the not so young, all over the industrialized world, not only to the excitement of Negro music but to the rebellious jargon of city streets that goes with it . . . the new Bohemians are vehement in rejecting Ford and Edison, the inventors, the explorers, Teddy Roosevelt and his Rough Riders, all those Americans who by aggressive self-reliance and guts have made modern America what it is. To take the side of the Negro is, for them, to take the role of protest and freedom," *The Times* remarked.

The sociologist Horace Cayton added weight to this observation when he pointed out that "jazz fans and rock 'n roll youth really have joined the Negro underground." Europe's strictures drove the first settlers to this continent to find freedom. Curiously, the freest art form ever developed in America, and obviously the most original, had to go to Europe to be recognized. Duke Ellington played for royalty in Europe before he ever got on the stage of Carnegie Hall in New York.

THE NAZIS COULD NOT STOP IT:

Even Nazi Germany was unable to suppress jazz. Lectures and re-corded concerts of jazz were given all through the Hitler era by German jazz critic Dietrich Schulze-Koehn. During the occupation of France, Django Reinhardt and the Hot Club of France continued to play and Radio Paris to broadcast Louis Armstrong records saying, "ici, une jazz."

Today, jazz is taught by jazz musicians in the school system in Po-land, where, despite the rigors of the Iron Curtain, there are almost 20,000 members of the Polish Jazz Federation who met in cellars to play contraband albums during the years immediately after World War II.

Three American jazz groups have appeared in Russia. Benny Good-man toured there (his men suspected of being C.I.A. agents by some Russians, a thought that was greeted as a value judgment by caustic American jazz critics) and Earl Hines, the Chicago pianist toured there with great success. In 1965, Charles Lloyd, the modern jazz alto saxo-phonist, took his quartet to the Talinin Jazz Festival (even Russians have jazz festivals!) and made international headlines with his success.

Jazz groups from Czechoslovakia and Poland have recorded and there have been jazz festivals in those countries as well as in Russia. Voice of America jazz programs have the most attentive audiences of any U.S. broadcasts. When Dave Brubeck's Quartet played in Poland in the late Fifties, crowds of young people ran after the train when he left from the Warsaw station.

Today only China remains impervious to jazz. Everywhere else, in Japan, Australia, South America, India, Pakistan, Turkey (the Bolshoi Ballet, playing in Istanbul, came backstage to hear the Dizzy Gillespie orchestra), Finland and the Scandinavian countries all hail America's music in the most enthusiastic terms.

SOMETHING WORTH STUDYING:

Yet, in America, the American Federation of Musicians classifies a jazz concert as a variety show rather than allowing it the "concert" classifica-tion it gives to a string quartet or a symphony.

Until very recently in America, jazz was all but ignored in the curricula of American colleges and universities. A professor of music at the University of California answered the question why there were no courses in jazz by saying, "We don't have courses in plumbing, either."

Today as the black American's drive for wider recognition gains momentum, black jazz musicians are beginning to be in demand for positions in black studies programs. Archie Shepp, the tenor saxophonist, has served on the faculty of New York State University at Buffalo and John Handy, the alto saxophonist who played with Mingus, has taught at San Francisco State College. But these are exceptions. Professional jazz musicians have not entered the faculty group in any number, though there are indications this may be changing. Julian Adderley, whose quintet is one of the most successful in modern jazz, now offers a weekend seminar as part of a concert proposal to colleges and includes lecture demonstrations on various instruments as well as a discussion of the sociological and cultural aspects of the music. John Lewis of the Modern Jazz Quartet is now on the Board of Manhattan School of Music. Both Tulane University and Rutgers have extensive jazz archives.

There is no point in claiming that jazz is the only valuable music in America. But it is the only music completely original to this society, child though it is of the black portion of that society. When we think of American music, we ought to think of those great artists whose names we have not known in the past though the rest of the world knew them very well. When we hear America singing, we might think of it as does Julian Bond, the black Georgia State legislator who wrote the following verse with its multiple references to artists and compositions in the paper of the Southern Student Non-Violent Co-ordinating Committee—SNCC:

I, too hear America singing
But from where I stand
I can only hear Little Richard
And Fats Domino.
But sometimes I hear Ray Charles
Drowning in his own tears
Or Bird

Relaxing at Camarillo
Or Horace Silver doodling.
Then I don't mind standing
A little longer.

Jazz could do worse than that for an epitaph.
And for prophecy, one might settle for Baby Dodds' 1944 statement,
after a concert:

This ain't the last night! This stuff will be heard all over the world.
I mean all over the country. I mean every night will be the last
night and that ain't never gonna become! And the thing about it,
ain't gonna be no finish on this stuff, 'cause it's gonna be done and
heard for years and . . . Oh, I mean a long time . . .

Amen.

[*Lithopinion* #1, Fall 1969, winner of ASCAP/Deems Taylor Award
for Excellence in Music Journalism]

Perspectives

■

With jazz music being the business that it is, musicians have a problem of commercialization versus artist taste. You hear it 1000 times if you hear it once—how can I play what I want to.

Yet few want to face the fact that when you are good and have something valid to say, if you have the conviction of your own worth and of the rightness of your message, you eventually will find a way to play what you want and get paid for it.

And if, after years and years, you do not, it just might be possible that what you have to say isn't worth hearing.

ERROL FOR INSTANCE

Errol Garner—not only is he his own favorite pianist (and mine, too) but he always has played what he wants to play. If they ask him for the Hut Sutt Song, he plays it but in his own way. There are other pianists who sound like Erroll from time to time, but Erroll never sounds like anybody else, thus pointing out another major rule—be yourself.

There have been few greater commercial successes in jazz then Garner. This was demonstrated again in San Francisco this summer when the Black Hawk, after what seemed one long string of never-ending bombs, booked Erroll for three weeks.

"He came just in time. He saved us," said Guido Caccienti, the owner.

EVERYONE PLEASED

Garner plays Garner every minute. And what pleases him, pleases the public. One of the reasons for this, of course, is that he enjoys himself so much you can't help but like him for it. Then, too, he never is playing down to the audience and never playing over their heads.

When he does something complicated, he still has a line of simplicity running through it that can be grasped by the average listener. You don't have to have your hip card punched to dig Erroll.

Five or six years ago, he was playing the same as today and just working in joints for a little over scale. Today, he's a headliner.

It can happen. It's happened to Nat Cole, too. If you meet someone and expect them to dislike you, the chances are he will. It's like that with music, too, in case you never thought of it. Walk out on the stand, stick out your chin and announce you are going to play a ballad and imply—you'll fight anyone who doesn't give you the proper respect, and nobody but the hippies will dig you.

Go your own way, play your own style, because you like it that way, and if you have it, the public will recognize it. It's awfully hard to bury a real talent. But it's too easy to make a lot of noise about a little talent and then wonder why nothing big ever happens.

[*Down Beat*, September 22, 1954]

Perspectives

There probably isn't a more modest guy in the whole music business than Woody Herman. For a man who has really contributed much more to the stream of jazz history than many a more loquacious musician, Woody has always been oddly reticent, reluctant to claim very much for himself and letting the public and the critics do it instead.

Off and on now for several years, I've been gathering little bits of comment on jazz from Woody, things he says on disc jockey shows, interviews, and occasional asides. Without shouting, without fanfare, and without pretense, Woody is a pretty solid thinker about jazz, and what he has to say is fundamental and worth mulling over.

Let's go:

The spirit of jazz is abandon. If you present it too grimly serious, you lose naturalness. The basic thing about jazz is that the music is meant to have a ball to—music to enjoy and to be happy with. Any time you weaken that, you lose. Many young musicians today are too serious. Too grim.

Take jazz out of the saloons? It won't be jazz. It's hard to keep that naturalness in a concert hall and you can't work concert halls 52 weeks of the year anyway.

The first thing in jazz is to swing. And if you don't swing you are not in the jazz field. When you stop swinging you are competing with the classical musicians and to tell the truth, Toscanini cuts you.

We have proved a very important point with the Third Herd. We found you can please people who don't know anything at all about jazz and still play jazz.

The cool cats went too far and erected an Iron Curtain between themselves and the audience. We want to play for ourselves, sure; but we also want to play for the audience, and if we don't reach them, what we do is only half done. But whatever we do, we first want to swing it. We want to keep the spirit of naturalness and freedom and having fun that made jazz great music.

Other bands? Well, the Duke has always been the greatest in his style, color and that particular kind of feeling. And Count Basie, especially his new band, is the greatest, too. And I guess we go after what's left!

[*Down Beat*, October 6, 1954]

The San Francisco Jazz Scene

■

San Francisco has always been a good time town. For periods it has been a wide-open town. And no matter how tight they close the lid and no matter that 2 AM closing is mandatory in California, it is still a pretty wide open town.

A high-priced call girl, flush from the Republican convention and an automobile dealers conclave and happily looking forward to the influx of 20,000 doctors, 8000 furniture dealers and divers and other convention delegates, put it simply. "San Francisco is the town where everyone comes to ball, baby," she said.

This spirit of abandon goes hand-in-hand with a liking for jazz, because jazz is, no matter how serious you get about it, romantic music by and for romantics. What could be a better place for it to flourish than a town where everybody comes to ball, baby?

Because San Francisco is a small town with the charming lines of a big city, concentrated on the tip of the peninsula in an unnaturally air-conditioned dream world (it never gets too hot, nor too cold) there is a perpetual springtime air about searching for jazz. The fog is friendly; the clubs—dirty, dingy, crowded, smoky and badly run like jazz clubs everywhere—somehow seem warmer. The audiences—Nob Hill slummers, bearded Bohemians, crew-cut University of California sophomores and the casual tourist, gaping at the "big name" jazz stars—are friendly. They want to tell you why they like the city, why they like its music and what Stan Getz said to them last time they heard him and do you remember the time Duke played the Fillmore Street ballroom and Al Hibbler sang "Trees"?

The San Francisco native is not suspicious. Here, his jazz excursion seems safer, though still a glimpse of a different world, possibly because he can get back to his flat in the avenues, his Berkeley home, his Palo Alto patio or his Sausalito barge, in half an hour and let the babysitter go home.

It's an easy audience. The color line, though strictly drawn in prewar San Francisco (pre–World War II, that is) and still occasionally drawn today, is quite relaxed for a city so close to Mason and Dixon's line—it runs just south of here. The large Negro population has mixed for years with no tightening of lips or stiffness of necks at the jazz clubs.

These are some of the reasons why San Francisco has been for years and still is one of the best jazz towns in the country. Back before World War II, San Francisco radio boasted jazz programs where Ma Rainey records were played and Anson Weeks' band at the Palace Hotel had Ivie Anderson as vocalist. Paul Whiteman got his real start here, and the first explorers from New Orleans, Jelly Roll Morton, King Oliver, Bunk Johnson, Kid Ory and Mutt Carey, impregnated the area with a feeling for real jazz that was never that strong in any city outside New Orleans and Chicago.

One of the first jazz clubs (an organization, not a nightclub) began in San Francisco in the late Thirties and begat the Lu Watters band whose splinter groups, led by Bob Scobey and Turk Murphy, today are the kings of revivalist jazz. One of the first modern jazz radio programs— Jimmy Lyons' KNBC show at the end of the 40s and lasting into the 50s (back on the air now, incidentally, at the same spot)—paved the way for the cool sounding Stan Getz and the swinging Gerry Mulligan style. Lyons' show started Dave Brubeck on his rise and was the genesis of a score of other jazz programs throughout the area. The *San Francisco Chronicle*, as far back as the 30s, did frequent interviews with jazz performers and since 1950 has offered thrice weekly coverage of recorded and in person jazz on the same editorial basis as its coverage of classical music. For a decade, Bay Area universities and colleges have offered jazz courses, sponsored jazz workshops and graduated a generation of jazz fans. It is no coincidence that Anson Weeks is still a bandleader here nor that his son, Jack, is a modern bassist with his own group. Succeeding generations of northern Californians have supported them both. Families whose 60-year-old senior citizens went dancing to Anson at the St. Francis or the Mark, and whose 40-year-old second-generation drank beer to Lu Watters' Yerba Buena Jazz Band at the Dawn Club, have 20-year-olds today who attend Sunday afternoon sessions at the Black Hawk or drop in to hear Jack Weeks at Fack's II.

Digging jazz today in San Francisco can be a capsule history of the music if you want it that way; or it can be all in one style. Down on the waterfront there are two jazz clubs catering to traditional fans and exploiting all the atmosphere of a dockside saloon it is possible to concentrate in one spot, including sawdust floor and old three-sheets. The Tin Angel, with a circular fireplace and the stage built by Turk Murphy, is home to George Lewis, Murphy, Kid Ory and now and then Bob Scobey with the diehard traditional jazz fan rubbing shoulders with the sack-suited Nob Hiller down for a night on the town and bitterly resenting him. Across the street (actually the Embarcadero with the railroad switch line and the silhouettes of Matson liners as a backdrop) is Pier 23, a sailor's bar, where Burt Bales, a fine traditional pianist and one of the few dedicated jazzmen of that style left, plays as he pleases. The Sail 'N is a few blocks away and a host of other beer-and-wine or beer-only storefronts, such as the Hug-A-Mug, the Honey Bucket, and Burp Hollow, offer varying brands of Dixieland ranging from faithful imitations of Lu Watters (and if there is a San Francisco style in traditional jazz it is Watters' style with touches of Turk Murphy) to fraternity house Dixieland sans striped coats and straw hats. (San Francisco jazzman, traditionalist style, are more apt to be in shirtsleeves or Brooks Brothers suits, than uniforms.) In the middle of the downtown area (the business district and the hotel district is "downtown") The Hangover has been a West Coast Nick's for a decade with a good deal of the ad agency "it's deductible" atmosphere. In recent years, the music has been the product of various versions of a house band selected by the owner and led, for almost two years now, by Earl Hines with such traditional "names" as Pops Foster, Muggsy Spanier, Joe Sullivan and Meade Lux Lewis involved from time to time.

Modern jazz in San Francisco centers in and around the Black Hawk, a one story, drab looking club (once called the Stork Club, it lost a suit to you know who and changed its name, though the original is still etched in cement under the doormat) in the middle of the Tenderloin. The Hawk deals in modern jazz exclusively with names like Mulligan, Miles Davis and Shorty Rogers. For several months each year, Dave Brubeck, who got his real start there and still lives in the Bay Area, returns to the Hawk for an extended series of appearances, playing for consecutive weekends, sometimes for three months at times. Sunday afternoon sessions at the Black Hawk offer blowing time to young modernists. It is always a shock to come in out of the bright sunlight of a California Sunday afternoon to the dustiness of the Black Hawk, which, with the franker light of day time, shows a frowsiness hidden by night—the mark of a true Tenderloin resident.

The other stronghold of modern jazz is The Cellar, a sort of homemade night club in a converted Chinese restaurant. (Several San Francisco clubs have had a history of conversion from Chinese restaurants or clubs.) It is located deep in the North Beach section—the Greenwich Village of San Francisco, close by Telegraph Hill. The Cellar has recently experimented with a series of jazz-and-poetry evenings in which San Francisco poets Kenneth Rexroth and Lawrence Ferlinghetti read their own poems while the jazz group improvised in the background. The result of this, while far from aesthetically satisfactory to the performers involved, has been astounding in terms of attendance. Turn away crowds were at the first two sessions and brought considerable heat from the local representative of law and order, a squaresville type who hates jazz, hates musicians, poets and bohemians, and seems only to love his own authority.

Oddly enough, the only successful emergence of a big band in the Bay Area in recent years has taken place in Oakland, not San Francisco. Rudy Salvini, a young trumpeter and quondam high school teacher, has had a rehearsal band for some time which, under the wing of Pat Henry, Oakland disc jockey, has made a series of appearances at an Oakland ballroom to a curious young-old crowd. The band has been a workshop for local jazz arrangers and has recorded for San Francisco Jazz Records, one of the two local firms offering recording opportunities to young jazzmen. (The other is the exceptionally successful Fantasy Records, home label of Cal Tjader and Paul Desmond, and original recorder of Dave Brubeck.)

One of the curious aspects of San Francisco jazz is that, although the traditional jazz groups of Lu Watters and Turk Murphy have inspired considerable imitation, the modern jazz group of Dave Brubeck, despite its completely San Francisco personnel and its international reputation, has inspired no imitation at all. In the little hideaways where traditional jazz—second and third line—is played, there is always an overtone of Watters or Murphy and sometimes an outright copy. Obviously these men have made a tremendous impression on the musicians interested in that style.

On the other hand, at the Sunday afternoon sessions, at junior college and college amateur jazz concerts, at sessions near the University of California campus—the spots where the budding modern jazzmen sharpen their axes—no one steps up to the piano in a Brubeckian mood. There are however, numerous saxophonists in whose playing there is a definitive stamp of Paul Desmond, Brubeck's star boarder.

But on an even greater number there is the stamp of Sonny Rollins, Charlie Parker, Stan Getz, The Modern Jazz Quartet and other Eastern jazz groups. The pervading influence in San Francisco modern jazz is Eastern, with the exception, if you can count it as such, of Gerry Mulligan.

A lot of jazz experimentation in the Bay Area never is heard in public at all. Instead, the young musicians gather in apartments, garages (Lu Watters used to play in the Oakland hills) and hotel rooms for rehearsals. The recreation hall in the Musicians Union building is a favorite spot for blowing and there are several YMCA halls where jazz is encouraged. What is sadly needed, though, is some official union encouragement of the sort that is given the musicians in Seattle where the local AFM unit has sponsored a jazz workshop. In the Bay Area the jazz musician is on his own.

This may produce a hardy crop of survivors, but it has also resulted in many potentially good jazzmen abandoning music or seeking the shelter of what few steady musical jobs there are. Another disappointing aspect of modern jazz in San Francisco is that it has brought forth no young singer of any stature. While traditional jazz has Turk Murphy and Clancy Hayes to sing its songs, there is a horrible shortage of modern singers.

Despite this, the Bay Area is alive with jazz talent. There is a constant struggle for new ideas and new concepts and a continuing experimentation that suggests more interesting developments in the future. Jazz concerts have always been successful here—the big traveling shows rack up huge grosses. Perhaps in future years more attention will be paid to local artists. In any case, the jazz fan, local or visiting, can find whatever type of jazz makes his pulse beat faster, intrigues his brain or merely causes his feet to tap. It's all here.

[*Evergreen Review,* No date]

Jimmy Witherspoon,
At the Monterey Jazz Festival

■

The slight, wispy strings of Pacific fog were beginning to come in over the fence at the Monterey County Fairgrounds the night of October 2, 1959. The Second Annual Monterey Jazz Festival's opening concert was coming to an end and there was a momentary pause. Some of the audience thought the show was over.

They knew differently a moment later because a stocky, dignified man strode out on the stage, slapped the piano twice with his hand, shouted "Down Home! 'A' flat!" to pianist Earl Hines and then grabbed the microphone and gave the 6000 people a lesson in the blues.

Jimmy Witherspoon, after a decade of singing in dingy nightclubs and Jim Crow bars all over the country, had finally gotten a break in the big time and he made the most of it.

If fish can love underwater,
'N worms can love underground,
If rats can love in a garbage can,
WOMAN! You better not turn me down!

Witherspoon's warm, husky, sometimes rough voice rolled out over the crowd and those who were preparing to leave sat down. Mop! 'Spoon's very presence was commanding and his voice, with the classic "cry" in it completely dominated the arena. You couldn't leave. It was a great, dramatic moment.

Jimmy Witherspoon's presence at the Monterey Jazz Festival was no accident. Earlier in the year he had an LP produced by Dave Axelrod and released on World Pacific. Jimmy Lyons, the disc jockey who is the master-mind behind the Monterey Jazz Festival, heard it, flipped and made up his mind to have 'Spoon at Monterey.

Finding him was another matter. 'Spoon had just been through California but Lyons had missed him. Finally phone calls all over the country tracked 'Spoon down in Cincinnati where he was offered the Monterey date.

Jimmy Witherspoon had the closing spot on the first evening's program at Monterey. He had been preceded by the Earl Hines Trio (Earl, Vernon Alley, bass; Mel Lewis, drums). They had broken it up. Then Roy Eldridge, Ben Webster, Coleman Hawkins, Urbie Green and Woody Herman joined the Hines Trio for an All-Star set. Then came 'Spoon.

There were no rehearsals and no program. "How will it go?" Witherspoon was asked before the set. "Don't worry," he said, "Ben and I used to do this all the time and Earl's a swinging piano player."

Witherspoon was so right. "Down Home! 'A' Flat!" was all the instruction the band needed. As you hear on this LP, they fitted with Witherspoon like ham and eggs. Earl Hines in person—just as on this LP—really astonished people who had written him off as an old timer, lost in a swamp of dixieland. Witherspoon is a real take-charge guy and he took over at Monterey that night.

Midway through the set, Jimmy halted the proceedings and introduced his mother, Mrs. Eva Witherspoon of San Francisco. A devout church woman, Mrs. Witherspoon had never heard her son sing in public before, since she would not enter the nightclubs and bars where he usually sang. "I guess the Festival will be different," she said. A moment like this could be awkward, even a bit corny but it was genuine and true when 'Spoon asked for a hand for "one of the greatest persons in my life—my mother!"

During the course of the set Jimmy Witherspoon sang at Monterey there were many moments that remain in my memory. Most of them are on this album. For instance, there's the great introduction Earl Hines plays on "Ain't Nobody's Business" . . . Roy Eldridge's muted trumpet on the same tune . . . 'Spoon crooning "rain, rain" later in the song and then Ben Webster's magnificent solo.

Ben started to blow on that solo and a thrill ran through the audience. "Awrite, Ben," Witherspoon said and then at the end added "Lovely." Backstage later, Witherspoon summed up the entire audience reaction to Webster's solo. "Ben wrote his name tonight," he said.

Earl Hines' beautiful sound on "When I Been Drinkin'" is here, too, and 'Spoon's rollicking "There's Good Rockin' Tonight" ("well, you'll hear Dizzy Gillespie along with Bird/Everybody'll be jumpin' even J.C. Heard/You'll hear all the cats, even ole Sonny Criss/If you don't come down you won't know what you've missed . . .").

Witherspoon set off a great wave of emotion that lasted through the entire Festival.

"This is the greatest thing that ever happened to me," he said afterwards as he hugged Jimmy Lyons. "I'm proud tonight," his mother said, her grey hair shining and her glasses misty as she posed for pictures with her son.

The next afternoon, 'Spoon sent a note to Lyons volunteering to sing at the Saturday night show as well. Free. In appreciation. "You don't find guys like that," Jimmy Lyons said. "'Spoon is not only a great singer, he's a great gentleman."

Amen!

[Liner notes, Hi-Fi Jazz Recordings—J421, December 1959]

John Coltrane, *Olé Coltrane*

■

That John Coltrane is one of the most important musicians in jazz is no news, of course, to those that have been intimately concerned with jazz music, as laymen or musicians, in recent years.

Sometimes, however, it seems as if great sections of the public have the idea that men like Coltrane exist in a vacuum, a musical vacuum in which they merely get on the stand and play, with never a thought in their minds about the problems of their art or their personal style.

In the case of a shy, reticent man like Coltrane, this can be accentuated. It may surprise some to learn that John Coltrane is not only a major jazz musician, but a man who is constantly involved in an agonizing reappraisal of his approach to his art.

Only a short while ago, when he was playing with Miles Davis, people found his solo playing too much to take. He was criticized heavily by a nationally syndicated columnist who heard him at a concert, and now and again people would even get up and leave when he played.

Today, his group has won all the honors it is eligible to compete for, his audience is among the most faithful and numerous in jazz and he is firmly established on that lonely plateau of achievement, a box office success and an artistic success at one and the same time.

Early in 1961, I had the opportunity to record some of John Coltrane's reflections on his music that seem to me to be particularly pertinent to this album. Here are some extracts from that interview:

> I like to play long . . . the only thing is, I feel that there might be a need now to have more musical statements going on in the band.

I might need another horn, you know. I ran across a funny thing. We went into the Apollo and the guy said, "You're playing too long, you got to play twenty minutes." Now, sometimes we get up and play a song and I play a solo maybe thirty, or at least twenty, minutes. Well, at the Apollo we ended up playing three songs in twenty minutes! I played all the highlights of the solos that I had been playing in hours, in that length of time. So I think about it. What have I been doing all this time? It's made me think, if I'm going to take an hour to say something I could say in ten minutes, maybe I'd better say it in ten minutes! And then have another horn there and get something else.

I've been soloing for years and that's about all, I feel a need to learn more about production of music and expression and how to do things musically, so I feel a need for another horn for that reason. I could really go on just playing like I am now, I enjoy playing that long. It seems like it does me a lot of good to play until I don't feel like playing anymore, though I've found out I don't say that much more! At the Apollo, My Favorite Things, which runs 13 minutes, we played that about seven minutes long. Cut it right in half.

On My Favorite Things my solo has been following a general path. I don't want it to be that way because the free part in there, I wanted it to be just something where we could improvise on just a minor chord and the major chord, but it seems like it gets harder and harder to really find something different on it. I've got several landmarks that I know I'm going to get to, so I try to play something in between that's different and keep hoping I hear something different on it. But it usually goes almost the same way every night. I think that the 3/4 has something to do with this particular thing. I find that it's much easier for me to change and be different in a solo on 4/4 tunes because I can play some tunes I've been playing for five years and might hear something different, but it seems like that 3/4 has kind of got a straightjacket on us there!

I try to pick a song that sounds good and that might be familiar and then try to have parts in the song were we can play a solo. But it seems like we are into this thing where we want to solo on a modal perspective more or less, and therefore we end up playing a lot of vamps within a tune. I don't know how long we're going to be in that, but that's the way it's been. So the song is usually picked primarily as a vehicle to blow on.

About his own composing, Coltrane said:

I've been going to the piano and working things out, but now I think I'm going to move away from that. When I was working on those sequences which I ran across on the piano, I was trying to give all the instruments the sequences to play and I was playing them, too. I was advised to try to keep the rhythm section as free and uncluttered as possible and if I wanted to play the sequences or run a whole string of chords, do it myself but leave them free. So I thought about that and I've tried that some, and I think that's about the way we're going to have to do it. I won't go to the piano anymore. I think I'm going to try to write for the horn from now on, just play around the horn and see what I can hear. All the time I was with Miles I didn't have anything to think about but myself so I stayed at the piano and chords, chords, chords! I ended up playing them on my horn.

I tell you one thing, I have done so much work from within now what I've got to do is go out and look around me some and then I'll be able to say I've got to do some work on this or on that.

This album was made some months after the conversation from which these extracts were taken. The music on it in many ways reflects some of the work John Coltrane's been doing along the lines he indicated here. Each new album he produces, it seems to me, in all likelihood will be a major exhibit in the continuity of his artistic growth. There are very few artists in any field whose every work is of interest. John Coltrane is one.

[Liner notes, Atlantic Records—SD1373, 1961]

School Jazz Has Quality

■

One of the most interesting sociological changes in the jazz culture is going on all around us these days practically unnoticed.

Until the last decade, jazz musicians came from low economic and minority groups for whom the prospect of a quick reward in music, as in sports, was attractive. Relatively few, and these were rebels, forsook the security (and risked the censure) of the higher levels of society to make a career in jazz.

Jazz musicians served their apprenticeship in the big bands before launching their own careers in the pure jazz idiom of the small groups and the recording studio.

Today, high schools in the Bay Area and throughout the country are changing all this. Many of them have "stage bands," i.e., big jazz bands which rehearse, give concerts, conduct workshops and, in short, provide the experience no longer available via the big swing bands. And they are producing a generation of jazz musicians who come to the music from the widest possible social and economic backgrounds.

The University of Nevada for two years has sponsored a "Stage Band Festival" during the winter and a "clinic" during the summer. Similar affairs are held in other places in the U.S.

And right here in San Francisco, Gus Hassapakis five years ago founded the Riordan High School's Bay Area High School Dance Band Tournament which, Friday night, presented its fourth annual concert. Nine high school bands participated and I must say, after a lifetime of listening to big bands, these kids knocked me out.

To begin with, the Riordon students (under the leadership of Ray

Lagger) presented a concert that was as well staged and lighted as many a professional one. It was impressive.

But even more impressive was the calibre of musicianship of the bands. When I was in high school outside New York (in the Pleistocene age), we couldn't have hired professional bands, aside from the big names, who were as good as these kids. I mean that literally. And when I was at Columbia the famous Dartmouth Barbary Coast Collegians and the Columbia Blue Lions were not a bit better than these high school students.

The youngsters didn't take the easy road of the simple arrangements. They played things with overtones of Kenton and the Berklee School of Music and they played with delicacy, feeling and swing.

The winners were South San Francisco, Berkeley and Balboa in that order. Lauri Verhagen won the vocal honors (she's from South S.F.) and another good singer, Terri Cole, should have won a consolation prize. Two of the many outstanding soloists were exceptional. They were Jeff Jones, an alto saxophonist from South S.F., and John Kipp, an alto from Berkeley.

Both players have already won scholarships to the Lake Tahoe Music Camp this summer.

Everyone connected with this affair deserves congratulations. The evening's listening was more interesting, enjoyable and exciting than the lineup of dance bands New Years' Eve on the radio.

The San Mateo Junior College orchestra, which gave a short recital at the end of the evening, was a pleasant surprise; a good, swinging, highly professional band with a number of outstanding soloists.

[*San Francisco Chronicle*, March 18, 1963]

Louis Plays the Claremont

■

Louis Armstrong's appearance at the Claremont Hotel this weekend was the occasion for a sort of mass worship rite in which couples from 16 to 60 packed the uncomfortable Garden Room to hear Pops.

Parents with their children, middle-aged couples who stood in silent contemplation, sharp looking college students, all came to hear a man who is—if ever there was one—a legend in his own time.

For Louis seems to have been there since our earliest memories. His presence on the stage is, somehow, reassuring; the sound of his horn one of the purest and most beautiful sounds of our time.

But Louis is 63, or will be in July. He keeps talking of taking a year off, of resting. But he keeps on working. Tonight he plays Castro Valley High School, last night it was Oroville, tomorrow Sacramento and then on to Salt Lake City, Casper, Wyo., and then Chicago.

He flew here after a week in Honolulu, which followed a long tour of Australia, Hong Kong and Japan. How long can it go on? How long can Louis walk on that stage and, whether or not he wills it, be the symbol of the world before Birmingham? When everything was under control, when progress was being made quietly, if slowly?

Louis has traveled all over the world in the past 15 years, quite possibly appeared in as many cities and as many countries as John Foster Dulles and with better effect, for wherever Louis has been, he has made friends.

I do not presume to know what is in his mind, but his heart must be in Birmingham. And it is a very special heart. For all these past 15 years, wherever Louis has gone, in Africa, in Asia, in Europe, he has been faced with Little Rock and Montgomery and Nashville and Birmingham and Greenwood and with the hypocrisy of the North.

He seldom plays the South anymore. For even Louis, the epitome of the patient man, must balk at coming from a foreign capital where he is treated as a king, to some Jim Crow hotel in the back of town.

Once before he revolted and in a front-page story blasted Eisenhower over Little Rock. I won't be surprised if he blasts Kennedy over Birmingham. And if and when he does, he will be criticized, as he was then, by the pious Jim Bishops who want him to be always smiling, always "giving some skin" and cracking jokes.

If you have imagination, think of how it must be with him, getting out of a plane in Hong Kong, where the non-white masses are crowding the limits of the city, and being asked his opinion on the state of affairs in his native land. It is not in Louis' heart to say, as Les Spann, the guitarist, said in England, that he was happy anywhere outside the United States. That's not Louis' style.

But don't think for an instant that the hurt and the pain are not there. Louis can read and Louis can hear and the newspapers and the airwaves have been full, the world over, of our disgrace. "The respect for the United States has never been lower overseas," a member of the Armstrong troupe said the other night. Think about that.

And think, too, of what James Baldwin said the other evening; that we are all guilty, if the only Negro we have ever known "was Billie Holiday, when she was drunk," I suggest we're all guilty, too, if the only Negro we have known is Louis, smiling and blowing that beautiful horn, and laughing and signing autographs. There is no hiding place from this one.

[*San Francisco Chronicle*, May 13, 1963]

This Year at Monterey

■

"You have to learn to close your ears and wait for the good things," Miles Davis remarked backstage, and that summed up the sixth annual Monterey Jazz Festival neatly.

It was necessary to close one's ears to the dull and the overly ambitious portions in order to appreciate the good things this festival really offered.

The dull moments were more frequent than usual this year, the exciting moments fewer. But there was still enough to make Monterey worthwhile. Certainly the 27,000 ticket-holders who paid a record-breaking $113,000 at the box office for five concerts seemed to think so.

But this year, for the first time since the initial Monterey Jazz Festival in 1958, the well-publicized Monterey attention to rehearsal, new music, and planning was not in evidence. There was no new music. Still, the appearance together Sunday afternoon of Laurindo Almeida, the Brazilian guitarist, and the Modern Jazz Quartet was at least a sensitive and lyric interlude of bossa nova, Bachianas Brasileiras, and John Lewis compositions in new arrangements.

Most of the rest of the festival consisted of good jazz groups performing their usual repertoire of set pieces and conventions for improvisation.

Except . . . And that "except" tells the story. It was the spur-of-the-moment, unplanned events that made the festival the artistic success it was and provided the real spice.

On Saturday afternoon, for instance, 17-year-old Tony Williams, drummer with the ultramodern Miles Davis Quintet, joined a trio of veterans led by banjoist Elmer Snowden. It was a quiet demonstration of the unity of jazz and the timeless ability of jazzmen of all ages to swing together. Snowden's banjo playing was warm and swinging. The clarinet solos by Darnell Howard, another venerable jazzman, were sprightly and provocative, and the solid bass of 71-year-old George "Pops" Foster (old enough to be Tony Williams' grandfather and a veteran of jazz wars even before the time of Louis Armstrong) was delightful. It made for a rare jazz moment.

Baritonist Gerry Mulligan, who stands four-square in favor of music and against categories, played a set with Jack and Charlie Teagarden, Pee Wee Russell, and the brilliant pianist Joe Sullivan. Although not Mulligan's responsibility, he had organized the set and improvised a blues duet (clarinet and baritone) with Russell that was paradoxically delicate yet earthy, while swinging along with the loping ease of a Greyhound. Musically it was more rewarding than many of the performances by long-established groups.

Again, on the Sunday afternoon program, the Gerald Wilson bigband, the unit from Los Angeles that served as house band for the weekend, opened its set in its usual competent but uninspired style when Dizzy Gillespie suddenly came on stage and began to blow in the trumpet section. He was followed by John Lewis, who took over on piano, and Connie Kay, who sat in on drums. Heady with the presence of these major players, the band took off for a wild, exuberant thirty minutes of big band jazz. Blues singer Jimmy Witherspoon, half a day early for his scheduled appearance, then sang with the band, accompanied by blues guitarist Roy Gaines, who master of ceremonies John Hammond spotted in the audience and brought on stage. None of this was planned. All of it was excellent.

There were other surprises. The Gildo Mahones Trio, which accompanies the vocal group of Lambert, Hendricks and Bavan, filled in as intermission act between stage set changes almost the entire weekend and never failed to come through with performances that lifted the audience emotionally. In bassist George Tucker and drummer Jimmy Smith, as well as in pianist Mahones himself, this unit has highly proficient individual players. They have melded together in a remarkable example of jazz cohesion and even out swung the big band on occasion.

Thelonious Monk, making his first appearance at Monterey, played with his quartet on Saturday night and again Sunday afternoon. Both times he was a total success, playing with that curiously mesmerizing style he develops on his own compositions and with his slapstick humor on ballads. Monk's sidemen, drummer Frank Dunlop, bassist Butch Warren, and tenor Charlie Rouse, seemed to play with unusual emotional intensity Sunday afternoon and attracted a huge backstage audience of musicians.

Miles Davis, also making his Monterey debut (and his first U.S. festival appearance in some years) was hampered by the overlong opening-night program. He did not begin until after midnight. Nevertheless in the few numbers he played, Davis displayed sparkling virtuosity in a series of trumpet-drum duets with Tony Williams. The audience stood and cheered him, as it did the Mulligan Quartet later in the weekend.

Carmen McRae and Jon Hendricks, who appeared on Sunday night, were excellent examples of superior jazz singers. Miss McRae was so effective in her performance of "What Kind of Fool Am I" that the 6,000 people in the Sunday night house were hushed to almost total silence. She is obviously the Edith Piaf of this art, with the capacity to communicate lyrics as an emotional experience that has not been heard in jazz since Billie Holiday.

Jon Hendricks twice gave moving vocal performances. On opening night he sang the Miles Davis trumpet solo from the Davis record of "Bye Bye Blackbird," making it into a taut essay on emancipation, and on Sunday he brought back the ancient popular song "I Wonder What's Become of Sally" in a performance that should revive interest in this long-dead composition.

But unquestionably the lack of planning hurt several of the concerts. Saturday afternoon was allowed to drown in sentimentality, with a cloying Teagarden family reunion, brothers Jack and Charlie, sister Norma and their mother, all of whom occupied the stage for an interminable length of time.

Helen Merrill, a singer of doubtful quality, contributed an achingly dull set Saturday night, the Japanese saxophone star, Hidehiko "Sleepy" Matsumoto, was interesting only as a curiosity. There were numerous unexplained cancellations. The proposed panel on "What Happened to Dixieland" was dropped at the last minute, and neither trumpeter Lu Watters nor singer Mel Torme ever appeared.

Nonetheless, Monterey was a success, even if aesthetically less so than in previous years. The atmosphere was benign and the musicians were eager. Typical of the thoughtfulness that characterizes this festival—a community project of the city of Monterey—were the several moments of silence in memoriam to the Birmingham victims, the inclusion of John Hammond as a master of ceremonies (an implicit recognition that without the Newport Jazz Festival there would not have been a Monterey), and the attention to musicians' personal and artistic comfort.

As a natural festival setting, Monterey is unsurpassed. The community nature of the event results in social amenities and a lack of discrimination in any form. The musicians reciprocate by playing at their highest levels most of the time. They enjoy themselves and it shows in the music.

One may hope, however, that Monterey's success will not tempt it to follow the standard procedure of American business of building a superior product and then cheapening it. If next year Monterey returns to its previous dedication to planning and new music and retains its spontaneity, it will fully justify its claims to pre-eminence in this field.

[*Saturday Review of Literature*, October 12, 1963]

Billie Holiday, *The Golden Years, Vol. II*

■

I got my manner from Bessie Smith and Louis Armstrong,
honey. Wanted her feeling and Louis' style.

That was the way Billie Holiday once described her singing and she kept saying it over and over in one way or
another whenever they asked her, and they asked her a
lot. For Billie Holiday's singing style is one of the most
unique and personal in all of jazz music.

That's what history will remember of her, solidly supported by the un-
debatable evidence of the records. She was a singer of jazz, the greatest
female jazz voice of all time, a great interpreter, a great actress and the
creator of a style that, in its own way, is as unique and important to jazz as
the styles of Louis Armstrong, Charlie Parker and Lester Young. The fact
remains that after all the lurid stories of her star-crossed, self-destructive
life, she did something no other woman has ever done in jazz. Today, if
you sing jazz and you are a woman, you sing some of Billie Holiday.

There's no other way to do it. No vocalist is without her influence.
All girl singers sing some of Billie, like all trumpet players play some of
Louis. She wrote the text.

The first time anyone was asked to describe her style, it was disc
jockey Ralph Cooper, then emcee at the Apollo Theatre in New York,
and he said, "It ain't the blues. I don't know what it is, but you got to
hear her."

That description hasn't been topped yet. It ain't the blues, but the
blues is in it. In some strange, arcane, witch-like way, Billie made blues
out of everything she sang.

But Billie's forte was the ballad, the pop tune. That she could take these frequently banal and generally trivial numbers and make them into something lasting, something artistic (most singers at best are artful) is a tribute to the way she was, for her time, the voice of Woman.

"I've been told that nobody sings the word 'hunger' like I do. Or the word 'love,'" Billie remarked in her autobiography, "Lady Sings the Blues" (a story made all the more tragic and poignant by the little-girl-turned-hip-kitty style in which it was told), and this may be true. But it is the way Billie pronounced another word that always symbolized, for me, the role in which she was, for better or for worse, cast in her life: the idealized sex symbol for an American generation just starting to recognize what jazz was all about, four letters and all.

You can hear her do it numerous times in this collection but nowhere does she achieve quite the promise, the assumption and the wild longing that she does in "Them There Eyes" when she lets out that deep-throated, magnificently sexual cry, "Ahhh, baby." For in Billie's world, which represents the introduction to the twentieth century's social upheaval if we look at it sociologically, "baby" had become the word for "lover" in the most intimate, perhaps even Freudian, sense. And Billie, born in the city and raised in town, was the symbol of a sexual reality that transcended all the celluloid make-believe of the glamour queens of Hollywood. She was real and she was alive and you could hear her and she spoke to you in that sulphur-and-molasses voice—the epitome of sex.

The story of her life, in all the grisly, tawdry Sunday supplement detail from illegitimate birth, through prostitution, jailhouse, junk, jailhouse again and the final deathbed scene—under arrest in a hospital room for narcotics, gasping out her final breaths, $750 in $50 bills strapped to her shrunken leg—has been told over and over and over. Please God, let her rest in peace at last; she was tortured enough in life in her own all-too-public hell.

Let us deal here with what will live on as long as there is anything left alive in this culture—her music—and forget for now the rest of it, which even carried over into graveyard quarrels as to who paid for her tombstone. Billie needs no tombstone, ever. These records—and her others—are a monument to her that no stone can ever equal. She is in this album, just as surely as in life, all of her, the good and the bad and the beautiful. It's here in her voice, in the songs and in the titles and the lyrics. You can't miss it.

I heard her say "baby" once, offstage and not in song. It was twelve years ago as these notes are being written, but I hear it yet. She had opened at a San Francisco nightclub and she was with her then man-ager, John Levy. She was wearing a brown turban, a full-length blue mink coat, green wool suit, brown crepe shirt with a Barrymore collar, pearl earrings and a Tiffany diamond and platinum watch. She had waited for Levy to come out of the club and had finally gotten into a car with a group of us. Then he arrived, slipped into the front seat, and she leaned forward and said, "Baaaaaaby, why did you leave me?" In that line was all the pathos of "My Man," "Billie's Blues" and the rest. Nobody could say a word for minutes and she didn't even know what she had done.

It's very possible Billie never knew what she did to people with her voice when she sang. Carmen McRae, in "Hear Me Talkin' to Ya," spoke vividly of Billie the singer. "I'll say this about her—she sings the way she is. That's really Lady when you listen to her on a record . . . singing is the only place she can express herself the way she'd like to be all the time. Only way she's happy is through a song . . . the only time she's at ease and at rest with herself is when she sings."

And Bobby Tucker, her long-time accompanist, gave us a terrifying hint of Billie the woman: "There's one thing about Lady you won't believe. She had the most terrible inferiority complex. She actually doesn't believe she can sing . . ."

Musically, Billie herself had the most illuminating things to say of her own style. First its origin in Bessie Smith and Louis Armstrong and then, "I don't think I'm singing. I feel like I'm playing a horn. I try to improvise like Les Young, like Louis Armstrong, or someone else I admire. What comes out is what I feel. I hate straight singing. I have to change a tune to my own way of doing it. That's all I know."

Listening to the performances on these albums, which is like living over again the best years of our lives for those of us who were lucky enough to have heard her then, the memories are so strong, one is struck by several things. First, how little, in terms of departure from the melody, Billie actually changes the tune. What she does, as Miles Davis was later to work out for himself, is to take a limited canvas and paint exquisitely upon it. She had no tricks, no vocal gymnastics. She may have hated straight singing, but her way was to sing it almost straight but with a special accent on articulation, phrasing and rhythm. Phrased as she phrased, the words mean something. Many lines in drama are banal on their own, but in context and in performance take on meaning. She did this with pop songs because they held meaning for her of a world she never made and never knew, except when she sang.

The samples here are overwhelming. The way she says "this year's crop just misses" on her very first record with Lester Young ("This Year's Kisses," Vol. 1, Side 2), for instance. They became not lyrics, but Billie's own expression.

The other thing is how, in retrospect, she really did sing as Lester Young played. Just listen to the way she comes in on "Them There Eyes." You hear it again and again as she starts a number, as she comes back in for the second chorus or the bridge and in the way she phrases multi-syllable words. It's no wonder that from the time she made her first record date with Pres, in January of 1937 ("This Year's Kisses" is from it), there is an entirely new feeling. Billie was home, musically, at last.

For me, at any rate, aside from all the intense and very personal memories evoked by all of these numbers, it was a delight of the highest order to hear the three tracks, previously unreleased, that are included here. They are air-checks of Billie Holiday singing with the Count Basie orchestra. For my money they rate not only as three of the very best Billie Holiday performances, but as three of the great jazz vocals of all time. I am particularly attracted, for numerous reasons, to "I Can't Get Started." Not only does Billie here, as in her other two sides with the Basie band, have a sound of pure, unadulterated joy in her voice, but she and Pres in the second chorus indulge in what can only be described as an unsurpassed duet. With Billie singing and Pres talking to her on his horn, this must be ranked as one of the most exquisite jazz moments preserved for us on recording, and we may thank John Hammond for it.

The sides with Basie and the ones from the studio dates around that time are the end of a period of Billie's sound, if not development. Afterwards, she had many things, but never again, or hardly ever, that joyous thrust to her voice.

So in a strange, twisted way, symbolic perhaps of her strange, twisted life, it was an anticlimax when Billie Holiday died.

She had been dying by inches for years. You could hear it in her voice—the ugly sound of death—all the way back to her early days at Cafe Society. It was, perversely, part of her charm, like that of Pres and Bird.

Drink, dope and dissipation were really only the superficial aspects of what was wrong with her. She suffered from an incurable disease— being born black in a white society wherein she could never be but partially accepted.

"You've got to have something to eat and a little love in your life before you can hold still for anybody's damn sermon," she wrote in her autobiography.

There was plenty to eat in the later years, though in her childhood as a classic juvenile delinquent she was hungry for more than food. But money never helped Billie, nor did men. She had plenty of both and she died alone and thin, her great body wasted by disease and deliberate starvation, with a police guard on the door.

She was ridden by devils all her life. In the beginning she was in control most of the time. Those were the days when she made the great records, the classic jazz vocals that comprise this collection.

But Billie was more than a singer. She was a social message, a jazz instrumentalist, a creator whose performances could never be duplicated. It's been tried by a whole generation of singers whose inspiration she was. None of them came any closer to it than sounding like Billie on a bad night.

There were plenty of bad nights, too. In the later years her voice and her sense of time would desert her. At nightclub performances, listeners who remembered her when she was not only the greatest singer jazz had produced but also one of the most beautiful and impressive women of her generation, choked up and cried to see and hear her so helplessly bad.

Billie Holiday, when she was in her prime, in the years covered by these performances, was simply the most magnetic and beautiful woman I have ever seen, as well as the most emotionally moving singer I have ever heard.

I remember when she opened at Cafe Society in December, 1938, for her first big nightclub break. She was simply shocking in her impact. Standing there with a spotlight on her great, sad, beautiful face, a white gardenia in her hair, she sang her songs and the singers were never the same thereafter.

She really was happy only when she sang, it seemed. The rest of the time she was a sort of living lyric to the song "Strange Fruit," hanging, not on a poplar tree, but on the limbs of life itself.

Just as Chaplin never won an Oscar, Billie Holiday never won a "Down Beat" poll while she was living, but for jazz and its fans her music is unequalled and as indispensable as Louis' and Duke's.

The fall before she died, I saw her sitting stiffly in the lobby of the San Carlos Hotel in Monterey, the morning after the festival finale. The jazz musicians tried to ignore her. Finally, in that hoarse whisper that could still (after 30 years of terrifying abuse) send shivers down your spine, she asked, "Where you boys goin'?" And when no one answered, she answered herself. "They got me openin' in Vegas tonight."

"They" always had Billie opening somewhere she didn't want to be. That's over now and all that's left are memories and the records and the poor, misguided singers trying to sound like her, God save them.

There's really too much and too little to say of someone like her. We have the memories and we have the records. As for myself, I feel like the young man in Colin MacInnes' novel, "Absolute Beginners," who says, "Lady Day has suffered so much in her life she carries it all for you." It was a long, long road from "Your Mother's Son-in-Law" to "Gloomy Sunday," but Billie traveled it for all of us. We owe her a great deal.

It is sad beyond words that she never knew how many people loved her.

[Liner notes, Columbia Records—C3L 40, 1966, Grammy
Award–nominated for Best Album Liner Notes]

The Greatness of Carmen McRae

As my close relatives and all three regular readers of this column know, on the subject of Miss Carmen McRae who is currently singing at Sugar Hill, I am outrageous.

Well, I am not really so outrageous. At least to myself. It may appear that way to others and I know that to at least ONE other singer, my reaction to Carmen McRae is considered gross critical maladjustment.

The trouble is that every time I hear Carmen McRae sing I am knocked out of my mind, even when it isn't as good a performance as she might wish, or as good as on other occasions.

And because of my great basic humanity and love for all of you, I want to share my joy.

Far from being critically maladjusted, it seems to me that it is not only the critic's job but his moral obligation to yell and scream to everyone when something sounds as good to him as Carmen McRae's singing sounds to me.

After all, would you have me leave the residents of this city in a state of cultural impoverishment due to their ignorance of the incredible beauty of Carmen McRae's vocal gifts?

She opened Monday night at Sugar Hill and it was a rough opening night, as most of them are. A drunk in a porkpie hat yakked all through every number she sang and stopped talking when she stopped singing, as is the way of drunks in nightclubs.

The telephone rang in the quiet moments of a tender song. (The telephone never rings during drum solos.) And then to cap it all, the microphone went dead. Simply went dead. For several numbers Carmen McRae just stood there vocally au naturel and sang.

Carmen McRae

It was a strain on her (it's physically hard to do this) and a strain on the audience, because when she whispers, Carmen McRae whispers. Then the microphone mysteriously returned to life and she was able to manipulate her own voice, and the emotions of the audience, like the master mesmerizer she is.

I heard two sets and they were lovely. She sang a lot of tunes I had never heard before from her, as well as several of the numbers she has made into minor masterpieces. One of the new ones, "How Did He Look?" is one of those tears-of-regret and mourning-for-lost-love emotional ballads that bring out the best in Miss McRae's personality.

She has the ability to depict the broken hearted lover, that cliché of prose, poetry and music, with frightening reality. When she asked the title question, "How did he look?" And then threw in as an aside the self excusing phrase, "not that I care," she was not a girl singing songs in a nightclub but a woman sick at heart from the sad lover's blues, grasping at vicarious straws.

Among the other numbers new to her repertoire were "Come Sunday" and "The Music That Makes Me Dance," which is a song Barbra Streisand sings in "Funny Girl" (Carmen McRae thinks Barbra S. is one of the greatest of singers, I should add in all honesty since I have been notorious for a different view).

"Come Sunday" is one of the melodies from Duke Ellington's "Black, Brown and Beige" suite which was first sung by Mahalia Jackson in an important performance on record a couple of years ago. Carmen McRae brings to it an entirely different sound, if not a different emotional approach, and just from one hearing I am convinced it will become one of her greatest numbers. She sings it magnificently.

I have never heard Carmen McRae without wondering why it is that she is not rich, starred in films and Broadway shows and taking her pick of the best jobs, from the Fairmont to the Waldorf-Astoria. She deserves it if talent ever got its full reward in our world.

[*San Francisco Chronicle*, May 14, 1964]

Guaraldi and Sete — A Happy Union

∎

For pure musical enjoyment, the two best concerts so far this year have been given by the Vince Guaraldi Trio and guitarist Bola Sete.

Saturday night, Guaraldi and Sete constructed again the magical aura that made their appearance earlier this year at the San Francisco Museum so memorable. The scene this time was the Berkeley Little Theater, a lovely hall adjacent to the huge Community Center. They appeared there in a benefit concert for the Berkeley High School Stage Band.

Guaraldi has been concentrating recently on taking as subjects for his improvisations current popular songs of high melodic content and structural adaptability.

For the first part of his program, Guaraldi, accompanied by bassist Fred Marshall and drummer Jerry Granelli, played a dozen numbers including "Hello Dolly," "Green Dolphin Street," "In Other Words," and "What Kind of Fool Am I." In each of them the fluidity with which Guaraldi improvises on the lyrical statements was the outstanding feature. He has the ability to control the dynamics of his playing so tightly that when he plays a run in the right hand, he can get a perfect glissando effect, almost as if he were using a slide instrument. This, combined with the strong rhythm foundation of everything he plays, helps give his music a rare combination of liquid beauty and strong pulsation. It is particularly evident in songs like "Green Dolphin Street" or his own haunting original "My Loneliness."

Bassist Marshall and drummer Granelli have worked with him long enough now so that the group moves, breathes and plays together as a unit. Given the excellent acoustics and the responsive audience of Saturday night, it really expands and glows.

After Guaraldi's opening set, guitarist Bola Sete came on for a solo program of his own compositions and excerpts from the classical literature. His selections included Brazilian folk music as well as orthodox musical sources. Bach, Villa-Lobos and traditional Brazilian melodies were all treated to the patient, lapidarian touch of the guitarist.

Bola Sete programs all of this with dramatic contrast, plays it with fire and flair and communicates a combination of deeply serious classicism and potentially explosive folk to the audience.

At the end of Saturday's program, he was joined by Marshall and Granelli for music from "Black Orpheus," and eventually by Guaraldi himself. This group—the Guaraldi Trio with guitarist Sete—is one of the most pleasing and effective combinations of recent years, with a solidly jazz feeling, bright contrasts and the effective projection of diverse personalities. It is indicative of the quality of their performance that one forgets about time. And it is indicative of something else about the Bay Area that this group is only playing weekends at the Trois Couleur.

Prior to the Guaraldi and Bola Saturday appearance, the Berkeley High School Stage Band, directed by Bob Lutt, went through a series of big-band arrangements with plenty of fire, considerable skill and great charm. The band boasts two good drummers in George Newcombe and Robbie Williamson, two good trumpet soloists in Allen Park and Peter Hansen, and an excellent trombonist, John Ritchie.

Paul Pipkin, the outstanding soloist of the band, not only plays tenor but also writes, composes and arranges. Two other good saxophonists were displayed—alto Steve Keller and tenor Ralph Kahn.

The BHS band was quite enjoyable and should be a strong entry next semester in the various local stage band contest competitions. Dr. Herb Wong, principal of Chabot school, was master of ceremonies for the evening and displayed precisely the same quality of articulateness that he does on his KJAZ show.

[*San Francisco Chronicle*, May 18, 1964]

John Handy, *Recorded Live at the Monterey Jazz Festival*

■

This album is the latest in a sequence of events which, for me at any rate, is a perfect illustration of what the poet Philip Whalen was talking about when he referred to those moments of sudden enlightenment which cause "distant galaxies of nerve ends, never before contemplated, to light up."

My experience with the John Handy group has been one long delight of just this kind, going back a few months to the very first time I heard them play at the Both/And, an experimental jazz club in the Divisadero Street section of San Francisco.

John Handy has long been known in San Francisco, if not in the rest of the country, as an exceptionally able composer of jazz, and as a strong and moving soloist on tenor and alto, both with his own groups and with Charles Mingus. But, with the brief exception of a remarkable unit known as the Freedom Band, none of his San Francisco groups had ever, really, gotten off the ground. They were good, but they were not consistently exciting and never took off to fly with a life of their own.

After playing with Charles Mingus at the Monterey Jazz Festival's historic session in 1964, he went to Vancouver, B.C., and met two Canadian musicians, bassist Don Thompson and drummer Terry Clarke. On his return he told everyone about them and how he hoped to bring them to San Francisco. Eventually, it worked out and eventually the group opened at the Both/And. I was not there on opening night; I didn't get there for a couple of weeks, and people kept telling me that I was missing something.

Finally, one night I decided to make a tour of the Divisadero Street section, which is becoming a new jazz area in San Francisco. I stopped at the Half Note, run by Herbert and Norma Warren, who used to operate Sugar Hill in North Beach. Thus, I eventually got to the Both/ And, in the company of Herbert, a rival nightclub owner, to hear John Handy. There was almost no one in the club, but the band was on stage and the Canadians were there, and so was Mike White, a violinist who had long had an underground reputation as an exciting soloist, and pianist Freddie Redd, once again in a period of San Francisco residence.

They started to play. I was stunned within moments. I simply couldn't believe it. The power and excitement that flowed from that band was overwhelming. I looked at Herbert Warren and he looked at me, and we shook our heads in disbelief. It was one of the great moments of a lifetime of listening to jazz.

So I wrote a column about it in the *San Francisco Chronicle*, a column filled with exuberance, hoping to reflect some of my own excitement at the band's performance.

Some weeks later, on the San Francisco educational television station, KQED, we did a Jazz Casual show (which one day I hope will play on the rest of the National Educational Television Network). We made a tape of that show, and I wrote a note to John Hammond at Columbia Records to tell him I was sending it. I don't know if this is ethical for a jazz critic, but I couldn't keep from screaming about this band.

Hammond expressed immediate and firm interest. Soon, we took Jimmy Lyons, general manager of the Monterey Jazz Festival, out to the Both/And. He, too, was knocked out by John Handy's group and signed them to appear at the 1965 Monterey Jazz Festival on the afternoon avant-garde program.

Monterey, before an arena packed with 7000 people sitting in the blazing sun, John Handy turned the band loose (guitarist Jerry Hahn had replaced Freddie Redd by then) and broke it up. They played two numbers—the performances in this album—and they were the hit of the festival. People gave Handy a standing ovation and talked about what they had heard for weeks. They are still talking about it. I get calls every week asking when "the Monterey performance" will be released.

These unexpected delights, these sudden enlightenments are what those of us who listen to jazz as a way of life live for.

John Handy, who was born in Texas, and Mike White are both alumni of McClymonds High School in Oakland, a spawning ground of much talent, and their schoolmates included basketball star Bill Russell and baseball's Frank Robinson.

"I first played with Mike in 1964 at events around here," John says "and we only recently got together in the group. I wrote 'Spanish Lady' a few months ago. I had kept 'hearing' something I wanted to do, and when I took the train to the date in Vancouver, I figured the twenty-four hour trip would be good for writing. But I waited until the last half hour! There's really only eight measures of it written out, the rest is improvised. There isn't any real 'Spanish Lady'; it's just a conglomeration of a lot of people. I was just groping for a name."

We started playing it right away in Vancouver at the Flat Five. Don Thompson was playing piano in that group, and he brought Terry in on drums. It was my first visit up there. It was quite a thing, meeting them. I didn't know anything about Vancouver at all. Neither Don Thompson nor Terry Clarke had worked much with groups. They had accompanied a lot of people and Thompson doubled on piano and bass.

"If Only We Knew" dates back to a composition class at San Francisco State, where John Handy was a student in 1956. "It was something for the class to play," he says.

Jerry Hahn, the guitarist, came to San Francisco from Wichita, Kansas. "I first heard him at Jack's, an old San Francisco nightspot on Sutter Street, in a jam session," John says. "Later, he worked with me in The Freedom Band. He's had all kinds of experience, in hotel and country and western bands. It shows the value of having a varied background. He can play anything—flamenco, Spanish guitar, blues. Anything."

Mike White, to my personal taste, is one of the most interesting musicians to record in some time. He plays an electronically amplified violin, and he plays it in the contemporary idiom; hearing it is an entirely new experience. And there are Hahn's solos and those of Handy himself which, although he always seems to feel he has not played his best, are consistently exciting.

I have heard the band on numerous occasions—in concerts and at clubs and elsewhere—and it never fails to get off the ground. The presence of those two Canadian troopers, Terry and Don, is one of the reasons. They work together magnificently as a rhythm section. Don is a virtuoso on bass and sometimes even sounds as if he is playing flamenco guitar in his solos! And Terry Clark has the kind of fire and drive that drummers lust for. It's an exciting group and one that will make jazz history.

Nothing new is happening in jazz, they say. Oh, really? Just listen to this.

[Liner notes, Columbia Records—CL 2462, 1966]

"Soul Sauce"—A Hummer's Hit

■

Cal Tjader, the vibraphonist and bandleader who is currently at El Matador, is the latest San Francisco jazz musician to taste the delights of having a hit single record.

Cal's Verve single, "Soul Sauce," is currently 94 in the Billboard Magazine top 100 best-selling discs, and the album of the same name from which it comes is 71 on both the Billboard and Cashbox charts of the top 100 best-selling albums. In addition, "Soul Sauce" has been listed for several weeks in the top ten of the rhythm and blues bestsellers.

"Soul Sauce" is a composition by trumpeter Dizzy Gillespie and Latin drummer Chano Pozo, well-known to jazz fans from the original Gillespie big-band recording on RCA Victor back in 1949. It was then called "Guachi Guaro" and was in the series of Gillespie-Pozo big-band numbers which Dizzy featured with his exciting big-band of that period.

Cal recorded it almost 10 years ago for Fantasy in his "Tjader Plays Mambo" album, and a single from that LP was released with the title "Wachi Waro" in the reasonable belief that disc jockeys wouldn't be able to pronounce "Guachi Guaro." Creed Taylor of Verve followed the same line of reasoning, only he re-named the tune "Soul Sauce," which seems to be okay by everyone. Disc jockeys can pronounce it, Cal has a hit and Gillespie has the pleasure (and financial rewards) of seeing one of his compositions catch on 17 years later.

Chano Pozo was the greatest of all the conga and bongo drum players in jazz, and he was a sensational performer with Gillespie's big band before his tragic death in the early 50s. "Chano hummed the tune to me," Dizzy says, "and I wrote it down and added a little and gave it to Gerald Wilson to do the arrangement. I don't know what the title means. I haven't the slightest idea," he added chuckling.

Cal heard the record when he was just starting out in jazz and also heard Dizzy's big band do it during their historic engagement at The Barbary Coast.

"We didn't think it would be a hit," he says. "We needed a strong Latin album and we put that in it and Creed Taylor, of Verve, wanted to put it out as a single so after we cut it and were gone out of town, he overdubbed Willie Bobo playing jawbone and singing harmony to the vocal. A kid down the block came up to me today and said 'I love your record of "Wa."' That's how it goes."

The number is the biggest hit Tjader has had to date. "It started selling in New York but now it's out all over. You know you've got a hit when the long-distance operators say are you the one who did 'Soul Sauce'?" Cal added.

The usual increase in pressure and activity is beginning to hit Tjader now. "We had a chance to play the Al Hirt show but we couldn't stay in New York long enough. We did do the Merv Griffin show, it will be shown here Wednesday," he says. On the Merv Griffin show, Cal, who has known Griffin since the second grade will be seen in a dancing role in addition to playing his hit. Merv Griffin enticed him into doing a soft shoe dance. "I haven't done anything like that for 20 years," says Cal, a former vaudeville hoofer.

[*San Francisco Chronicle*, June 14, 1965]

Mingus Mail Album a Huge Success

■

Charles Mingus, whose album, "Mingus at Monterey" was not only the best jazz album of last year but one of the best jazz albums ever issued, says he has been so successful with his sale of it via mail order that he is forming a company for this purpose.

"Mingus at Monterey" sells for $10, which is a lot of bread for any jazz LP. The album can only be obtained from Mingus at 128 E. 56th St., New York City. It is not available in stores. No free review copies were sent out (which may be why *Down Beat*, the magazine which purports to cover the jazz world, has yet to review it) and yet it has made money.

Mingus is setting up mail order facilities for this LP and for future recordings in association with musician Buddy Collette of Los Angeles, basketball star Wilt Chamberlain and other investors. The new corporation hopes to record at the Monterey Jazz Festival this year and Mingus hopes to be able to work out a deal to record his own group there, if he is invited to participate in the program.

Negotiations are also underway for European distribution of the records and Mingus is now on a coast-to-coast trip setting up the corporation with the musicians who will be participants.

Chief motivating factor for Mingus' leap into the record producing business was his experience with the Monterey album. "What would you do if you made more money in four months by mail order than you did in eight years with regular record companies?" Mingus says.

Miles Davis will not play the Newport Jazz Festival this year and possibly will not play the Monterey Jazz Festival either. Miles' leg is still in a cast from his recent, successful operation and the cast won't come off until mid-July, hence Newport is out.

Meanwhile, Davis is working on the music for two film scores and his group is filling in the time until he returns to work playing with other New York musicians including tenor Charles Lloyd.

Davis, who was originally announced for Monterey as one of the two features of the Sunday night show (the other being the Harry James big band), says he doesn't want to play it but would like to hear it! Meaning the weekend schedule of trumpet players spanning the history of jazz, from Louis Armstrong to Freddie Hubbard.

Despite Miles' reluctance, Jimmy Lyons, Monterey general manager, is still hopeful of convincing him that the Sunday night spot on the Monterey show is worth having.

Denzil DeCosta Best, surely one of the most ill-starred of all modern jazzmen, is dead. The drummer-trumpeter-composer died last week in New York after a lingering illness. He was 48.

Originally a trumpet player, Best was forced to give up playing wind instruments because of a lung ailment and became a drummer instead. He was active on the New York scene in the beginnings of modern jazz, composed some of the best of the early bop tunes such as "Move" and "DeeDee's Dance" and then joined the George Shearing Quintet with which he made a worldwide reputation. His ill luck pursued him there. An auto accident almost killed him and it took several years for him to recuperate.

After a short time with Errol Garner and Artie Shaw, Best remained in New York in recent years working intermittently. A bright, personable man, his death is a real loss to music.

[*San Francisco Chronicle*, June 16, 1965]

B. B. King, *Completely Well*

∎

Thumbnail They called B. B. King "King of the Blues" and even though titles may seem out of place in a democracy, B. B. King has earned his because he is simply the best blues singer of his generation.

If that is not enough, he is truly the man who, for all practical purposes, invented the electric guitar. You can't walk into a rock concert, sit in a nightclub, dance at Fillmore West or turn on any one of the hundreds of stations throughout the country playing rhythm & blues and rock 'n roll and not hear B. B. King.

It isn't that you will hear his records twenty four hours a day on the air, it's that he invented a style of guitar playing that is so influential there must be, literally, hundreds of other people playing his style every minute of the day.

B. B. King is to the blues guitar what Ernest Hemingway was to the novel and Miles Davis is to the trumpet. You simply can't escape them. He is the King.

Royalty has not always been known for its modesty but B. B. King is a modest man. When we did the National Educational Television program [*Jazz Casual*—Ed.] with him in 1968, all the staff at the studio were amazed at how little he would claim, and how he insisted he wasn't really able to play what he could hear and at how he worried about people praising him too much. It was an unusual and a beautiful thing to find a man so gifted who was so modest in what he felt about himself.

"I come from B. B. King, man," Mike Bloomfield said one night at a concert when a young guitar player asked him, and what holds for Bloomfield holds for nine tenths of the guitar players in the world, almost.

B. B. calls his style "the B. B. King twinging guitar style" and admits that it is an original contribution. "I think so," he says, "because I hear so many guys, guys since I've started playing, play that way and I don't remember ever hearing anybody before that!" Amen!

The people that B. B. listened to on guitar, he will tell you, as well as for their singing were first "My cousin Bukka White . . . then the people who influenced me the most were T-Bone Walker, Lowell Fulsom, Elmore James . . . Johnny Moore and the Three Blazers. They were the people that had that bluesy feeling that made me feel so good." But he listened to jazz players, too. "Maybe it was an intermingling of these that created the style that I play, because I was crazy about Charlie Christian . . . and one of my real favorites was Django Reinhardt and if you listen to my playing you'll hear a little bit of all of them."

And B. B. also listened to Jimmy Rushing with Count Basie and Al Hibbler with Duke Ellington and he put it all together and made it come out his own.

You'll hear it on this album. The same quality—and quality is the word to apply—that marks the difference between the original and the imitation, the real artist and the sham, B. B. King has it. When he touches the guitar, it is with the sounds that no one else can get, just as when he throws back his head and sings, his voice is unforgettably unique.

For years, B. B. King starred on the rhythm & blues circuit; the Regal Theater and the others where the blues artists could play, plus the endless round of what Lou Rawls has called "the chitlin' circuit."

The blues explosion of the past two years has brought him out into the mainstream of American music, for which we should all be grateful. "I thank God that today I can stick out my chest and say, 'Yeah! I'm a blues singer!'" B. B. says.

This album will show you, if you don't already know, just why B. B. King is King of the Blues and if you know him already, it will bring you more of what you love.

I dig it, all of it, but then I dig B. B. King because he has the power to take me out of myself and into his music whenever I hear him, and that's the mark of a true artist. As George Bernard Shaw once said, anybody can make a beginning, the thing to do is to do something that can't be bettered and nobody has bettered B. B. King in the blues since he first came up.

There is one track especially on this LP I want to point to and that's "Confessin' the Blues." Jay McShann, the Kansas City pianist and bandleader, wrote that song with his vocalist Walter Brown in the late Thirties and it was a big hit for them. So big was its impact that it was on the jukeboxes of all the joints in all the ghettos of America. And, as an historical note, Chuck Berry sang "Confessin' the Blues" when he made his first public appearance as a high school student in East St. Louis singing in an assembly and it was a hit then, too! And another historical note: on the Jay McShann–Walter Brown original disc of "Confessin' the Blues" the alto saxophonist was Charlie "Yardbird" Parker making his recording debut.

At the end of the TV show after B. B. had played and sung the blues and we had talked about what it all meant to him, I asked him what he wanted to do with his music and he said "Play the best I can, reach as many people as I can, in as many countries. In other words, I'd like the whole world to be able to hear B. B. King sing and play the blues."

It is coming to pass, I do believe.

[Liner notes, Bluesway Records—BLS 6037, 1969]

The Rewards in Mingus' Music

■

There are a handful of artists in every genre every single bit of whose work is not only of interest but rewarding.

Charles Mingus is such an artist in the world of contemporary music and he is playing these nights with his quintet at the Both/And, the Divisadero Street nightclub. Mingus's current group is composed of trumpeter Bill Hardman, tenor saxophonist Billy Robinson, alto saxophonist Charles McPherson and Mingus's perennial drummer Dannie Richmond.

Individually Mingus's players are strong, adequate soloists in the bebop or progressive jazz style of the early 50s. Hardman is distinctly influenced by the late Clifford Brown and McPherson's main influence is Charlie Parker. Robinson is not so easily bagged. He is not consistent (or wasn't when I heard him) but he can play and he did several solos that were both imaginative and rhythmically moving. Richmond is a humorous drummer. He plays most of the theme within the framework of the stylized 1950s jazz, letting the structure of the tune rather than the soloist's line determine what he does. His drum breaks are satirical and he is capable of great humor in his playing.

When I heard the group, Mingus did not take a single solo (he did at the U.C. Berkeley concert; a beautiful "Sophisticated Lady") but chose to hold the group together with his incredibly dexterous playing. He and Richmond worked, as is natural seeing how long they have played together, as one.

In the two long Mingus compositions I heard, however, the whole group moved from the bebop style out into the overwhelming emotional impact and musical modernity that marks Mingus's work.

He writes orchestral music. Whenever he plays his music with a small group, the feeling and concept of the orchestra is there and frequently it is so strongly implied by what is played that one almost hears it. Ellington is the only other one, it seems to me, that does this.

Why Mingus is restricting himself so much at the moment is an enigma. I was struck by the contrast between his compositions and the free blowing session nature of the bebop material that made up the other numbers the group played. Mingus intentionally or unintentionally offers us not only a refresher course in bop but a dramatic demonstration of how much of it, no matter what fun it is to play it and listen to it, is dated, whereas his own music, like that of all the major artists, is outside the boundaries set by time. He has created a musical language for his own compositions that exists on its own terms altogether.

At the Both/And, before the set began and in the intermission, the house sound system played several free form modern jazz albums. The debt these people owe to Mingus is quite apparent; just as his music is inextricably entwined with the music of Duke Ellington, so is theirs with Mingus.

Anyway, he will be there this weekend and all next week. He is an exceptional player and an unusual and influential composer. Go hear him.

[*San Francisco Chronicle*, October 10, 1969]

Miles Davis, *Bitches Brew*

■

T here is so much to say about this music. i don't mean so much to explain about it because that's stupid, the music speaks for itself. what i mean is that so much flashes through my mind when i hear the tapes of this album that if i could i would write a novel about it full of life and scenes and people and blood and sweat and love.

and sometimes i think maybe what we need is to tell people that this is here because somehow in this plasticized world they have the automatic reflex that if something is labeled one way then that is all there is in it and we are always finding out to our surprise that there is more to blake or more to ginsberg or more to 'trane or, more to stravinsky than whatever it was we thought was there in the first place.

so be it with the music we have called jazz and which i never knew what it was because it was so many different things to so many different people each apparently contradicting the other and one day i flashed that it was music. that's all, and when it was great music it was great art and it didn't have anything at all to do with labels and who says mozart is by definition better than sonny rollins and to whom.

so lenny bruce said there is only what is and that's a pretty good basis for a start. this music is. this music is new. this music is new music and it hits me like an electric shock and the word "electric" is interesting because the music is to some degree electric music either by virtue of what you can do with tapes and by the process by which it is preserved on tape or by the use of electricity in the actual making of the sounds themselves.

electric music is the music of this culture and in the breaking away (not the breaking down) from previously assumed form, a new kind of music is emerging. the whole society is like that. the old forms are inadequate. not the old eternal verities but the old structures. and new music isn't new in that sense either, it is still creation which is life itself and it is only done in a new way, with new materials.

so we have to reach out to the new world with new ideas and new forms and in music this has meant leaving the traditional forms of bars and scales, keys and chords and playing something else altogether which maybe you can't identify and classify yet but which you recognize when you hear it and which when it makes it, really makes it, it is the true artistic turn on.

sometimes, it comes by accident. serendipity. with the ones who are truly valuable, the real artists, it comes because that is what they are here to do even if they can say as miles says of this music i don't know what it is, what is it? they make this music like they make those poems and those pictures and the rest because if they do not they cannot sleep nor rest nor, really, live at all. this is how they live, the true ones, by making the art which is creation.

sometimes we are lucky enough to have one of these people like miles, like dylan, like duke, like lenny here in the same world at the same time we are and we can live this thing and feel it and love it and be moved by it and it is a wonderful and rare experience and we should be grateful for it.

i started to ask teo how the horn echo was made and then i thought how silly what difference does it make? and it doesn't make any difference what kind of brush picasso uses and if the art makes it we don't need to know and if the art doesn't make it knowing is the most useless thing in life.

look. miles changed the world. more than once. that's true, you know. out of the cool was first then when it all went wrong miles called all the children home with walkin'. he just got up there and blew it and put it on an LP and all over the world they stopped in their tracks when they heard it. they stopped what they were doing and they listened and it was never the same after that. just never the same.

it will never be the same again now, after in a silent way and after BITCHES BREW. listen to this. how can it ever be the same? i don't mean you can't listen to ben. how silly. we can always listen to ben play funny valentine, until the end of the world it will be beautiful and how can anything be more beautiful than hodges playing passion flower? he never made a mistake in 40 years. it's not more beautiful; just different. a new beauty. a different beauty. the other beauty is still beauty. this is new and right now it has the edge of newness and that snapping fire you sense when you go out there from the spaceship where nobody has ever been before.

what a thing to do! what a great thing to do. what an honest thing to do there in the studio to take what you know to be true, to hear it, use it and put it in the right place. when they are concerned only with the art that's when it really makes it. miles hears and what he hears he paints with. when he sees he hears, eyes are just an aid to hearing if you think of it that way. it's all in there, the beauty, the terror and the love, the sheer humanity of life in this incredible electric world which is so full of distortion that it can be beautiful and frightening in the same instant.

listen to this. this music will change the world like the cool and walkin' did and now that communication is faster and more complete it may change it more deeply and more quickly. what is so incredible about what miles does is whoever comes after him, whenever, wherever, they have to take him into consideration. they have to pass him to get in front. he laid it out there and you can't avoid it. it's not just the horn. it's a concept. it's a life support system for a whole world. and it's complete in itself like all the treasures have always been.

music is the greatest of the arts for me because it cuts through everything, needs no aids. it is. it simply is. and in contemporary music miles defines the terms. that's all. it's his turf.

[Liner notes, Columbia Records, 1970, Grammy Award winner for Best Album

The Sunlight and Beauty of Johnny Hodges

■

When the ambulance arrived at Harlem Hospital the evening of May 11, Johnny Hodges was dead. He'd been stricken in the dentist's office and like the tough, independent man he was, he hadn't said a thing, but had gone out to the head. That's where they found him.

Most of you have never heard of Johnny Hodges—his full name was John Cornelius Hodges and the musicians and his old friends called him "Rabbit." He played the alto saxophone for Duke Ellington's orchestra and most of the time since 1928 when he joined Duke, he sat there in the reed section.

He played with love and with beauty and if ever a man made an instrument sing and talk, Johnny Hodges did. He played so well and with such an individual sound and concept, that for the purposes of jazz, he really invented the alto. He really did. Even after you pass the horn through Charlie Parker and then Phil Woods to come out with the Fred Lipsius solo on the Blood, Sweat & Tears album, there is still in it some of the sunlight and beauty of Johnny Hodges.

He was a master musician—one of the most incredibly prolific improvisers that has ever existed and his strong and personal style on the alto influenced generations of musicians and set the stage for others to develop on their own.

He believed in music—as many of his generation did—not only as a way of life but as a mystic force for good. He played for people and he would help people and the last time I saw him he was posing with some 12 or 14-year-old youngster who had taken up the alto and Hodges was giving him pointers on its use.

Duke Ellington wrote for Johnny Hodges to play. So did Billy Strayhorn and the magnificent, warm, flowing tones of Hodges' solos were
an outstanding characteristic of the Ellington orchestra.

Hodges began as a drummer. Sidney Bechet, the master of the soprano saxophone, had him briefly on that instrument but there was
really no room while Bechet was there (no one did anything with the
soprano until 40 years later when John Coltrane took it up) and Hodges
switched to alto.

In 1951, after 22 years with Ellington, Hodges split and formed his
own small group which he led for four years and with which he recorded his instrumental R&B hit, "Castle Rock." Then he went back
to the Duke and had been there, looking like the chieftain of some
ancient tribe, ever since.

Hodges recorded innumerable times with Ellington, for his own
groups and with other people. He never played a wrong note. Extravagant as that might seem I mean it and it's true. Hodges could improvise endlessly and perfectly. He had a unique and mysterious ability
to conceive of phrases to play which not only fitted together into perfectly constructed architectural lines but which, when you heard them,
seemed so logical they were inevitable. He played the blues like he
had invented it. Like B. B. King plays it. As though it was a personal
possession.

He would swing a room full of lead balloons, he was so powerful.
Chorus after chorus on the blues would flow out and fill whatever hall
he was in, each phrase adding to the next to make a longer, perfect
structure and each structure building on the others to create waves and
waves of emotion that flowed with the pulse of life itself.

Musicians always listened when Hodges played. Even the musicians
in the band who had heard him for 40 years. He never played a wrong
note and he never had a bad idea. Ellington featured Hodges a great
deal, it was like having a Heifetz in the string section, and one of the
numbers he played a lot was "Things Ain't What They Used To Be."
Years ago some salty-minded musician had said the line that fitted the
opening phrases of that number and from then on it was always in my
head, incongruity of context notwithstanding. "All the boys in the band
eat pussy" the words would come as the music sounded out and Hodges

played. And no matter how many times he played it, he made it new and fresh each time. That is magic. Truly.

When Hodges played the soft, dreamy songs with what Ellington called his "slurpy" tone, it was disgraceful what it could do to you. His specialty were songs like "Warm Valley" and "Passion Flower" and you didn't have to have too vivid an imagination. All you had to do was remember that the Ellington music is basically about women.

Back in the 30s, Hodges did a little swinging blues instrumental which he titled "The Jeep Is Jumpin'" and from that song they named the Jeep. No kidding.

Hodges on stage was beautiful. Not only did he look like a prince, but he had the most incredibly bored facial expressions. He could look out under his eyebrows with the pain of infinite patience at some nut in the hall. When he got up to play it was an exercise in time: Hodges never rushed. He was as deliberate as an ocean swell. He would get up, walk out from his chair and get to the microphone in time to adjust it and start to play. Not an extra second. But, my God, how he could play! Rocking those blues out line by line with the horn singing to you and the ends of the phrases giving him time to take it out of his mouth and run his tongue across his lips, put it back and sing out another line.

"All the boysintheband eat puss-eeeeeeeeeeeeey!"

All my life, since I got the measles in high school and discovered the Ellington band on the radio from Chicago, I have had the sound of Johnny Hodges in my ears. I got goose pimples (as Dizzy Gillespie said) when I first saw him with the Ellington band. I will never forget it. There they actually were! They were really and truly alive and I was going to hear them do this wonderful thing right there in front of me! I shit.

One night I heard the band when Wellman Braud, who hadn't played with them for 15 years, came in with Barbara Dane and sat in. Braud was the original bassist with Ellington and he took them back to tunes Duke had forgotten. But not Hodges. Braud would play a bit of the bass and then Hodges would stick the alto in his mouth and play the line for Duke and they'd be off. He could smile when he played. I saw him do it one night at Monterey when Jimmy Rushing (the blues singer who did that line "don't the moon look lonesome shining through the trees"

40 years ago) came on stage. Hodges turned to him, still blowing, and smiled.

In the intermissions he used to walk around, stocky, rolling, like a banker. Dignified and almost somber. Beautiful deadpan sense of humor.

In the educational TV film of Ellington's Sacred Concert, there is a short bit when Hodges steps up to take his solo in the beautiful "Come Sunday" portion. He stands there in the area in front of the altar of Grace Cathedral and lets his eyes roll up . . . up . . . to the top of the Cathedral while he plays. Wow!

Like I said, I have had the sound of Johnny Hodges in my ears all my life. And I can tell you that things ain't what they used to be now that he is gone and they never will be again.

Johnny Hodges was a real musician and a real man. I was always proud when he recognized my face.

[*Rolling Stone*, June 11, 1970]

God Bless Louis Armstrong

■

When James Baldwin wrote his classic *The Fire Next Time*, an editor of a leading daily paper noted for its liberal, sometimes even mildly radical but always civil libertarian viewpoint, remarked, "If they felt this way, why didn't they ever tell us?"

Daniel Louis Armstrong, a trumpet player and international figure for decades, "told" *them* once in plain English how he felt. Though the music he played for over 50 years has told and retold his feeling and his story to the world.

You have seen him periodically on Ed Sullivan or during the past year on the TV talk shows, clowning with Dick Cavett late at night and playing a few notes or singing while he wiped the sweat away with a gleaming white handkerchief.

He would sit there, when he wasn't singing or playing, and tell stories of the old days in New Orleans, of street marches and funerals, of tail-gate trombones and Buddy Bolden, of Mississippi River steamships with bands playing all night long and of the time in Chicago when he showed up carrying his trumpet in a paper bag, a 21-year-old green youth from New Orleans making his debut in the big city.

And Louis' appearances on those shows, just as his thousands of concerts and nightclub performances and his hundreds of records over the years, reaffirmed the insecurities of WASP America because Louis was safe. Louis was like a kind of musical Rock of Gibraltar, always there, always smiling, singing, playing and never rocking the boat.

So the first time Louis ever rocked the boat he really raised hell.

Gov. Orville Faubus (whom Charles Mingus immortalized in "Fables of Faubus") had just fought integration to a standstill in Arkansas.

President Eisenhower, rather than take the step the world longed for and lead a little child by the hand up the steps to one of Little Rock's schools to inspire humanity, instead deciding to do nothing at all and in such a situation, doing nothing was tantamount to encouraging the racists. Louis, on one of his interminable road tours of the US (he worked without respite playing night after night on the road all over the world right up until his final illness which came upon him last year), blew his stack.

It was September 18, 1957, and Louis was in that cultural center of the Great Plains, Grand Forks, North Dakota, for a concert. "The way they are treating my people in the South," he told a reporter for the Grand Forks Herald, "The government can go to hell!" Pres. Eisenhower, Louis said (unknowingly echoing the sentiments of many others), "has no guts."

And then Louis promptly canceled a tour of the Soviet Union which had been set up by the US State Department, refusing to go on the road for a government led by such a president. Louis, a veteran performer on the European concert circuit, plaintively said, "The people over there asked me what's wrong with my country. What am I supposed to say? I have had a beautiful life in music, but I feel the situation the same as any other Negro. My parents and family suffered through all of that old South and things are new now."

The White House, naturally, refused to comment. Louis' road manager, an ancient white named Pierre Tallerie, told all the media Louis had been "led" into saying those things and didn't mean them, but Louis told everybody yes he did so mean them, Tallerie was prejudiced, and then added "What I've said is me!"

It caused quite a ruckus. Jim Bishop, a Hearst Newspapers columnist, attacked him viciously for an ingrate and the University of Alabama canceled a concert despite a petition by students to let the show go on.

Louis, however, like the Mississippi, just kept rolling along, making those incredible one-nighter jumps from Tokyo to Toledo, from London to Los Angeles. And now and then in the years following, he opened his great mouth and growled some nitty-gritty truths about the country in which he was born. To the Associated Press in Copenhagen during the 1965 Selma, Alabama, march, Louis burst out again. He was sick to his stomach, he said, after watching the TV news coverage of the event. "They would beat Jesus if he was black and marched," he told an interviewer.

But that was about the end of it. Louis never again opened his mouth publicly to discuss anything but music, food, the old days in New Orleans and his panaceas for health.

Well, almost.

Some years ago I ran across a short interview Louis did with Max Jones in England. Louis' band, which for years has been an integrated unit, had run into trouble in Louisiana. The state had a law against "mixed race" public performances and Louis was sore. Louis is a Louisianan, born in New Orleans in 1900, and he said, "I don't care if I ever see the city again. Honestly they treat me better all over the world than they do in my hometown. Ain't it stupid? Jazz was born there and I remember when it wasn't no crime for cats of *any* color to get together and blow. I ain't going back to New Orleans and let them white folks be whipping me on my head!"

Something about the juxtaposition of Louis and London and New Orleans clicked in my mind and I started rooting around in all my files and books until I found what I was looking for.

A Belgian writer and jazz critic named Robert Goffin wrote the first book about Louis Armstrong, based on interviews and his own personal experiences living with Armstrong on tour in Europe and for a while in the US.

In it, he told about Louis' return to his home city of New Orleans in 1931. Hundreds of people met him at the train. Members of his family, musicians he had grown up with, all paid him tribute in a parade down Canal Street with a banner stretched across the street—WELCOME TO LOUIS ARMSTRONG—THE KING OF PERDIDO. It was an orgy of nostalgia because, of all the musicians bred in that musical city, Louis was the one who had really made it in the outside world and they were welcoming him home. His band was to play a week's engagement at the Suburban Gardens and a crowd of almost 10,000 blacks had gathered outside the club, across the parking lot behind the fence, hoping to hear a note of his music when he played.

"It was a white man's place," Louis had said. "No Negro band had ever played there before. Opening night came and the place was packed. The folks knew I had been up North, and been a big hit there and had even been out to Hollywood."

All of New Orleans high society was there. The Suburban Gardens had its own radio program. They had a mic in front of the bandstand, which used to broadcast only for white bands. There was a lot of excitement in the air. 50,000 colored people were on the levees, close to radios.

At the last minute the southern radio announcer said, "I can't announce that nigger man." My manager rushed over to me with a worried look. "The announcer refuses to announce you." I turned to the boys on the bandstand and said, "Give me a chord." I got an earsplitting chord and announced the show myself. It was the first time a Negro *spoke* on the radio down there.

Within a year of that day, Louis Armstrong was playing to standing room only at the Palladium in London, the talk of Europe, sought after by royalty, idolized by musicians, given a golden horn by members of the London Philharmonic. And after England and the continent in 1932, back to the USA. Let Louis tell it again:

We used to tour the cells in a big Packard. Lots of times we wouldn't get a place to sleep. So we cross the tracks, pull over to the side of the road and spend the night there. We couldn't get into hotels. Our money wasn't even good. We play nightclubs and spots which didn't even have a little boy's room for Negroes. We have to go outside, often in the freezing cold and in the dark.

When we'd get hungry, my manager, Joe Glaser, who's also my friend, Jewish and white, would buy food along the way in paper bags and bring it to us boys in the bus who wouldn't be served. Sometimes even this didn't work. So most of the time while touring the South, we used to stock up in a grocery store. We'd come out with a loaf of bread, a can of sardines, big hunks of bologna, cheese and we'd eat in the car. Sometimes we'd go to the back doors of restaurants where there were Negro chefs. They'd give you what you wanted. Many are the times I've eaten off those big wooden chopping blocks.

Louis Armstrong saw his face on the cover of both *Time* and *Life*. He was the first jazz musician *Time* did a cover story on (February 2, 1949), and when *Life* did its cover story (April 15, 1966, the only cover *Life* has ever done on a jazzman) they ran a huge foldout picture of Louis, eyes popping, blowing his horn right out at you from a cover that carried the headline "Vietnam—Week of Wild Uncertainty" right over "The Louis Armstrong Story—As Only He Can Tell It."

Edward R. Murrow did a full hour CBS-TV program on him which was then expanded into a film called *Satchmo the Great*, released in 1957. Four one hour interviews with him were broadcast on National Educational Television in the early 60s in addition to innumerable other network shows (including one in the R.J.G. series, *Jazz Casual*, in 1962). Magazines all over the world would've done in-depth interviews and articles with and about him. His second autobiographical book, *Satchmo*, was issued in 1954 and parts of it were printed in several national magazines including *Holiday* ("Stoned In Rome," Louis once scrawled on a postcard of the Coliseum). And he appeared on so many TV variety shows that it is impossible now to tabulate them all.

There is probably only a handful of concert halls in the Western world where he had not appeared and the *New York Times* once ran a front-page story on the hysteria at the Zürich airport when Louis arrived. When he played in the Berlin Sportspalaast, fans slipped across the border from East Germany to hear him and he came close to causing a revolution by his appearance in Yugoslavia and other Iron Curtain countries.

After his appearance in East Berlin, reporters asked him how he felt about re-unification of Germany. "Unify Germany? Why man, we've already unified it. We came through Germany blowing this old happy music and if them Germans ain't unified this ain't old Satchmo talking to ya!" Louis then said he'd like to warm up the Cold War by going to Russia. "They ain't so cold but what we couldn't bruise them with the happy music."

Medals and awards from all over the world graced the walls in his

Corona, Long Island home but his native country honored him only with money.

In the late Fifties, the *Vancouver Sun* noted that Congress had, on occasion, honored civilians with special Congressional Medals and suggested, diplomatically, that Louis Armstrong be given such an award. Congress gave one to George M. Cohan for writing "Over There" during World War I. President Kennedy instituted a program of such awards and although an atomic scientist made the first list, Louis did not. After John Kennedy's murder, a campaign was mounted by several writers and elected officials, including myself and Sen. Javits, to get a special award for Louis, or at least to have him included on the presidential list.

We wrote letters to congressmen and officials. I even got from the US Information Agency the list of people on the President's Commission to make the awards and wrote individually to them.

The response was polite but noncommittal. Daniel Moynihan wrote an ominous note saying sometime when he was in San Francisco he would tell me all about what had happened, but he never did, and only recently, from a source that begs anonymity, did I learn that Lyndon Johnson, emulating that now anonymous New Orleans radio announcer, just couldn't bring himself to approve the award. And apparently, rather than give one to Louis, the whole award system was dropped and there has not been, as far as I know, any other such honors for anyone since.

Louis made, literally, thousands of records. He had tapes of them all, having transferred them from the original discs long ago. "I got it all down on tape," he told me once. "My records, Bessie, Joe Oliver, my concerts. They're all lined up against the wall. I look forward to going through them and listening to them. That's my hobby. It's all there—my side of the story and it will keep. Think of what it would be to have them transcribed and arranged for a symphony, even. Me blowing them with a symphony orchestra!"

Although his recorded output was probably greater than anyone else's, and certainly greater than any jazz player, he had few hits in his 50 years in disc, though dozens of people have themselves made hits out of songs Louis first made famous. A perfect example is Bobby

Darin, whose "Mack the Knife," as close a duplicate of the Armstrong version as Bobby's gift for mimicry could make it, sold infinitely more than Louis'. Another is "Fats" Domino's "Blueberry Hill," cut long after Louis' original version. Louis' only big top 40 hit was "Hello Dolly," which in 1965 was the first disc by an American artist to break the Beatles' monopoly of the top rung of the Hit Parade ladder.

Louis' version of "Mack the Knife," incidentally, was an early victim of radio censorship. Its sales, which were thus inhibited, were still substantial and the only time I know of when a single disc became any kind of a hit at all without extensive airplay.

Louis' version was largely barred from radio, both in the US and in England, because of the so-called bloody lyrics. But the disc has endured and Louis' version became a standard and, while he was still performing, an integral part of his program.

It is a fascinating song for Louis to have chosen. George Avakian, then a producer at Columbia Records, had heard it in the off-Broadway production of the Three Penny Opera and had jazz trombonist Turk Murphy, long a Louis Armstrong admirer, make an arrangement of it for Armstrong.

The song, you may recall, was a litany of corruption, a musical account of a pimp called Mac "The Knife" McHeath who stabbed a man to death, robbed him and spent the money on whores. It was written by Kurt Weill and Bertolt Brecht out of the miasma of vice, decadence, corruption and despair that marked the underworld of Berlin in the early Twenties. Armstrong sang it with the kind of conviction that made it seem it was written for him. And in a sense it was, because "Mack the Knife" is about all the people Louis Armstrong grew up with, his boyhood was a black version of Brecht's song. And his natural affinity for the lyric tells us a great deal about Louis and provides a glimpse behind the mask.

And the mask was a lifetime cover for the real Louis. Generally, what the world saw was Louis on the Dick Cavett show, Louis on Ed Sullivan singing "Hello Dolly" or laughing and showing his teeth and slapping somebody's hand. Sure, he was a great trumpet player and one of the greatest of all jazz musicians. And undoubtedly he was a show business personality of the highest level. His fame was worldwide. A couple of years ago an American composer walking through Moscow Airport heard Louis' voice on a record over the loudspeaker.

The world knew him well in his public personality. But Louis was a lot more than that. Before he was a trumpet player he was a juvenile delinquent with a police record.

He was arrested twice in New Orleans when he was a teenager and eventually was sentenced to a year in a place called Jones Orphanage, a kind of detention home for black youths. Louis Armstrong came from the ghetto of New Orleans. In his autobiography he tells of his early life with the same kind of frankness Charles Evers displayed when he recently announced his candidacy for the Governorship of Mississippi and told of his career as a bootlegger, gambler and pimp. Like Evers, Louis offered no excuses. He told it like it was.

After his father disappeared, Louis wrote, "my mother went to a place at Liberty and Perdido streets in a neighborhood filled with cheap prostitutes who did not make as much money for their time as did the whores in Storyville. Whether my mother did any hustling or not I cannot say." She would, however, Louis recalled, be gone for days and his childhood was filled with a succession of "stepfathers." "I remember at least six," he wrote.

> When I was about four or five—still wearing dresses—I lived with my mother in a place called Brick Row—a lot of cement, rented rooms. . . . And right in the middle of that on Perdido Street was the Funky Butt Hall. Old, beat up, big cracks in the wall. On Saturday night mama couldn't find us 'cause we wanted to hear that music. Before the dance the band would play out front for about a half hour and us little kids would all do little dances.
>
> Then we'd look through the cracks in the wall of Funky Butt. It wasn't no *classified* place, and to a tune like 'The Bucket's Got a Hold Of It [Hank Williams' version of the song, recorded in the fifties, carries Hank's name as composer!], some of them chicks would get way down, shake everything, slapping themselves on the cheek of their behind. . . .

As a teenager, "the boys I ran with had prostitutes workin' for them. They did not get much money from their gals, but they got a great deal of notoriety. I wanted to be in the swim, so I cut in on a chick. She was not much to look at but she made good money, or what in those days I thought was big money. I was a green inexperienced kid as far as women were concerned, particularly when one of them was walkin' the streets for me. . . ."

Louis' career as a pimp lasted a short time until the girl stabbed him in the shoulder. But he worked as an errand boy and go-fer in and around the brothels of that classic brothelized city and played in them, too. Eventually he married a whore whom he met in a brothel called The Brick House. He tells of this, too, in his autobiography. She named her price and he accepted and later married her.

> Everybody wanted to know was mama satisfied that her son's marrying a prostitute 21 years old. She say, "I can't live his life, he's my boy and if that's what he wants to do, that's that."

So that's why, when Louis sang of Mack the Knife, of Louis Miller and Sukey Tawdry and Jenny Diver he sounded like it was real because it *was* real, Louis' teenage world was filled with true life characters called Dirty Dog, Steel Arm Johnny, Mary Jack the Bear (a tough whore who fought like a bear), One-Eye Bud, Cocaine Buddy and Egg Head Papa. Threepenny Opera as true story, in fact.

And when Louis moved out and up to Chicago, he stayed mostly in the ghetto—Chicago's Southside with the real-life mobster prototypes of The Untouchables enforcing contracts with guns.

But New Orleans, when Louis was coming up, was unique. "There was over 100 bands then," Louis says. "Most of them six pieces, and most of them working. Now, on Sundays, the band would be out on the wagons, doin' the advertisin'. See, in those days, there were long wagons, pulled by maybe one horse or two mules. They hauled furniture weekdays."

On Sundays, a dance hall owner would hire a wagon for his band. And the wagon would go around the streets. Bass fiddle player and the trombone man sit on the tailgate, so they won't bump the others. Rest of the boys—drums, guitar, trumpet, and so forth sit in the wagon.

So, on Sundays, the musicians who wanted to work, not lay around and drink, went "on the wagon" and that's maybe where that saying come from.

You see, they always had the big dances on Monday nights, and you did the advertisin' the day before, Sunday.

For instance, one gentleman is giving a dance at Economy Hall tomorrow, and another gentleman is giving a dance at the Funky Butt Hall. The hall where—well, everybody, they named this kind of dancing they did there, Funkybuttin', and the hall was famous by that name.

Anyhow, these two gentlemen each are giving a dance and they want, each wants to draw a big crowd. So they send out their wagons, paradin' and advertisin'.

Now finally these two wagons meet at a corner. Their wheels are chained together. Then the two bands blow it out. And the one that gets the big ovation from the crowd, that's the one gets most all the people Monday.

Musicians used to help each other in those days. I mean, the older ones would help the younger ones. Now, I was just a kid, 16, but Joe [King] Oliver, was a powerful man. The *top* trumpet. I could play a whole lot of horn in my little way, but Joe was *The King!*

But Joe told me, "Now, if you ever get on the corner with a wagon, and *my* wagon comes up, you stand up, so I can see you. That'll be our signal, you know. I'll just play ordinary and give you the break."

But one Sunday, I didn't stand up and oh, man, he like to blow me out of the business.

It was good money according to the times. At the better places, like the Economy Hall, we'd get $2.50 a night. Easter Sunday was our big day. We'd make $3 at the Easter Sunday picnic, and then we'd play that night for $2.50.

Remember, that was Economy Hall, a big place. Now, all of

them great musicians down there in the Red Light District, which they called Storyville, they only got a dollar a night. Joe Oliver got $1.50 and that was top money for the leader.

Thing is, in 1915 I got a dollar a night at Henry Metrango's honky-tonk and I could make a living and still have enough money to buy a suit of clothes.

I was very young when I first heard Joe Oliver. He was in the Onward Band, a brass band they had down there in New Orleans —a good brass band. About 12 pieces: with three trombones and three cornets. Joe was playing cornet at the time. Two of them would play lead; there was Joe and Manny Perez. I used to play second line behind them. When Joe would get through playing, I'd carry his horn. I guess I was about 14. Joe gave me cornet lessons, and when I was a kid, I ran errands for his wife.

Joe used to come by Liberty and Perdido. I used to play in the honky-tonk and he used to come from down in Storyville though and come up there where I played, as he got off at 12 o'clock at night and seein' they threw the key away where I worked, he'd come up there and sit down and listen to me play and then he'd blow a few for me, y'know and try to show me the right things. At that time I didn't have no idea he would send for me to come to Chicago. I was playin' in the Tuxedo Brass Band with Kid Ory and I just had left the excursion boats and I was playin' with the Tuxedo Brass Band, and that's when King Oliver sent for me to play the second trumpet with him at the Lincoln Gardens. Was I surprised? I was happy, couldn't nobody get me out of New Orleans but him! I wouldn't take that chance.

I hadn't heard his band till I got to Chicago. When I heard it at the door, I said, "I ain't good enough for *this* band, I think I'll go back . . ." That was one of my life's biggest moments. It was the same setup as New Orleans but, see, we didn't have no pianos in New Orleans, we had git-tars and Lil [Armstrong, his second wife] was on the piano here, see what I mean?

And they was wailin'! I fit right in there, sitting with Joe, because I admired him so anyway, y'know. I just went to work. No rehearsal. I knew all the guys and I just sit in there and went to work the next night. I played second trumpet to everything he played. Second cornet at that time, 'cause we both was usin' cornets.

"Snake Rag" was one of the ones he just made up for the record. Gennett Records. When he started making records he started being a writer, ha ha ha. We'd rehearse it on the job and when we got to the studio, all we had to do was cut it up and time it. Was no trouble at all to make them records, we'd just make one after the other. They wasn't as particular then as they was today. No drums at all at that time. They was scared it would throw the needle off.

Louis was talking on National Educational Television where I had been playing him some of his first records. I had always wanted to ask him how he and Joe Oliver were able to improvise the fabulous two- and four-bar breaks they played simultaneously. It has always been a feat of astonishing virtuosity.

Louis smiled and told me, interspersed with sly chuckles and the demonstrations of Joe Oliver's fingers on an imaginary horn.

I put notes to his lead, whatever he made . . . We didn't write it, he'd tell me while the band was playin' what he going to play on top, wa wa wa wa and I'd pick out my notes and that's why all the musicians used to come around to hear us do that, y'know. They thought that was a secret we had, heh, heh, heh! Bix and Louis Pancio and Paul Whiteman and all the boys used to come around, y'know, and they thought that was sumpin'! Whatever he was gonna do, he let me know about four, five bars ahead while the band was jumpin,' heh, heh, heh.

Playing with King Oliver was easy, Louis said, and so was making all those incredible records accompanying the classic blues singers of the Twenties—Ma Rainey, Bessie Smith, Clara Smith, Maggie Jones. "All we had to do," Louis recalled, "was play the blues and fill in them gaps! Like Bessie Smith. I remember she just stayed in the studio and wrote the blues there. She finish one, she write another."

I don't know who was first, Ma Rainey had been singin' a long time. But Bessie came a little later and out-sang them all!

Making the great Hot Five and Hot Seven records for Okeh—still classics of jazz—was easy, too, Louis recalled. "We just make up them things! Make 'em up in the studio. One time there where I dropped the paper and started scatting, we used to do that in the quartets in New Orleans. Sound like an instrument, or somethin'."

And in Chicago, Louis doubled from the Oliver band to bigger orchestras. "Playin' for silent pictures. Big old symphony orchestra for soundless pictures! After the curtain go up, you play an overture. Then a hot number. That's where I came in!"

Louis went to New York in 1924 to join a band at Roseland Ballroom (still the palace of dance in Manhattan). "When I went with Fletcher Henderson's band in 1924, why, that was sumpin' else! The minute I got up on the stand, there is a *part* in front of me! Y'know? Well, I wasn't used to *that*."

Louis took up the horn in Jones Orphanage in New Orleans. And all over the world in the years since then, he played "When the Saints Go Marching In," the spiritual that the orphanage band played when the boys marched to church on Sunday morning.

When he got out of the orphanage, Louis hung around the New Orleans clubs and dancehalls listening to the great players of the first days of jazz. "Louis was always worryin' me and worryin' me to carry my horn," Bunk Johnson, the veteran who played with Buddy Bolden's Original Superior Band, has said, and told how Louis learned— "anything he could whistle, he could play."

In those days, after the reign of King Buddy Bolden as chief musician in New Orleans, Joseph "King" Oliver was the man. Oliver played so strong he would blow a cornet out of tune in a few months and Bolden could be heard across Lake Pontchartrain, old-timers recall. But Joe was Louis' idol. Oliver went to Chicago while Louis was still in short pants and working the local gigs. Armstrong stayed behind, playing with Kid Ory's band and then on the Mississippi River steamboats with Fate Marable.

The Oliver band was the band which scored the big success in Chicago. It had the legendary Johnny Dodds on clarinet and Johnny's brother, Baby, on drums and when Joe sent for Louis, the young Armstrong packed his trumpet in a paper bag and took the train to Chicago.

The Oliver records were and remain marvels of collective improvisation. Louis and Joe's breaks would be thrilling. Armstrong was soon the sensation of Chicago's black community but Oliver, who acknowledged Louis' ability, insisted "He can't hurt me when he's with me," and they stayed together for a long time. But eventually the virtuosity of Armstrong drew him away from the Oliver band into recording sessions on his own, accompanying blues singers such as Ma Rainey and Bessie Smith, and with the Hot Five and Hot Seven.

These latter groups were studio groups assembled from the Chicago musical cadres and including the best sidemen in the city with players such as Kid Ory, Earl Hines and the Dodds brothers, and in a short period in 1926 they made the series of jazz records that included some of the greatest solo instrumental performances ever put on record. Many of the tunes were old New Orleans street songs and blues and musicians' warm-up tunes and others were things the band or Louis made up in the studio.

It is hard today to imagine the original impact of those records. There was simply nothing remotely like them at the time. Okeh was a reasonably big record company with national distribution (it later became part of Columbia) and the thick old shellac 78 RPM discs were available in the ghetto record stores all over the country. They were never played on the air then, at all, incidentally. Few, if any, records were played on radio at that time and actually the old discs carried a legend plainly stating "Not licensed for radio broadcast."

But all over the country, in that mystical way in which the underground has always worked, musicians, white and black, heard those discs. It was like the Second Coming of Christ. They could not believe their ears. That such sounds could be made! Columbia has had most of these available in an Armstrong package for years and is re-issuing more this year.

Louis spent some time in New York with Fletcher Henderson's big band. The era of the big bands was just beginning and Henderson was the man whose book of arrangements was to be the basis for the original Benny Goodman orchestra's success a few years later, and then he returned to Chicago.

A man named Joe Glaser, who managed dance halls and nightclubs in Chicago during that Prohibition era, hired Louis to lead the band at the Sunset Café, a favorite spot for Chicago black and white nightlife. Glaser recognized the importance of Louis and became his lifetime manager and friend. He once told *Life Magazine*, "Louis has always been inclined to feel he's got to go on and blow his brains out . . . So I used to say, 'Louis, forget all the goddam critics, the musicians. Play for the public. Sing and play and smile.'"

At first in Chicago, Louis was always very, very shy, very quiet. When I hired him at the Sunset, I used to act like the coach on the football team. I'd say, "Louis, sing and make faces and smile. Smile, goddammit, smile! Give it to them. Don't be afraid!"

Glaser really changed Louis' life. From then on Louis smiled and made faces and played and sang and even years later, when he was asked about his reaction to the way young musicians in the bebop era were breaking away from his style, Louis went right back to the Glaser formula. "I'll play for the old-time people," he said. "They got all the money!"

Glazer, who died in the late Sixties, became one of the biggest booking agents in the country as head of Associated Booking Corp., which he founded. Louis was always his first line attraction even when he was booking Noel Coward and other stars. Once Glaser, a tempestuous and profane man, was asked by a leading folk group whom he wanted to book, to guarantee them he would give them as much attention as he gave Louis. "Goddammit!" he yelled in a hotel lobby when he was telling me the story. "How in hell could I give them as much attention as I could Louis? I'm Louis and Louis me. We grew up together. We're a part of each other."

Yet Louis (he has always been Louis and not Louie) always called Joe Glaser "Pops" or "Mister Glaser" just as he called the white trombonist

Jack Teagarden, himself a jazz virtuoso who played in Louis' band for a number of years, "Pops" or "Mister Jack."

In the mid-Thirties, Armstrong led a big band himself and made scores of records for various companies of current pop tunes. His great thing was to take the lyrics of some silly song, "Stardust" is a good example, and treat those insipid lyrics in such a fashion that they became a work of put-on art. At the end of "Stardust" where the lyric goes, "a memory of love's refrain," Louis would growl out, in a vocal riff, "Oh memory! oh memory! oh memory of love's refrain!," breaking down the banal lyrics more and more until they became something else altogether.

His endurance and his power was legendary. His lips were iron and his lungs had the strength of a hurricane. During one of his periods in New York, he held down three jobs. He played downtown in the Hudson Theater for a show with the Connie's Inn Hot Chocolates Review. Then he went uptown at midnight for a late show at the Lafayette Theater in Harlem and then after that played a breakfast set at the Connie's Inn Cabaret!

It took strength but Louis always took good care of himself, He catnapped whenever he could and he always slept on his back after heavyweight boxing champ Max Baer told him that was the best way to relax. "He taught me how to relax one muscle at a time."

But it was to the care of his lips that Louis gave the most attention. The lips are crucial to the trumpet player since they control the entire horn blowing operation and Louis took great pains not to split a lip. Once when he did, at a show in a Baltimore theater, he continued to play, blood dripping down his chin, while members of the orchestra literally cried to see him put himself through such agony for the sake of the show.

Years later, Louis talked to a reporter about staying in condition.

You got to stay in shape, man. To me, it ain't the money in this business; I could've been a millionaire four times. I just want to blow the horn as long as I can. All those musicians trying to get famous, so they can have yachts and swimming pools and all that

. . . I come through life trying to get more joy out of staying healthy, so I can blow. And so, if I get a million dollars, I don't have to have nobody wheeling me around in a chair.

You see, most those fellows in the old days in New Orleans, they wouldn't relax ever.

Around 1916, I'd see those boys play all night, then go to the Eagle saloon at seven on Sunday morning when they got a parade coming up at nine. Instead of taking a two-hour nap to break their tiredness so they could tough the day out—no, they'd stay up and drink!

And at 2 o'clock in the afternoon, when that sun beat down on them, I've seen them drop dead in the parade.

So I learned my lesson early. Some of them didn't believe in going to the dentist every so often, for a checkup on their chops. Joe Oliver, that great trumpet player, played till his teeth got so loose you could pull them out with your fingers. Take Buddy Bolden. He was a great trumpet way back in 1910 to 1915, but he blew too hard.

You take a cat who's blowing, and he's got a tough high note coming up. He don't figure he can make that note no more, so he'll make 100 notes just to get around that one.

But Buddy Bolden, he would *try*. He would blow sooooooo hard . . . well, you could see the veins. Finally, he just blew his brains out.

Not long ago, I sat in with Count Basie's band in Florida one night, just having fun. Count says, "Damn! I ain't never heard that much strong horn played in all my life!"

Now, Basie's trumpet players are all good musicians, but they run away from their notes. Why? Because they don't keep their chops fortified; their lips are sore.

Everybody wants to know why I play stronger than any other trumpets. Well, it ain't nothing mysterious. Ain't no witch doctor, two-head stuff. If you take the soreness out of your lips, you can put pressure on the horn.

How to do it? I bathe my lips every night, soon as I leave the stand, with witch hazel and lip salve and sweet spirits of nitre. And I bathe 'em again before I go to bed.

Sweet spirits of nitre will take the soreness out of anything, man. Oh, it stings! You put it on and then grab a chair for about five minutes, and too many trumpet players ain't got the guts to stand the ache.

Or they won't use the salve, 'cause it's greasy. It's not bad, smells like strawberry.

Now, when I get up to work, I put witch hazel and sweet spirits of nitre on again, and by the time I get to the club tonight, I'm okay again.

Sure, my lips are scarred up—I been playin' that horn 50 years—but they're *relaxed* at all times, and that's it. If your lips swell up a fraction on the mouthpiece, you're in trouble with your notes.

Louis always used a special salve from a special factory in Holland, and during World War II musicians conspired to break the wartime blockade and get the salve to Armstrong. For years he has been a devout believer in the efficacy of a laxative called Swiss Kriss, even giving out samples of it to friends and preparing a special instruction sheet on how to stay healthy and lose weight, "The Satchmo Way."

At Bedtime—

P. S. Your first dose will be real heavy, in order to start blasting right away, and get the ball to rolling. After you get over your surprises and whatnot, you'll be very happy. The first week, take a tablespoon of Swiss Kriss. Put it into your mouth and rinse it down with a glass of water. Fifteen minutes later, drink a large glass of orange juice. Don't eat no food before going to bed. After the first week, cut Swiss Kriss down to a teaspoon every night.

At Breakfast Time—

Large glass of orange juice and black coffee or tea, etc. . . .

At Lunch Time—

Eat whatever you want . . . As much as you want . . . Just have slices of tomatoes with lemon juice over it . . . , Mmm, it's good. In fact you may choose any salad that you like . . . just see that you have the same kind, any kind. Coffee, tea, or, etc. Twenty minutes

later, take a tablespoon of Bisma Rex. Stir it in a glass of water . . . Stir real good . . . And drink it right on down. Chase it down with a half a glass of water.
Between Meals —

If you should get a little hungry between meals, just drink a large glass of orange juice, two glasses if you should desire.
Supper Time —

You can eat from soup to nuts . . . Eat as much as you want to. Please see that you have, at least, either sliced tomatoes (with lemon juice) or your favorite salad. All kinds of greens are good for the stomach. So . . . eat to your satisfaction. Of course, the less you eat is in your favor . . . hmmmm?? Twenty minutes later, after you have eaten your supper, take a tablespoon of Bisma Rex . . . in a glass of water. Don't eat before bedtime.
Comments 'n' Stuff —

It's a known fact, while eating your meals, if you feel yourself getting full, it's in your favor to leave the table with a satisfactory stomach. It's better to have a satisfied, full stomach than to have an overstuffed stomach . . . Aye??? P. S. That's where Bisma Rex steps in . . . It's really great for overstuffed stomachs, or people who suffer with gas, etc. Yea . . . it's a Gassuh! In case you do get gas, Ol' Bisma Rex will straighten you. That's why she's on the mound . . . To cut gas, grease and a lot of discomforts from a lot of foods and liquors that won't act right in your stomach, lots of times.

Orange juice is so delicious . . . You should never get tired of drinking it. P.S. it's a sure thing . . . If you dig this set-up here in this chart, you will automatically lose all the weight that you don't need. And, no one should want a lot of excess weight when here's an easy way to get rid of it. Just like I've said before . . . It takes time, but not as long as an old strenuous diet would drag you, trying to cope with . . . [meaning, to dig] . . .

I always could see the wonderful things that orange juice did . . . And it tastes so good . . . Yum, yum. P.S. When you buy your Bisma Rex, inquire about those Bisma Rex tablets. Always carry a package in your pocket, pocketbook, or your purse so in case you're out someplace away from home . . . You can still keep up your routine that you have at home by putting one Bisma Rex tablet into your mouth 20 minutes after you finished. Or, two tablets if you should feel it necessary. Don't get frantic because you have to trot to the bathroom several times when you first get up [awakened]. P.S. You won't need an alarm clock to awaken you . . . No-o-o-o. Relax, if you feel a little tired from the Swinging Actions of your dear old Swiss Kriss . . . Ha ha.

So, that's about it . . . I have explained to the very best of my knowledge . . . So I'll be like the little boy who sat on a block of ice . . . My tale is told . . . tee hee. Have a good time. P.S. In case you're wondering as to how much Swiss Kriss do I take . . . Well, even though I've always taken a heaping tablespoon every time I go to bed to rest my body, I shall do the same every night for the rest of my life. Because, when you and Swiss Kriss get well acquainted, then you'll dig . . . He's your friend.

Swiss Krissly,
Louis Armstrong

P.S. When the Swiss Kriss Company give me a radio show, my slogan will be . . . "Everybody, this is Satchmo speaking for Swiss Kriss. Are you loosening??????" . . . Wow.

So on through the Thirties and Forties, and yes the Fifties and the Sixties, Louis made those one-nighters, those concerts and nightclubs and shows from Korea, where they booked him to open some gambling house in Seoul, to the opera houses of Europe.

Wherever he went he was always good copy for all the media because he kept saying things in that personal, colorful style in which he always spoke.

When he played for England's King George V, he dedicated the number thus: "Here's one for you, Rex." And 30 years later when he played for King George's granddaughter, Princess Margaret, Louis blew "Mahogany Hall Stomp," a rousing number named after the raunchy old dance hall in New Orleans. "We really gonna lay this one on the Princess," he growled.

People always ask him to define jazz. What is it?, they'd ask, and Louis' standard answer has become one of the legends of the music world. "Lady," he is reported to have once told a bejeweled dowager, "if you got to ask what it is, you'll never know." Pure Zen. Even if Louis never heard of Dr. Suzuki.

Over and over, down through the years, he has blown the fuses of jazz critics and fans by giving unexpected answers. What records did he listen to when he was a kid? "The Original Dixieland Jazz Band," that's who, and the disc of "Tiger Rag" by that group of young white New Orleanians, Louis insists, is the all time best performance of that classic.

What was his favorite band? He has determinedly insisted for decades that it is Guy Lombardo and there's no trace of put-on in his statement.

"I haven't heard no band that plays more perfect music than Guy Lombardo *yet*. That's the way I feel and I don't let my mouth say nuthin' my head can't stand," he told *Life*. "Any time I walk up on the stage with Guy Lombardo, I'm relaxed. That's the music I've played all my life." Those of us who have listened in vain for some clue to what Louis hears in The Sweetest Music This Side of Heaven (as Lombardo has always billed his work) have just had to accept the fact that he digs them and to hell with it.

He even rankled the big anti–rock 'n roll crusade back in 1957 when they thought they could get the Old Master to put rock down. "It's all right," he surprised everyone by saying. "Ain't nothing wrong with rock 'n roll. The cats have fun with it. It's nuthin' new. I been doin' it for years."

He even dug folk music, but again he wasn't surprised by it. Louis said something profound when he uttered his famous comment about folk music in the Peter, Paul & Mary–Kingston Trio era. "Folk music?" Satch said. "Why, daddy, I don't know no other kind of music *but* folk music. I ain't never heard a hoss sing a song."

His bitterest words about music were directed against the late Forties, early Fifties bebop or so-called modern jazz. Chuck Berry sang "I got nothing against modern jazz" but Louis wasn't so benign.

What bothered Louis about modern jazz was its disrespect for the old-timers and the implication that nothing important had happened before the young beboppers came on the scene. "I remember every note I ever played," he said, "I got some respect for the old folks who played trumpet before me. Then," he added murkily, "the trumpet is an instrument that's full of temptation."

You got to like playing pretty things if you're ever going to be any good blowing your horn. These young cats now, they want to make money first and the hell with the music. And they want to carve everyone else because they are full of malice, and all they want to do is show you up and any old way will do as long as it's different from the way you played it before.

So you get all them weird chords which don't mean nuthin', and first people get tired of it because it's really no good and you got no melody to remember and no beat to dance to. So they're poor again and nobody is working and that's what that modern malice done for you.

Louis, of course, was a very philosophical cat. For instance there was his attitude towards "Sister Kate," a song which has been recorded and performed for decades, most recently by Taj Mahal and the Kweskin Jug Band.

Once I was promised $50—more money than I'd ever seen all at once—for a tune I wrote called "Get Off Katie's Head." I sold it to A. J. Pirón and Clarence Williams [two early black songwriters, musicians and publishers] . . . They wrote some words and called it "I Wish I Could Shimmy Like My Sister Kate." They never did pay me for it, never even put my name on it. I didn't holler about it. You can't get everything that's coming to you in life.

"I fell in love with that horn and it fell in love with me," he once said. "Man, I ain't leavin' this old horn *nowhere*, not even when I go to heaven, because I guess them angels up there are waitin' to hear old Satchmo's music, too. I'm my own audience. They put a stop sign on my head, I take it right down. Me and my horn ain't never going to stop."

"I'm not the ambassador, the music is," he said on TV apropos his effect upon jazz fans in the Iron Curtain countries. "They hear a lot of things, some good, some bad, but I know one thing—this ain't no cannon!"

In Yugoslavia they called him "Satchmovic" and in Africa "Okuka Lokole." In New Orleans they called him Satchelmouth (a reference to his huge mouth) and usage shortened it universally to "Satch" or "Satchmo." But Louis says, "Call me anything at all. Just don't call me too late to eat! I been blowing the horn for 50 years and I never looked back once."

> You can live on this earth without pouting all the time. I bet I made a million dollars, but I don't know. I just blow my horn and let my manager count the money. When a man's in love, what else can he want?

Louis was married four times and, as far as we know, had no children. "I'm a Baptist, married to a Catholic and I wear a Jewish star all the time for good luck. I'm a good friend of the Pope's," he added. Louis visited the Pope once and one of the great apocryphal legends about him concerns their exchange on that occasion. The Pope reportedly asked Louis if he had any children and Satch replied, "No father, but I sure had a lot of fun tryin'."

Louis' fourth wife was Lucille "Brown Sugar" Wilson, a chorus girl from the old Cotton Club in New York. They were married more than 25 years. A handsome, dark woman, she was the first to break the "high yaller" color standard maintained by the Cotton Club chorus line for years (Lena Horne is also a graduate of that chorus line). "I like my women beautiful, dark and tender—the blacker the berry the sweeter the juice," Satch said. "But I love my trumpet, too. I always made it plain to all my wives that that trumpet must come first before anybody or anything. That horn is my real boss, because it's my life!"

Always a sharp dresser by show business standards, Louis sometimes had as many as 16 suits in his road tour luggage and he always carried his trumpet mouthpiece in his coat pocket. Since he would use up so much energy playing and singing, Louis sweated profusely and one of

his road manager's chores was to have 60 clean white linen handkerchiefs ready for every working day. During his heavy road touring days,
Louis had "Satchmo" embroidered on his handkerchiefs and used a
cológne with the same name.

For years on the road he spent his time in the dressing room between
shows pecking out letters on the typewriter to friends all over the world,
in his own inimitable style replete with "ha has" as asides for laughter
and always signing off, "Red beans and ricely yours."

Louis Armstrong's dressing rooms over the years had changed only
in one respect—he would play a better class of place in recent years.
There's always the old friends from New Orleans. Musicians, people he
knew when he was a kid (New Orleans must've had millions of black
jazz fans; they showed up everywhere he worked). The people associated with whatever show he'd be playing, fans from all over, young
and old, and his musicians and personal staff. Louis frequently received
visitors sitting in the dressing room wearing nothing but his shorts and a
handkerchief wrapped around his head and as he talked or signed autographs, he rubbed his lips with his special salve and chuckled.

Louis was dedicated to his fans. I remember once seeing the young
producer of a concert stopped cold by Louis when he tried to tell the
line of autograph hunters Louis was too busy to sign their programs.
"No, no," Louie was almost salty, "them's my people." And he dutifully
signed them all, program after program, "red beans and ricely yours."

I've been going to hear Louis Armstrong at stage shows, concerts and
nightclubs and dances since I was a kid in college and dug him at the
Apollo theater, standing there with his gleaming trumpet and the white
handkerchief in front of that big band.

I remember him walking into a club one night to hear Kid Ory's
band and as soon as they saw Louis, Ory and Papa Mutt Carey (the
trumpeter in the band and a contemporary of Louis') broke into "Mahogany Hall Stomp." Then there was the time at the Monterey Jazz
Festival when he was scheduled to appear on a panel discussion with
Dizzy Gillespie and arrived late. When Louis walked in, Dizzy stood
up applauding and the room was Louis'. Just as Dizzy sat on the stage at
another Monterey Festival night at Louis' feet while the Master played.

Back in 1962 after the show at a big hotel, Louis told me he had something to announce and then took me to his room and talked about his plans to retire. "I'm tired," he said, and went on to describe how he wanted to travel slowly, and for fun, and to listen to all kinds of other music. "Let them young fellas play for a while," he said while his wife, echoing his plans, said, "I got 12 big rooms [in their Corona, Long Island, home]. I don't need 'em. What's home without him?"

But Louis didn't retire. His manager, Joe Glaser, told me not to pay attention to what Louis said. Louis wouldn't know how to stop, goddammit. And Joe was right. Louis didn't stop until he was too sick to travel.

Despite all the ironies of his life ("I can have lunch with the president of Brazil," he once said, "in the presidential mansion, but I can't walk into a hotel dining room in the South and order a steak or a glass of water as any ordinary white man can do"), Louis refused to become bitter or depressed.

It had only been in the years since jazz achieved some acceptance, the late Fifties, that Louis stayed at a downtown hotel even in such a cosmopolitan city as San Francisco. Before, he stayed out in the ghetto boarding houses and hotels. When he was making his early pictures in Hollywood (he was in over 30 flicks, including *New Orleans*, that classic of jazz history), he couldn't stay in the downtown hotels in Los Angeles but stayed out on Central Avenue. And at the parties he went to in Hollywood, he quickly tired of people, with a couple of drinks in them, coming up to him and starting a conversation by saying, "Ya know, I used to have a colored mammy."

As late as 1960, Louis could say he didn't go out with the Hollywood movie crowd. "Even though I've played with a lot of them . . . Danny Kaye, Sinatra. I don't even know where they live. In fact, I've never been invited to the home of a movie star, not even Bing's."

Louis has been called an Uncle Tom. Kenneth Tynan, the British critic, even quoted Billie Holiday once as saying (in admiration and love), "Louis toms from the heart." And he would make jokes about one of his musicians being "Bing Crosby in Technicolor." And he once traumatized network TV bosses when, making a guest appearance on the Dorsey Brothers show (the same summer series that presented Elvis Presley for the first time), he gave his instructions to the band: "Don't play too slow or too fast — just half fast."

But then Louis never was one to hide anything. Take, for instance, his classic record of "You Rascal You." The lyric went like this:

I'll be standing on the corner, high
When they bring your body by,
I'll be glad when you're dead
You rascal you.

When Louis made that disc back in 1931, even though grass was still legal the song swept across the underground of the time like a rumor about Mick Jagger today.

Black people had it on their jukeboxes and in their homes and a handful of white record collectors bought it in the record stores of the ghettos where "race records," as they were pejoratively known then, were sold. The "downtown" or white stores did not carry them.

Jazz was still an underground music then, in many ways, but curiously enough, bands like Armstrong's would broadcast almost nightly from wherever they were on the late-night radio network shows and when Louis laid down that one word, "high," the aficionados all over the country fell out. White and black. And they used to listen for it. Just as they listened for other special messages like his line about "smokin' a Louis Armstrong special see-gar." They had the kind of impact in the underground then that "Everybody Must Get Stoned" had 40 years later.

Louis has always been one of the mythological heroes of the grass culture. He figures heavily in Mezz Mezzrow's autobiography *Really the Blues*, just as he figured in the lives of all the jazz musicians of the Thirties and Forties. Mezzrow was a big dope dealer, an early Owsley, with the same quality control and, like Owsley, he gave his name to his product: the "Mezzerole," made with the golden grass he specialized in. The Mezz. Alberta Hunter, the blues singer, sang, "Dreamed about a reefer, 5 foot long, the mighty mezz, but not too strong." Mezz sold his grass by the shoebox coast-to-coast, mail-order, as well as standing on 125th St. underneath the Tree of Life dealing with all who came by.

But Mezzrow is cautious about linking Louis to grass, though the implication runs throughout the book. And Louis himself has put grass down in recent years. Still, it is an interesting point that censorious officials never picked up on the drug references in the early Armstrong songs.

I never saw Louis light up a joint (though Mezz writes about the motto in his circle being, "light up and be somebody"), but I sure watched some of his sidemen blow some gauge. Louis had a pianist once who used to lean back from the piano and take a long toke from a friend standing behind the curtain and keep right on playing. And Big Sid Catlett, the drummer who played with the Armstrong All-Stars, once had a San Francisco club so stashed with grass that all he had to do, whenever he was in the joint, was run his hand along the top of the paneling near the ceiling and grab a roach.

Louis, though, was always Louis no matter where the gig and no matter what the audience. In the Oakland Auditorium the week he was on the cover of *Time*, when there were less than 500 people in the place, or in the Fairmont Hotel before a crowded room of bankers, it was still Louis. And he gave them all "Mack the Knife" and "Coal Cart Blues" and the rest, and they never—at least the audience in the Fairmont never did—picked up for even a second on what a slice of reality he was laying out before them. Louis' "Coal Cart Blues" was a folk song. No boss could sing it, true, but it came right out of Louis' own childhood, picking up coal along the railroad tracks coming into New Orleans, to feed the thin fire in his mother's shack. He worked for $.15 a day doing that and when he sang about it to the Fairmont Hotel audience, they thought he was charming.

I don't know how many times I saw Louis Armstrong perform. I've lost count. But I do know what was his most moving performance for me, and that was the night he appeared at the Monterey Jazz Festival in Dave Brubeck's *The Real Ambassadors*, the musical Dave had written for Louis. It was a cold night, but the stage and the audience were warm with love. Louis stood there in his ambassadorial costume, high hat and all, and he sang, "All I do is play the blues/and meet the people face-to-face . . . In my humble way/I'm the USA . . . though I represent the government the government don't represent some policies I'm for . . ."

It was a thrilling night in the fullest sense of that overused word. And when Louis ended the show with the lines "They say I look like God

. . . Could God be black?," *that* audience, at least, was ready and willing to believe it just might be.

Gene Krupa once described what it felt like to play with Louis. "It was like somebody turned the current on." It was like that on that Monterey evening and it was like that every time the stars were right for Louis because he did a truly original thing in art.

From the time he came on the scene at the beginning of the Twenties, until the first level of the modern jazz revolution (led by Charlie Parker, Thelonious Monk and Dizzy Gillespie) in the late Forties, Louis Armstrong's concept of improvising and of playing was the basis of almost all of jazz.

He took the tools of European musical organization—chords, notation, bars and the rest—and added to them the rhythms of the church and of New Orleans and (by definition) Africa, brought into the music the blue notes, the tricks of bending and twisting notes, and played it all with his unexcelled technique. He went as far with it as he could by using the blues and popular songs of the time as skeletons for his structural improvisation. He would take the 32-bar chorus of a song and build upon it, like a carpenter with scaffolding, building on upward and upward until the original 32 bars were (at least in his ears and hopefully in the audiences') supporting an incredible superstructure which could, theoretically, be divided down until individual elements all related directly to the original bar structure.

Louis as a trumpet player (cornet player before he took up trumpet) had astonishing speed of execution and he had a range that extended the possibilities of the trumpet beyond the concept of the time. Brass players from the Royal Philharmonic heard him in London and were awed by his range. He was said to be capable of hitting 300 consecutive Gs above high C.

But he could and did play simply, too. His sparse use of notes (listen to him on the sides he recorded with Bessie Smith, Ma Rainey, Clara Smith and Maggie Jones, for instance) became an extraordinarily effective device to transmit emotion because of two things: his intonation and his phrasing.

Leading the final choruses of a number by his big 17-piece swing band, Louis' horn would sail on up above the sections of the band not unlike the way B. B. King leads the ensemble on his guitar today. Louis would swing the band in the old and truest meaning of the term, using his horn like a long leash to pull them one way and then another, but never losing sight of the original chord pattern, melody and harmony.

It was not until the bebop era of Parker and Gillespie that the use of passing chords, classical dissonances and irregular rhythmic patterns added another dimension to jazz playing which was to bring it to the end of the path defined by European musical rules. After that, Coltrane and Ornette Coleman broke through and made music on those same instruments in an entirely different, non-European way for a New Morning in jazz.

As a singer Louis paralleled his stylistic originality on trumpet. Nat "King" Cole told me once Louis had a style rather than a voice in the formal sense. But in his way, Louis was the first singer in popular music in America to include, as a part of his language, sounds made by the human voice which were not merely the reproduction of notes on the scale. Louis growled and grated, grunted and wheezed for special effects. He bent notes as he sang just as he would bend them when he played. His singing was his own reflection of his trumpet playing.

Just as Ray Charles was later to make the phrase "All right" into an almost universal ritual in vocal performances, Louis made the phrase "Oh yeah" into the same kind of thing as a tag at the end of his songs and as a signature expression within them as "Amen," sung after two notes, is the preachers' sign off.

Along with Bessie Smith, he was the seminal influence on many of the popular singers of the Thirties and Forties. Not only Billie Holiday, but almost every other singer, directly or indirectly, who performed during the swing era and who was at all influenced by jazz (and most of them were) bore the mark of Louis' style.

George Bernard Shaw once wrote that "anybody, almost, can make a beginning; the difficulty is to make an end . . . To do what cannot be bettered." And that is precisely what Louis Armstrong did. He did his thing so well that no one else has been able to equal his achievement within his style and what he did was so good in and of itself that it has survived generations. Whole tunes and countless arrangements have been based on parts of an Armstrong solo. At least one band of the Thir-

ties, the Glen Gray Casa Loma Band, made up instrumental compositions which were simply phrases from Armstrong solos played by horn
sections, trumpets or saxophones and strung together in a full number.

Any night, the studio bands on the TV shows can be heard still, 50
years after Louis arrived in Chicago to join King Oliver's Creole Jazz
band, playing little bits of Louis' music in their charts.

An entire generation, no—two generations—of trumpet players
were ruined and frustrated by Louis' brilliance. What he did was so
right, there seemed to be no other way. Musicians abandoned the trumpet and took up other instruments. Others became alcoholics or junkies
trying to ape his style, his tone and his phrasing. Some of them did it so
well that on early records collectors thought they were, indeed, Louis.

Young black musicians copied his gestures, his clothes and his manners as well as his vocal sound both in singing and in talking. Young
white musicians got so far into his bag that they tried to do the same
thing. Young Italians from Chicago and New York growled and grated
away when they talked, trying to sound like the gravel-voiced original
from New Orleans.

His style was impressive enough as an original contribution that people who played other instruments were deeply influenced by it. Earl
"Fatha" Hines, himself a classic jazz player, adapted Louis' style to the
piano, playing what was termed "trumpet style," with octave runs in
the right hand that would sound, if one took the top or the bottom line,
like an Armstrong solo.

Even such an original musician as Duke Ellington borrowed from
Armstrong. Early Ellington records show his trumpet players, when
they were not utilizing the growling trumpet "jungle" sounds, tended
to play like the rest of the jazz trumpet players—straight out of Louis
Armstrong. They still do, for that matter. And the big successful (finan-
cially) swing bands of Tommy Dorsey, Benny Goodman and Glenn
Miller, always had trumpet players in them whose main virtue was their
ability to play in the Armstrong manner.

It was an overwhelming achievement and it made him known and
loved throughout the world. He invented no labor-saving devices, designed no terrible weapons of destruction and did not break the barriers into outer space. Yet Louis Armstrong will be remembered perhaps

longer than those who did these things, for his achievement was for all people.

"I'll explain and make it plain," he sang in *The Real Ambassadors*, "I represent the human race."

And that is precisely what he has done.

[*Rolling Stone*, August 5, 1971]

Duke Ellington, *The Pianist*

■

When Duke Ellington came onstage to open the show at a nightclub, he would walk out just as the band was finishing the theme, "Take the 'A' Train," welcome the audience, thank them, tell them the boys in the band all loved them madly, and then say, "And now we'd like you to meet the pianist."

Duke loved the effect he would get occasionally from some member of the audience uneducated in Ellingtonia. As Duke finished saying ". . . meet the pianist" he would put out his arm toward the piano, turn his hand palm up and look expectantly toward the empty piano bench. For a split second he was the master of illusion.

There was more than one nightclub patron over the years who saw a pianist on that bench when Duke made that gesture.

Then, of course, as the appreciative applause arose, Duke would smile his elegant smile and stride over to the piano. It always amazed me how quickly he could move when he wanted to. He could sure move faster than I could.

Once across the stage and on the bench, Duke would stretch out his arms again to remove any tension from a tight sleeve, sometimes touch his hands together and look down at the keys. Then he would play.

Make no mistake about it: in addition to all the other things Duke Ellington was, and was superbly, he was also one hell of a piano player. Anytime.

Duke dominated the keyboard. He played all of it, sometimes his long arms extending from the bottom of the bass to the top of the treble. He not only had the scope to play the entire instrument, but he understood, as very few pianists understand, the use of the pedals for special effects. Duke was a master at this.

He played the piano in a constantly shifting way. I don't mean he had different styles. He did not. He had his own, personal, unique style, and what is even more important, he had a personal sound on the piano. Let Duke strike a chord or a note and you knew it was Duke and no one else.

But what I mean is that sometimes he played the piano as if he were playing an orchestra or as if the sounds he made were parts of an orchestral sound. And sometimes he played it like a rent party bluesman at nine in the morning after a long night. And sometimes he played it like a lover with his guitar serenading under a lady's window. And sometimes he played it like a man possessed, as if there would not be time even to get out all he wanted.

Duke came up on piano in a tough school. When he was first in New York the city was full of hard-playing keyboard men and they played against each other—like Minnesota Fats and Willie Hoppe. Competition was not only the spice of life, it was the act of survival in a sense, as the musical underground grapevine established a pianist's reputation by the contests at Mexico's or other late-hour clubs, and that reputation was what got the jobs.

Throughout his long career after his orchestra became established, and after Duke himself became established as a composer, his gifts as a pianist were generally treated casually when they were not ignored. To a degree Duke's other talents obscured his piano playing and his role as pianist in the orchestra was not obvious at all much of the time.

However, there was a clue for all who wanted to see it. The Ellington orchestra in stage shows and in nightclubs always began to play before the Maestro appeared. Duke would enter from the dressing room and walk up to the stand as the band was playing. You could always tell the moment he came into sight. The musicians sounded differently instantly. It was like a change in the electric current. And the moment he sat at the piano and struck the first note, the whole thing tightened up into a cohesive unit.

Then, throughout the performance, Duke would subtly feed chords, drop in rhythmic figures, add a special sound to underline the soloists or the ensemble passages, and literally drive the band.

He rarely recorded as a soloist but when he did he showed that he could extend to an entire number the brilliance he exhibited in the short solos he took in the orchestra's arrangements.

Ellington's roots as a pianist went back to the era of ragtime and stride piano, to a time when both hands and all ten fingers were needed because the pianist played alone, hour after hour, without the aid of other instruments. And thus he had to supply it all—melody, harmony, and rhythm—himself. Duke did not, as some of the modern jazz pianists did, play the piano like a horn. He could play hornlike figures and he did, but Duke heard the instrument on a larger scale than that, and thus made it sound larger.

No one in my memory has ever had the ability to make the piano growl and rumble the way Duke could, with those low clusters of notes and that heavy rhythm. He could stomp, in the old-fashioned sense, and he could rock like the all-time swinging pianist. And, of course, he could be melodic and rhapsodic, sometimes playing melodic lines that truly seemed to sing almost as if they had words.

Many times Duke worked out ideas for compositions at the piano after the concert when the stage and the hall were empty. Many times he sat at the piano during intermissions in clubs, if the circumstances were right, and worked on some idea, letting the audience assume he was aimlessly doodling. But that was pure deception. Duke Ellington did nothing aimlessly. Ever.

The most amazing thing about his piano playing, to me at any rate, was the way in which he could switch moods. At one number he would be the suave, international boulevardier, and in the next tune he would be as down-home funky as the raunchiest back-room, after-hours piano player. He could become positively earthy in an instant.

Sam Woodyard, who played with the Ellington band on and off for a decade, used to call Duke "Piano Red." That was a tribute to his basic funkiness because Duke Ellington's drummers, who had to work with him night after night knitting together the rhythmic basis for the band, really knew as no one else could know, just how good he was.

[Liner notes, Fantasy Records—F-9462, 1974, Grammy
Award winner for Best Album Liner Notes]

Cal Tjader, *Los Ritmos Calientes!*

■

Cal Tjader, rather amazingly is a native North American, raised in California. For many years he has been recognized as both a master jazz vibist and one of the top Latin small-band leaders. These two landmark albums date back to the very beginning of his remarkable Latin music career—actually, the first was made when he was still working with George Shearing, just before Cal formed his first band. The passage of time has not only left these recordings stronger than ever, it has also (by bringing major success to men like Mongo and Willie Bobo) turned this into an "all-star" collection.

Ritmo Caliente

In the last few years the influence of Afro-Cuban music on American jazz has been pronounced. Stan Kenton and Dizzy Gillespie pioneered in the use of Afro-Cuban rhythms and today the Latin bands in turn are featuring jazz harmonies.

The great conga drummer Chano Pozo, who had come up from Cuba in the early 30s and played with many of the Latin bands in and around New York and was the author of a number of Latin popular tunes, brought the Afro-Cuban beat to jazz fans dramatically during the period of his association with the great Dizzy Gillespie big band.

Today, the Latin bands are beginning to dominate the jazz scene both on records and in person. In the East, Tito Puente, Machito and others have started a mambo craze that is going to affect materially our musical history. In the West Perez Prado has been a major influence.

So it was only natural that when young Cal Tjader—he was born in

1925—hit New York as the vibraphone player with the George Shearing Quintet, he would be tremendously influenced by the great Afro-Cuban bands. Tjader, who had grown up in Northern California, attended San Jose and San Francisco State colleges and was a vital force in the early days of modern jazz in San Francisco, was one of the original members of the Dave Brubeck trio and quartet. An accomplished drummer, he was offered a job with Lionel Hampton while still a student at San Francisco State. Cal had taken up the bongos and conga drums on his own in San Francisco. When he joined Shearing he seized the opportunity to study with bassist Al McKibbon, a thorough master of Afro-Cuban rhythms who had studied conga drum with Chano Pozo. As a result of his interest in Latin music, Cal is now leading his own Afro-Cuban group at the Macumba Club in San Francisco.

To make this album, Cal set up two recording dates, one in San Francisco and one in Los Angeles during the spring of 1954 as he was ending his tour with Shearing. The San Francisco session was held on March 6 and the personnel was Tjader, vibes and timbales; Armando Peraza, conga and bongos; Richard Wyands, piano and maracas; Jerome Richardson, flute; Al McKibbon, bass and conga. The Los Angeles session was held on March 25 and the personnel was the same except that Eddie Cano replaced Wyands on piano and there was no flute. Tunes recorded in San Francisco were: Alegres Congas, Mambo Moderno, Afro-Corolombo, Alegres Timbales, and Mueve la Cintura, while Ritmo Caliente, Mambo Inn, Bernie's Tune, Goza and Panchero Mambero were made in Los Angeles.

Al McKibbon, who appeared on both dates, has been the anchorman of the George Shearing Quintet for several years and before that was with Dizzy Gillespie's big band. He is one of the most underrated bassists of our time and, in Cal's opinion, one of the few American jazz musicians with a true understanding of the complex Afro-Cuban bass rhythms. He doubles on conga drum and was a close friend, as well as a student, of the late Chano Pozo.

Jerome Richardson, who plays the flute solos, is a San Franciscan who has played alto sax and flute with Lionel Hampton, Vernon Alley and Earl Hines. Armando Peraza, who joined Shearing when Cal left, is a young Cuban who has played with Machito and many other Latin bands and is possibly the most exciting bongo and conga drummer in jazz. Richard Wyands is a young San Franciscan, a graduate of San Francisco State music school, who has worked with Vernon Alley's group for several years and is heard with Charlie Mariano on Fantasy LP 3–10. Eddie Cano, a young Los Angeles Latin pianist, is the composer of Goza and numerous other Latin tunes. He was featured with the Les Baxter Orchestra on Capitol's *Le Sacre du Sauvage* album.

A word on the tunes: Goza features Cal on timbales and Cano on piano, and it means "have a ball." Pachero Mambero is another Cano composition featuring Cal on vibes; Allegres Conga is a short, happy display of Al McKibbon and Armando on conga drums in a Cuban dance beat; Mambo Moderno is Richard Wyands' modern jazz harmony on a slow mambo beat; Afro-Corolombo is a tune based on a rhythm used as dance music on the African Gold Coast; Cal heard it on some field expedition recordings as done by the original natives and adapted it for this album.

Ritmo Caliente features Cano on piano and Armando on bongos and conga and Mambo Inn features McKibbon's bass and Cal's vibes; Alegres Timbales is another happy Latin jam session giving Cal a chance to record the feeling of the timbales; Mueve la Cintura, Cal's own tune, gives the vibes and flute a chance to show off, the latter working between two chord changes in the typical montoona style; Bernie's Tune, which Gerry Mulligan popularized, is played here for the first time in Latin style.

Cubano Chant, Buhuto, and Lamenta De Hodi were recorded in New York on November 11, 1955, and these compositions feature again the talents of Jerome Richardson on flute; Al McKibbon, bass; Armando Peraza, conga and bongos; with Manuel Duran on piano.

Mas Ritmo Caliente

As Dr. Morrell, the eminent researcher into the mystique of Afro-Cuban drumming, remarks on Fantasy's LP *Going Loco* (Fantasy 3203) "the mambo is a rhythm . . . Somewhere between the beguine and a rumba . . . Which allows the musicians considerable latitude in what they do."

This LP is by no means a collection of mambos. Rather it is a collection of various Latin rhythms including the mambo, the cha-cha-cha, the nanigo, the guanaco (Afro-Cuban rhythms close to a medium tempo rumba) and some assorted jamming in rhythm, Cuban style.

It is also spiced with the authentic flavor of jazz and blessed by the presence of some of the top Latin rhythm men in the United States— virile examples of the ultimate in authenticity in Latin rhythm, what Chano Pozo, the greatest of all the Cuban drummers to be heard in the U.S., called the trademark—"skin on skin!"

For some years now Cal Tjader has experimented with a blend of Latin rhythms and jazz with substantial success. And he has concerned himself more and more with the Afro-Cuban origins of these rhythms and he has frequently jammed with the top men in this field in Chicago, New York and Los Angeles. No "hill boy" himself, he has grown in stature as a vibes man through the years in both the Latin and the jazz field and this album, in his own opinion, is the best Afro-Cuban LP he has made.

For the dates from which this LP was taken, Cal used a variety of musicians. In Chicago, for instance, he was able to use Al McKibbon, that consistently fine bass player who was first exposed to the Latin influence while a section mate of the late Chano Pozo in the Dizzy Gillespie band and has continued it in the George Shearing group. With McKibbon came Armando Peraza, considered by musicians and fans alike the most consistently exciting bongo and conga drummer since Chano Pozo.

Armando is a veteran of the Machito orchestra, Slim Gaillard's group and in recent years has been featured with the George Shearing quintet. "I wanted to use a timbales player in Chicago," Cal says, "and I asked Armando and Mac if they knew of one and they did." It was Armando "Cuco" Sanchez, only in this country a short time from Cuba and, of all things, working in Chicago for the Fantasy distributor. Luis Kant, the regular conga drummer with the Tjader group, rounded out the rhythm section.

After the Tjader group played the London House in Chicago in the autumn of 1957, they went to New York to work opposite Dizzy Gillespie at Birdland. There they encountered a remarkable Cuban tenor saxophonist named José "Chombo" Silva. "I had heard him in sessions," Cal says "and he came in the club and played with us a couple of times. He was a tremendously exciting soloist. He has that definiteness that is so good to hear. He plays Latin music with an authentic jazz feeling and he loves straight jazz." Chombo is a veteran of the Machito orchestra and has spent some time in Europe.

The rest of the New York group consists of Tjader's regular pianist, Vince Guaraldi, a versatile pianist in any genre; Ramon "Mongo" Santamaria, an exciting conga drummer who has played with the big Latin bands in New York; Armando Peraza, in town with the Shearing group and again lending his exciting rhythms; Luis Kant, who this time played gourd and cowbell; Willie Bobo, the timbales player from the Tito Puente band; Bobby Rodriguez, bassist from the Puente band, and a fine alto saxophonist and flute player, Gerald Sanfino.

Of the tunes on this album, the opening selection, "Perdido," featured Chombo wailing away in an excellent example of his swinging tenor style in a real mambo groove with the authentic Latin jazz feeling. This is a side from the New York session and has solos by all the horns, Guaraldi and Tjader, too. "Armando's Hideaway" is done in the oddly insinuating guaguanco rhythm, closely associated with a major Cuban dance. "Cuco On Timbales," like the previous tune a product of the Chicago session, "is medium tempo to let Cuco improvise on timbales, sort of a Latin equivalent of a Basie blues," Cal points out. It is fascinating to hear the way McKibbon and Peraza worked together here with the bass under the drums. "Tumbao, Parts I and II" was recorded in San Francisco with Cal's regular group and was first recorded by Cal in a Universal short which he made in 1957. "Ritmo Rumba" is a fast dance with the three rhythm men from the Chicago date, McKibbon, Cuco and Armando improvising in exciting fashion. Note the staccato sound of Armando on bongos and the rapidity of Cuco's timbales playing. "Big Noise From Winnetka" is a favorite from the old Bob Crosby band with Cal doing the whistling.

The rest of it is a duet between McKibbon on bass and Armando on bongos. Listen again to the intricate and easy way they work together.

"Poinciana" is played as a slowed cha-cha with emphasis on prettiness in playing, particularly Tjader's vibes solo. "Mongorama" was made up on the spot to let Chombo and Willie Bobo improvise and it is an exciting number from start to finish. "Ritmo Africano" is done in the insinuating 6/8 time of the Gold Coast nano rhythm and "Perfidia," which runs eight minutes, is a cha-cha-cha. The band uses only four chord changes on "Perfidia," montoona fashion, and all the men, flute, tenor and vibes and piano, get a chance to wail. There's a fascinating passage with the flute playing behind the tenor that I especially liked.

As Chano Pozo said, the thing is authentic when it's skin on skin and you can tell it in an instant when you hear it. Whether you are attracted to this LP for the sound qualities and the kicks they give on hi-fi sets or for the Afro-Cuban rhythms or the merger of Latin and jazz, it should please you. This is not only the best Latin LP Tjader has made, but the most versatile as well.

[Liner notes, Fantasy Records—F24712, 1973]

Ben Webster

Another Giant Gone

◼

W hen, a couple of years ago, I did the notes on the back of Miles Davis' album, *Bitches Brew*, I said that there would always be time to listen to Ben play "Funny Valentine."

Ever since, people have been asking me—not jazz fans, because they know, but people from the rock audience—just who was Ben?

Well, Ben died recently of a heart attack. He was a tenor saxophone player and he had lived in Europe for most of the last 10 years. His name was Benjamin Francis Webster and if you want comparisons, he was to the tenor saxophone, perhaps, what Szigeti has been to the violin. What I mean is that Ben did not invent concepts and styles of improvisational playing on the tenor, but he developed a highly personal sound and the ability to phrase and to invent astonishing solos, all of them delivered with a special sort of high-voltage emotional content.

The analogy doesn't quite work, of course, because classical violinists are not composers; they are interpreters and Ben was both. Not that he wrote that many original compositions (though every one of his improvisations was in itself an original composition even if based on or inspired by someone else's work). Ben was a superb interpreter and a magnificent jazz instrumentalist, some of whose solos on Ellington records, for instance, have become in themselves traditional ways to play these compositions. Sometimes—once at the Monterey Jazz Festival—instrumental arrangers have scored a Ben Webster solo for an entire saxophone section, it had such originality and form.

The essence of jazz artistry is the ability, developed over years and years of assiduous practice, listening and absorption of music, to step to the front of the stage and, right off the top of the head, improvise enchanting melodies and moving variations on themes. Ben knew no superior at this kind of thing and the fact that he was able over a long, long career to do it every time in that astonishing combination of hard tenor tone and breathy, sensual sound, established him early on as one of the true kings of that instrument.

They called Ben "Brute" because he was built like a wrestler with a severe face and a scowl when he played. He looked like a black version of the guy who turns you down for credit at the used car lot. Yet he was gentle and romantic and sweet and it all came out in his playing.

He could be, in person, far from gentle and romantic and sweet as anybody who knew him was well aware. A few days after he died, Dizzy Gillespie and John Levy, who used to play bass in jazz groups before he became one of the top managers in the world of entertainment, were talking about Ben. When Levy put down the bass the world of jazz gained a businessman of stature but it lost a fine bassist. John told us that day about a night, years and years ago, when he was playing in a Harlem club. The club had a long bar and Ben came in "carrying that long, gold-topped cane he used to have, and he just swept it along the bar knocking all of the glasses to the floor," John said. "And then I got down from the bandstand and took him by the arm and walked him out around the corner to another bar and sat there and told him how he didn't have to act like that, how everybody really loved him. And it ended up with Ben sitting there crying."

"You always were the peacemaker," Dizzy said.

Ben was a man who needed a peacemaker because he was, for all his talent and his incredible musical gifts, a troubled soul. And when his trouble was deepest, he tended to let it erupt in such capers. But, as John Levy noted, Ben always knew who not to fight!

The reason Ben was a troubled soul was that he knew his art and he knew how little it was appreciated. In our world the innovator generally gets the attention and the interpreter may completely miss it. Many of us, myself included, tended to overlook Ben in our search for innovators and I know that hurt. But there was more to it than that; Ben was a black artist in a white society and it drove him to despair and eventually into exile. The first deep, poignant hint of that I had was when a British jazz critic who met with Ben in New York told me of the experience. He and Ben talked very frankly for an hour or more and then an American jazz critic, white, came into the room and right in mid-sentence, Ben began to change what he was talking about. That episode tells a lot of how it seems to a black artist here in the land of the free and so on.

Ben's life (he was 64 when he died) paralleled much of the history of jazz and the list of people he played with reads like the roster of the great. Ben started out as a violinist and switched to piano (self-taught) and then took up tenor when he went to work in a band led by Lester Young's father. He followed Coleman Hawkins in the Fletcher Henderson band and was a star of the big black bands in the Thirties, but came to his full fame with Duke Ellington in the Forties and rues the day he ever left. In fact I think if Ben had not wanted so badly to be back with "the Governor" he might have accomplished his dream. But the Duke digs cool and Ben was a flat-out unashamed admirer of everything Ellington did and knew where his true home was. After all, they never had a tenor in Duke's band until Ben joined them in Boston and when, a decade later, Paul Gonsalves took over that chair, what Duke dug the most was Paul's ability to play Ben's solos.

Ben made jazz history at the Monterey Jazz Festival more than once. He "wrote his name" there with a blues solo following Jimmy Witherspoon's ode to balling in the rain and he wrote it on the stages of many clubs and concert halls as well.

But he couldn't make a living at it in his native land. And his spirit, that glorious, loving spirit which imbued his playing with that incredible human quality, could not be nurtured in this society.

So he left.

Ben playing "Funny Valentine"? God yes. He played all of it every time he blew and he opened his heart to us and we let him down and so he went away. He's going to be hard to forget, though, as long as those albums last.

[*Rolling Stone*, November 8, 1973]

Frank

Then and Now

■

I t's hard to put into words now what Frank Sinatra meant to me
when I first got hooked on music. I can tell you that when he and
Woody Guthrie were both singing in the same city, I went to hear
Sinatra. I can also tell you that I had three singers I dug then:
Louis Armstrong, Billie Holiday and Frankie.

But that's not enough. At best it only lists my personal preference,
and it doesn't get at all into what it was about Sinatra that turned us
all on.

You read today about the Swing Era and the bobbysoxers swooning
at the Paramount Theater in New York when Frankie sang and all that,
but he reached out past bobbysoxers, believe me.

Sinatra had style in a time when style meant not only what passed
for sharp clothes, but included manner and, in his case, the sound and
use of his voice. He sang the pop songs of that time—those dumb, trite
ballads that Louis Armstrong treated as vehicles for comedy and Billie
Holiday made into tragedies—as though they were real stories. He had
the sound and the sliding grace of a good cellist and he phrased like a
horn player.

And far beyond the capability he had as a singer, he had a personal
sound. You knew it was him when you heard the first notes on the air
or on record. And, in another way, he *sang* as opposed to just mouthing
the words or making sound. He gave you the feeling of reaching out to
you, either speaking to you or for you, depending on the lyric. Above all
he did it with style.

It is simply weird now to see him all glossed up like a wax dummy, with that rug on his head looking silly, and the on stage movement, which used to be panther-tense now a self-conscious hoodlum bustle. It's even harder to see him with his bodyguards and hear all the gossip about his coterie of friends and their capers in this club or that hotel or that gambling joint.

He used to mean something to my generation and he probably still means something to some. But there are those of us who still dig his voice—that style he had was big enough and broad enough to carry the careers of half a dozen others—but for whom Ol' Blue Eyes is a drag that Frankie never was.

You see, he had the charm. He could turn it on and entertain, let the smile come out of those eyes and the voice out of that mouth and in 10 seconds he had you. Sometimes he could do it just walking on the stage. He didn't cheat. He gave a good show every time I ever saw him and you knew *he* knew what he was doing and you knew *he* knew he wouldn't let you down.

Back in the early years he got a lot of hard lines in the press for running with mobsters and visiting Lucky Luciano in Cuba and things like that. It didn't hurt him a bit. His insistence on picking his friends as he wanted to fell short of pure bravado and even had a touch of sincerity.

Today, he's swapped Charlie Lucky and the other mobsters for Spiro Agnew and Ronald Reagan and who is to measure the difference? All I know is that what seemed a useful bravado 25 years ago seems like angry perversity now. You used to think of him as a guy who could be Robin Hood, who could help some poor cat who was in real need. Today the guys he helps are millionaires and he behaves, if even only half the print is true, like an arrogant despot with a court of sycophants Uncle Tomming their asses off.

You see, somewhere along the line he stopped believing in the art he had. He hit the bottom of public acceptance, people did not come to his shows, his records were stiff right out of the morgue, and he was broke and had no future. He pulled himself out of that (guts he always had), and made himself into a good actor and then into a singer again and parlayed it all into his own record company and production company and $1 billion in nickels and dimes.

Now he can't spend his money in one lifetime even at his pace. His possible appearance on a TV show is the occasion for bodyguards and hush-hush phone calls and big security plans and a blanket of secrecy. Why? So the millions of Sinatra fans won't mob him and tear him to bits? So he won't be kidnapped and held for ransom?

You know, I swear to God I don't think anybody but he and those clowns on his payroll really think any of this panoply of power is necessary. For Frank Sinatra, whose voice made him the friend of millions of Americans, whose films made him even greater, to carry on like a Caribbean dictator holding back history with bodyguards and the secret police is simply obscene.

I only met him once. Back in 1941 when he was starting a three-nights-a-week CBS radio show which he did for a bit and then went with Harry James. He was as nice a guy as I ever met, sincere, decent, warm, human. I have dug his singing ever since and I did the liner notes to his first album on his own label.

But I know enough by this time to realize that he doesn't have to be a nice guy to be a great singer. And he is a great singer. And he doesn't owe me or you or anybody a damn thing. But by the same token, I can dig his singing and not dig his style anymore nor dig his friends nor his attitudes nor what they imply. I'd still go to hear him instead of Woody Guthrie, but the comparison is a little silly since the content of practically all Sinatra songs has had all the social significance of a good solid burp. Whatever Woody Guthrie may have been, he was no crooner.

Comparisons aside, and even granting his right to be whatever he wants to be, all I can say is that it just ain't the same. Somehow I know in my bones that Frank's not the guy he was that afternoon at 485 Madison Avenue. I'm not the same either but I think he went somewhere I would not go, somewhere that makes him alien now to me in a way he never was before.

The voice is good today. Those warm tones are there and the phrasing. He can really do it like a true professional. But I don't believe, anymore, that he is one of us. He is one of them now, singing from the other side of the street and I guess he doesn't even have a whiff of how power-mad and totalitarian it all seems, those bodyguards and the Rat Pack and all that egocentric trivia that has nothing at all to do with music. And he was once a thorough musician, right down to his toes. But then he didn't wear a rug, and I have the feeling he wouldn't have. All that came later when, in truth, he had lost a lot more than his hair.

[*Rolling Stone*, June 6, 1974]

Farewell to the Duke

■

Edward Kennedy "Duke" Ellington was three weeks and four days past his 75th birthday when he died last month in a New York City hospital.

He had played his music in almost every part of the world except China and Siberia. He had dined with presidents and kings, had a Prince of Wales accompany him on drums, played piano duets with a U.S. president, performed his music on TV in Japan, Sweden, England and the U.S. He scored Broadway shows, did a ballet with Alvin Ailey, conducted symphonies in various countries, wrote for Toscanini and the Paris Symphony, scored films for Otto Preminger and wrote special shows for TV.

His series of Sacred Concerts—among his most important works by his own estimation—was presented in cathedrals from Coventry and London and Barcelona to New York and San Francisco.

He composed approximately 3000 original works, many of them portraits of leading black artists, members of his own orchestra, friends and lovers and many others, and tonal histories of black people in America. His accomplishments defy cataloging and his honors are so impressively diverse and extensive that they are almost bizarre. He received honorary degrees from at least 15 colleges and universities including Yale, Columbia, Brown, Harvard and Wisconsin. Nixon awarded him the Presidential Medal of Freedom (highest civilian award of the U.S.), Lyndon Johnson gave him the President's Gold Medal, President Pompidou awarded him the Legion of Honor, and the city of Paris honored him with a special medal. Musicians' organizations around the world gave him special awards. He was made a member of the Royal Swedish Academy of Music and the American Academy of Arts and Sciences.

In 1964 the Poultry and Egg National Board elected him a member of the National Good Egg Club, and two countries, Chad and Togo, have issued stamps in his honor.

The list of prizes for him and his band (in magazine polls) comes to 77. Seven U.S. states gave him special recognition and he won nine separate awards from the National Academy of Recording Arts and Sciences.

The April issue of Schwann Record & Tape Guide, the reference work to recorded music, lists 72 Ellington albums in a special Ellington section.

But in the composer section immediately following, there is only one Ellington listing—of three of his longer works with the Cincinnati Symphony.

Ironically, in 1965 the Pulitzer Prize committee, rather than give him a special award in music, decided instead not to give an award in that category. Ellington, in a typical mocking comment said, "fate is being kind to me. Fate doesn't want me to be too famous too young." Two members of the committee quit in protest.

Something seems wrong here. America's greatest composer, in the opinion of so many musicians, never got the acceptance his art deserved from American intellectuals. In 1965 Dwight MacDonald wrote a long article in the *New York Review of Books* on the White House party for the arts, in which he mourned the fact that American composers were not present along with the writers, painters, actors and others. Yet, in the same article, he said the best moments of the whole event were when Duke Ellington's orchestra played the Ellington music. Obviously Ellington was not a composer in his eyes.

Until the day he died, Duke Ellington's appearances with that orchestra were governed by the American Federation of Musicians' rules that apply, not to so-called classical concerts, but to dance bands and entertainment.

Early in his remarkable career, Ellington knew he was more than a piano player, more than a songwriter and more than a bandleader. He knew he was a composer and an artist of the first rank, and the first time he took his orchestra into the studio in 1926 to record orchestrally, and not just as an accompaniment to singers or as a blues or a novelty group, he did two original compositions that stand as classics: "East St. Louis Toodle-Oo" and "Birmingham Breakdown."

In the years that followed, Ellington recorded more than 300 times, putting on disc a history of pop music of the Twenties, Thirties, Forties, Fifties and Sixties—from funky down-home blues to "Blowin' in the Wind" and his own symphonic compositions. One of the most consistent things about his original works was their reflection of the black culture from which he came. He celebrated life in the ghettos of New Orleans, Birmingham, Washington and New York. These compositions evolved only in the past ten years into the extended religious works of his Sacred Concerts. And even there he incorporated adaptations or revisions of other ostensibly secular material.

By the time Ellington went into the hospital early this year, the recognition black artists were achieving in other fields seemed somehow to be superfluous for him. He had won all the polls, his popular songs—from "Mood Indigo" and "Sophisticated Lady" to "Satin Doll"—were standards in the catalogs of record companies and in the libraries of performers, and his own music stands on its own, as a body apart from the rest of American music, so individual as to be almost a protest.

Nelson Algren once observed that "if society denies someone their reality, then they'll structure their own reality." That is precisely what Duke Ellington did. He knew what league he was really competing in ("Bach and myself both write and with the individual performer in mind"), even when the critics and the impresarios and the managers denied it. After his first Carnegie Hall concert in the early Forties, one manager dismissed his extended compositions as valueless (as did some critics) and is supposed to have told him to get back to "nigger music." He even had to fight at first to get his membership in ASCAP, the American Society of Composers, Authors and Publishers.

So Duke early on reached a decision. Let the symphonies and Philharmonic orchestras be supported by civic organizations and foundations. He had to have his music played and since he wrote for a special group of virtuoso players he would pay for his own orchestra by writing pop songs and playing in nightclubs. He did it for decades. His musicians received the most expensive payroll in the popular music or symphonic fields. He wrote its songs that earned him a guaranteed six-figure income for years, and he toured night after night. His was the only band that always worked 52 weeks a year and never disbanded.

Some of his people played with him long enough to have earned retirement pensions from General Motors. Harry Carney joined him in 1927 and was with him till the end. Johnny Hodges, Ray Nance, Cootie Williams, Lawrence Brown, Russell Procope and Jimmy Hamilton all spent upwards of 20 years playing the Ellington music. "I let them have all the money and I have the fun," he once explained.

He became so successful as a nightclub performer, as a songwriter, as a personality, that his serious musical efforts never got the attention they deserved. He mesmerized everybody with his elegance, his charm and his melodies, and then went ahead and wrote important music behind that screen.

He called it "skillapooping" and defined it as the art of "making what you're doing better than what you're supposed to be doing."

And so in nightclubs, he would introduce Johnny Hodges, the alto saxophonist, and, under the guise of having Hodges play some lacy, luxurious, bluesy melody, the band would proceed to perform a five- or 10-minute composition inspired by a Shakespeare play, a mountain in the Near East, a city in Japan or his memories of life in Harlem.

Duke was addicted to his own music. A prisoner of it, in truth, and some of his most casual efforts were so successful that audiences demanded them 20 years and more after Duke thought he had finished with them. The same was true of his musicians.

Ten years after one member had left, people would still ask for them and critics would compare Duke's immediate program with his early compositions and his current band with his original one. Duke was philosophical about it all.

This nostalgia for the gold days and our music is really a great compliment. To think that 25 years ago I had the good taste to select Barney Bigard, Juan Tizol, Wellman Braud, Harry Carney and all the rest. I'm just a victim of my own good taste.

The problem with Ellington was that he was so much more than he seemed, so many things at once. He confessed that he never could resist a challenge and deplored his own drive to move on to different things. Yet he was, beneath it all, always consistent in the quality of his music and no matter what bows he made to fad, from bossa nova to the twist, he was serious under the suave smile because, as he once said, "There has never been a serious musician who is as serious about his music as a serious jazz musician."

Duke lived well. He came from a family that lived well. He was never in want and never scuffled except for his first gig. In New York once, as he recalled, he and his band (then a small group) used to "split a hot dog five ways." He traveled in the Thirties on his tours of the U.S. not on a bus, but in two railroad cars: "That was the way the president traveled." The band lived and ate and loved and partied in those cars throughout the most prejudiced areas of the South. In fact as Ellington once remarked when a TV reporter tried to trap him into putting down the civil rights movement, he had his own freedom march in the Thirties: "We went down in the South without federal troops."

The public saw Duke on TV or in concert or in the nightclubs as a man who dressed his speech in all sorts of verbal circumlocutions, who changed clothes two or three times during a show or concert, who eternally smiled and blew kisses at the audience and accepted their applause with his standard line, "we love you madly," that he would sometimes deliver in a variety of foreign languages to accentuate his sophistication.

But backstage Ellington could be as funky and down-home as any human being. I remember standing with him one afternoon in the wings at the Paramount Theater in San Francisco while his band played. Duke listened, his legs spread apart, gently rocking from side to side, chewing gum (Juicy Fruit) and hitching up his belt from time to time. In the band at that period were two saxophonists who were dedicated to achieving nirvana through chemicals. While a long trumpet solo was in progress, the two sat in their chairs, heads drooping, nodding on the job. Duke shook his head and, out of the side of his mouth, said to me, "I don't understand it at all. I'm a cunt man myself."

And so he was. Ellington's nightclub engagements were especially notable for the appearance of ladies of all ages, colors and conditions. And Duke treated them all like queens.

When we were filming the documentary *Love You Madly* (nominated for an Emmy in 1967), Duke turned to the script girl the second night of the shooting. "Sweetie," he said, "I don't know your name. You must tell me right away because last night when I dreamed about you I could only call you 'baby.'" She almost fainted.

Another time I introduced a young woman to Duke saying, "she is in a class I'm teaching." Duke took her by the hand, smiled, and said to both of us, "and have you told her I'm giving classes every night in my hotel suite?" Duke's delicacy about romantic matters is legendary. Once when he called to ask if I could make a hotel reservation for him, he added, almost as an afterthought, "and a separate room for the young lady who is traveling parallel to me."

In his autobiography, *Music Is My Mistress*, Duke tells about the time at the White House when Nixon presented him with the presidential medal. Duke gave him double kisses on each cheek and he turned. "Four kisses?" the president asked. "Why four?" "One for each cheek," Duke responded smoothly and Nixon said, "Oh." I've seen that bit of choreography done with an aging society matron who then walked away dreamily after Duke's answer only to stop suddenly, turn around and blush as she finally understood the implications.

Old lady friends, those on one-night stands or those who settled in for longer engagements, never forgot. One night at a San Francisco club, a tall older woman who looked like the ghost of an all-American beauty of 25 years before came up to him. She was wearing a mink coat that dripped money and was bejeweled like an oil baron's wife. "Duke," she said, "can you play 'Birmingham Breakdown'? For me?" He smiled and turned away. She tugged at his coat and added, "don't you remember? Miss so-and-so's school in Dallas, in 1928?" Duke ignored her firmly, not because he didn't remember but because she reminded him of how old he was. The lady finally turned and walked to the back of the club, stood there for a minute fuming and then took off her expensive Italian shoes and threw them, one at a time, across the room at him.

Duke's music was as much about love and about ladies as it was about black culture. He would play "Satin Doll" and announce that a "Satin Doll" was one "which was just as pretty inside as outside." And "Passion Flower" he defined as "one better enjoyed than discussed." He never made small talk out of a description of "Warm Valley," another of his more romantic numbers, but then he didn't have to. Especially if you listened.

Duke himself was a listener. He claimed to be the best and said that listening was his pleasure. He had to keep that huge payroll of the band growing (some got over $600 a week) because that was the only way he could hear his music played right after he wrote.

Ellington was a facile composer who could write swiftly and on-demand. He spent large blocks of time in quiet solitude, either in airplanes or while driving from date to date with his baritone saxophonist, Harry Carney. He thought out his compositions carefully. Sometimes, he once told me, the most important things were thought out on the john. Then he wrote. Anything could inspire him. A pretty face, a sound in the city, the view of a mountain.

During the times he was producing, Duke would frequently write all night long in his hotel room after the concert or the nightclub job. He trained himself to do this, sleeping during the day. He needed to be isolated for think time and those late night and early morning hours were when it was easiest to come by.

At times his ability to write in quick bursts of creativity was astonishing. "Black and Tan Fantasy," he once told me, was written in 1927 in New York "in a taxicab. We used to stay in Mexico's juice joint all night long and would usually be there until time to go to the recording date which was at 9 o'clock in the morning . . . And there I was with a number to write and so I wrote 'Black and Tan Fantasy' in a taxicab on the way to the studio going down Central Park. And 'Mood Indigo,' I wrote it in New York in 15 minutes while I was waiting for my mother to finish cooking dinner. And 'Solitude' I wrote in 20 minutes in Chicago standing up against the glass office enclosure waiting for another band to finish recording. I wrote the whole thing standing up. 'Sophisticated Lady' is one of the things I struggled with for a month. In 1939 we did 32 one nighters in 30 days and I wrote a lot of things like 'Jack The Bear.'"

"I was the yearling," Duke recalled, "and played less than anyone and I had the best job at Mexico's on Broadway. We had some great sessions. There'd be The Lion [Willie "The Lion" Smith] and James P [James P. Johnson] to give the keys a dusting and I'd take a shot at it and Fats [Fats Waller] was there. He could play even then. There were some real jam sessions."

The Lion would put his cigar in his mouth and stomp over the piano and say, "Get up. I'll show you how it's supposed to be!" And he would.

If only we had tapes of those nights! And then there was the time Coleman Hawkins and Sidney Bechet tangled at the Candy Club. You should have heard that!

They used to have sessions every Wednesday night at Mexico's. One week they would have the trumpet players, the next week they'd have the tenor players, the next week the trombones. I never will forget the night they had the tubas!

It was a little joint and you couldn't get them all in it. They were backed up out into the street. There were four tubas on the curb waiting to get in and the tuba players inside were using pots and pans and plungers and anything they could lay their hands on to make that waa-waa effect!

Ellington chuckled at the memory.

And it was on the qui vive in those days. No gentlemanly give-and-take. They meant business. We had a small band—six pieces— and we'd run up against some of those big bands and Sonny Greer would walk over to their drummer before the set and look them in the eye and glare and growl out, "I'm gonna cut you!" We scared 'em to death!

And then there was the night that King Oliver met up with Fletcher Henderson's band. Oh, I wish we had a tape of that night!

"I wrote an entire show in one night," Duke told me once. "It was called 'Chocolate Kiddies' and though it never got to Broadway it ran for two years in Berlin with Josephine Baker and Adelaide Hall. I got an advance of $500 for it."

Ellington once wrote a composition called "Harlem Air Shaft" (you can hear echoes of it in Paul Simon's "The Boxer") and he described it as straight programmatic music. "So much goes on in a Harlem air shaft. You get the full essence of Harlem in an air shaft. You hear fights, you smell dinner, you hear people making love. Your intimate gossip floating down. You hear the radio. An air shaft is one great big loud-speaker. You see your neighbors' laundry. You hear the janitor's dogs. The man upstairs' aerial falls down and breaks your window. You smell coffee. . . . An air shaft has got every contrast. You hear people praying, fighting, snoring. I tried to put all that in 'Harlem Air Shaft.'"

The reference to Paul Simon's "The Boxer" is an illustration of how Ellington's music floats around in the air and crops up in the most unlikely places. Simon, for instance, says he doesn't listen to jazz. The author of "Night Train" certainly did. He's Jimmy Forrest, a tenor saxophone player who once spent a year or so working for Ellington. When he left, he took along a good memory of an Ellington composition called "Happy Go Lucky Local" (part of the Duke's Deep South Suite, which was never recorded in full). Ellington always claimed to have been flattered by the exact parallel of "Night Train" to the theme of "Happy Go Lucky Local."

There is a bit of Ellington's "Night Creature" (written for Arturo Toscanini and the NBC Symphony) in Leonard Bernstein's West Side Story and the Duke always claimed Count Basie's "1 O'Clock Jump" was the child of a phrase he played in an early blues. "Moonglow," the pop song of the Thirties that Steve Allen made into a hit in 1955 as "Theme From Picnic," is easily recognizable as a reworking of Ellington's "Lazy Rhapsody," first recorded in 1932. And then, of course, contemporary blues fans who dig Junior Parker's version of "Goin' Down Slow" are probably unaware that the instrumental blues figure in the background is an exact reconstruction of Adelaide Hall's wordless vocal on Ellington's "Creole Love Call" (circa 1927).

As far as I know Ellington never sued anyone for any borrowing of Ellington material. He professed to be flattered, and in a way he was. There certainly has been no lack of direct Ellington influence, something short of plagiarism, in almost every era jazz has gone through since he first came on the scene.

But in other ways, he could be very touchy about his prerogatives. He once lectured Dave Brubeck for allowing Dave's sidemen to share his dressing room. "You're a leader, a star," he told Dave—and stars don't share dressing rooms. And once when The Crescendo, a Hollywood nightclub, appeared to be giving top billing to comedian Mort

Sahl, Ellington refused to enter the club until the proper order of billing was accomplished.

Duke considered himself, at least in his show business personality, an equal with all the stars. And he certainly was. Duke was secure enough in this that he thought it funny when Hubert Humphrey stepped out of an elevator at the George V in Paris, looked at Duke and said, "Cab! Good to see you!"—thinking him to be bandleader Cab Calloway.

Ellington, as Stanley Dance noted when he delivered the eulogy at Duke's funeral, loved America. He was a patriot in a somewhat different sense from John Wayne. Duke fought racism all his life and he spoke out plainly in his autobiography, saying it was basically an economic disease. "Our major problem," Duke wrote, is "brainwashing of children and adults . . . [It] is the worst in the world . . ." There are educational institutions in the U.S. where we would still be barred from teaching because of opinions like that.

Duke's patriotism was not just based on his receipt of presidential honors. He felt this country had been good to him. When Franklin D. Roosevelt died, for instance, Ellington and his orchestra performed a singular service. While the presidential funeral train was traveling from Hot Springs to Hyde Park, the blue network (which was the predecessor to ABC) had Ellington on the air for hours, from the Radio City studios, playing a long program of his own compositions. Ellington was proud of the fact that his was really the only American music heard on the air that dreadful day.

He had done the same thing once before under slightly different circumstances. The night in the Thirties the Lindbergh baby was kidnapped, Duke was broadcasting from a Chicago ballroom and the network kept the band on the air into the early morning hours so that the lines would be open for bulletins about the kidnapping.

Sometimes the black press and his black audience thought he was less than outspoken in his support of the civil rights movement. Yet, as Duke told Nat Hentoff in 1965, "People who think that of me haven't been listening to our music. For the past 25 years, social protest and pride in the history of the Negro have been the most significant themes in what we've done. . . . We've been talking about what it is to be a Negro in this country for a long time."

All through his career, Duke's compositions reflected this, from "A Night In Harlem" in 1926 and "Black Beauty" in 1928 (long before Black was beautiful) down to his more recent "Togo Brava Suite," "Black Swan" and "Afrique." And back in Harlem in the Twenties, Ellington was trying to get other bandleaders like Fletcher Henderson to call their music Negro music, not jazz.

Yet, as I said before, Duke had his earthy side. If you hung out with him for a while, you saw it when he met the night people, the black doormen, the taxicab drivers and the street hustlers, each of whom had a word for him and many of whom he had known for years. They always dug him. He was a soft touch.

Backstage, he could bring off his elegant ambience under the most trying of circumstances. I remember him one night after a concert in a grimy old fraternal hall, standing in an improvised dressing room, just a sheet hung on a clothesline between some posts. Duke was in his shorts, a bandanna wrapped around his head, and he sat at a card table greeting one after another of his friends and making the whole shoddy room seem regal. Another time in a similar dressing room at a nightclub, an old friend apologized for thrusting himself upon the Maestro when the latter was changing clothes. Duke smiled beatifically and said, "I only take my clothes off with the people I love."

His humor could be sharp. When several of his best men left in the early 50s, he told me, "I'm just a young bandleader starting out again. I'm not old enough to be historical and I'm too young to be biographical."

Once when a new trombone player, who had been drinking a little more than he could handle, stumbled and fell down just as he had been introduced to take a solo, Duke turned to the audience and said, "This is not a lull. It's a dramatic pause."

Miles Davis has said, "Duke puts everybody on," and there was the usual Milesian truth to the statement. When I made the pilot TV show for the educational TV series *Jazz Casual*, Ellington was the guest artist. We were all set and waiting for a 5 o'clock taping. Came 4:45 and no Duke. Came 4:55 and no Duke and then he walked in.

The crew was in a panic. I was sweating like a grand jury witness. I went over to the Maestro and said, "Now Duke, the usual formula is. . . ." Duke smiled benignly at me and said, "Anybody can do it with a format, sweetie. The trick is to do it without one. Now I'll sit at the piano and start to play and you walk on and ask me what the tune is and we'll go from there."

I said "OK," weakly, did what I was told to do and we had a half hour of Ellington and Billy Strayhorn piano duets with the maestro talking up a storm about his music.

Duke could be perverse, too, to put it mildly. When he first appeared at the Monterey Jazz Festival, the same summer he had made a tremendous hit with a long up-tempo number at the Newport Jazz Festival called "Newport Up," Duke asked Jimmy Lyons, the manager of the festival, what he should play. "Anything you want to, Duke," Lyons replied, "except that number about the other festival." So Ellington opened his show with "Newport Up."

Ellington was a piano player and a great one, but his true instrument was his orchestra. One of his greatest abilities was his gift for creating tension with subtle rather than raucous sounds, as his son Mercer has noted. And he wrote, like Bach, for the performer, his performers, which is one of the reasons his scores are not published since they changed from player to player. "It's not the notes that are important," Duke said, "it's who they are written for. Before you can play anything or write anything, you must hear it. Some of the prettiest things on paper come off very drab. So you hear, you imagine, you see a note on a piece of paper and you hear it played in the tone personality of a particular musician.

For instance, here's a guy who uses a mute, and he finds he can get only seven good notes out of it. The problem is to use those seven. Personalized writing is very important. If I didn't know who I was writing for, I don't know what I'd do. When we first did "Black and Tan Fantasy" we found there was a mike tone created by using two horns close to the mike. The problem then, when we did "Mood Indigo" later, was to use that mike tone!

I always consider my problems opportunities to do something. Like Jimmy Valentine or Houdini. Necessity, in other words, is the mother! But I couldn't work without a deadline. If I retired to some luxurious home by the sea, you know what I'd write? Nuthin'!

And so Ellington spent his life on the road with his own self-financed orchestra, writing his music in hotel rooms, taxicabs and airplanes, making the final decisions in the john and hearing it played within hours by the collection of virtuoso musicians he paid so handsomely. Duke thought he was a lucky man to have that pleasure. Money was incidental. "I have to get a bang out of it, not just the money. I'm not worried about writing for posterity. I just want it to sound good right now."

The weekend Duke died, I watched the TV news shows from the funeral parlor and the church with all those thousands who came from all over to mourn him (singer Alice Babs flew in from Spain), and I could not cry for Duke. He was out there living every minute like a teenager right up to the last few months. He had been everywhere, seen everything, knew everybody, and all his adult life he had the one thing he wanted most—his orchestra ("an expensive toy") to play his music. And what music! As the French poet Blaise Cendrars said, "Such music is not only a new art form, but a new reason for living."

I am honored to have known him. His music gave me countless hours of pleasure throughout my life and I expect it will continue to do so. And it was not just pleasure, it was inspiration. Duke's mystery was inspiring. He made you want to know. As André Previn remarked one night after we'd seen Duke's band, "You know, Stan Kenton can stand in front of 1000 fiddles and 1000 brass and make a dramatic gesture and every studio arranger can nod his head and say, 'Oh, yes, that's done like this.' But Duke merely lifts his little finger, three horns make a sound and I don't know what it is!"

Previn's statement, really, says more than a Pulitzer Prize ever could. Duke was a musician's musician and a composer's composer. And one incredible man. Four kisses. One for each cheek.

[*Rolling Stone*, July 4, 1974]

FOLK, ROCK, AND POP

The Limeliters, *Through Children's Eyes*

Little-Folk Songs for Adults

■

The clear, innocent sound of children's voices raised in joyous song has an irresistible appeal all by itself. When you add to this the further advantage of the Limeliters with their full-throated good spirits, you would have to have a heart of stone not to be moved by the result.

This album was recorded during Christmas week, 1961, at the Berkeley Community Theater, Berkeley, California. The Christmas vacation of seventy children from the various Berkeley elementary schools had been utilized for numerous rehearsals.

The performance itself took place on the afternoon of December 29, 1961; it was a benefit for the music department of the Berkeley school system, as well as an opportunity to record the Limeliters in unusual and delightful circumstances.

"I cannot tell you what a kick it was to sing with those children," Lou Gottlieb says. "The sound of their voices was—and I know this seems corny but it is true—simply an inspiration to us. Dr. Blakeslee and Mrs. Wood of the school system were wonderful, cooperative and indispensable. If we were successful at all, great credit is due to them as well as the lovely voices of the seventy children."

The Limeliters, ever since they first sang together, have had fun and have been good fun. This album adds another dimension to the enjoyment we get from their music.

Dr. Earle Blakeslee, head of the Berkeley schools music department, labored far beyond the call of duty in setting up the program with Lou Gottlieb, Glenn Yarbrough and Alex Hassilev. Mrs. Harriet Wood, principal of the Emerson school in Berkeley, served unselfishly as choirmaster during the rehearsals and the final performances. (A second show was given in San Francisco at the Masonic Memorial Auditorium to share the pleasure of the children's singing with the residents of that city.)

[Liner notes, RCA Victor LSP-2512, 1962]

The Magic of Joan Baez

The street in front of Harmon Gym was packed with people in a wild array of rain gear, including one sun-helmet. Umbrellas made a wavy sea of black as the crowd pushed up the steps and on in to see Joan Baez.

A harassed ticket taker screamed, "Stop shoving!" A student laughed at the sign "No seat saving" and the usher inside the gym shrugged his shoulders and said never mind the reserved section, the best seats were in the bleachers.

The small stand at the north end of the UC gym was bare except for a microphone and a tall kitchen stool on top of which was a heavy white mug.

At 8:45, the lights dimmed and the young girl whose songs and personality outdrew the entire Charter Day ceremonies better than three to one, slipped along the bleachers and walked on-stage.

Joan Baez is slim, bird-quick and starkly simple in manner, dress and presentation. No stockings, low leather slippers, short, pleated skirt and a plain, short-sleeved white shirt, no jewelry but a watch. Her hair is extra long and hangs down the sides of her pale thin face. She brushes it aside continually in quick nervous gestures. Her voice is flat, almost metallic, as she makes her brief Salingeresque announcements.

"I'm a rambler, I'm a gambler and a long way from home, and if people don't like me, they can leave me alone."

The thin, reedy, throbbing voice filled the hall. She stopped and the applause roared. She stood there and let the late-comers enter, tuning her guitar.

"There are songs that make me feel like bursting," she said. "These are the songs that make me feel like bursting," and she sang in Spanish and Portuguese a medley that included a song from "Black Orpheus."

Then with quick wit, she did "She's A Trouble Maker," the rock 'n roll hit, all the way through. Entrance music for more latecomers.

"I'm just dying to find out what you sound like when you sing," she said, smiling. Her smile is suddenly beautiful like the smile of all serious people. The audience slowly and carefully rocked "Somebody Got Lost In a Store."

"I'd like to sing one of the saddest songs I know. It's for a friend of mine. It will make her very sad and then later on this evening, she can get happy."

She finished the song, a plaintive Western melody, and brushed back her hair. "I have to say something. I can't get away without a message. It's raining tonight and I can't help thinking that the rain has more fall-out than it ever had before. You can snicker if you want, but you don't like killing babies. I know you think about it, but it won't hurt to think some more."

Then she sang Malvina Reynolds' classic, "What Have They Done to the Rain?" In the hall that earlier that day had seen the science-oriented Charter Day Service.

Someone left her a note and a peace button during the intermission and she put it on when she came back. She asked the audience to sing again with her. This time it was "The Lord's Prayer" as a calypso with "Hallowed be thy name" as the audience's part.

And so it went. Afterward, as the 8000-plus people (she got more than 60 per cent of the net on a box office of more than $14,000) filed out, she sat in Alumni House before a roaring fire, a dark blue blanket around her, receiving a line of well-wishers like some pagan witch-Queen.

What do they hear? "I listen to her for all the poetry," one woman said. And that's as good an explanation of her magic as I've heard.

[*San Francisco Chronicle*, March 25, 1963]

Pete Seeger Is Here Tonight

A half-hour TV film featuring rare and almost forgotten footage of Leadbelly, the great folksinger, has been offered to the Columbia Broadcasting System for presentation in this country.

Pete Seeger, who produced the TV film for the Canadian Broadcasting Corp., offered the film to CBS in this country last week. "We'll find out the answer in a week or so, whether or not I'm really barred from their network," Seeger said the other evening in Los Angeles.

Seeger, who appears tonight at the Longshore Auditorium, did the program for the Canadian network earlier this year. "It turned out beautifully," he says. "I found some movies of Leadbelly done by two amateurs in Pasadena. The professionals said the unedited film wasn't any good. So it sat on their shelf for 17 years and I heard of it and wrote to them. It took a month to sync the sound to the pictures. I finally got eight minutes of Leadbelly synchronized.

"It was a terrible job. I called the show 'Two Links In a Chain.' Leadbelly would sing a song and then I'd sing one. I saw the kinescope again two weeks ago and it's really wonderful. I'm happier with it than anything I've ever done on TV. It ended with me saying to the audience, 'You can be the next link in the chain.'"

Regarding the widely publicized "blacklisting" of Seeger by the ABC-TV "Hootenanny" show, Seeger says "I feel with all its faults, 'Hootenanny' is still a good thing to break the ice with. It's a damn shame that it couldn't be better. The thing I feel worst about—I don't feel badly about myself—is that there's a lot of wonderful people they won't touch.

"People like Doc Watson, whom I believe to be one of the greatest musicians in America. An honest man and a good singer. And Bessie Jones and the Sea Island group. Magnificent. I regret that the show isn't presenting what I call the richness and variety of America."

"For myself, I don't feel bitter at all. I'm really an extraordinarily lucky musician. I'm able to make a good living singing the songs I like.

"But I'm outraged. I actually get hot and flushed just thinking about it, when I think that we have all this richness and variety in our country but a bunch of schmoes, out to sell soap, keep the whole country seeing the same dreary things night after night.

"As far as I'm concerned, if they wanted to find out what the reaction to having me on would be, they could've asked Channel 2 in Miami. I did a show on that station, a commercial TV station, with a professor who talks on books and poetry. He had me on and I sang and talked about folk music for an hour. They got four or five letters protesting before the show went on, but they got over 100 in favor of it after it was shown.

"What program will I sing in San Francisco? Well, it will be a combination of the old and the new. I find myself coming back to this formula. The program isn't complete unless I do some of the older as well as some of the newest. I'm particularly impressed these days by a young man, a true poet, who makes up songs about the things he sees in the world about him. His name is Bob Dylan and I'm convinced he's one of the greatest. I'm learning songs from him right now."

After tonight's performance at the Longshore, Seeger is slated to return to the Bay Area in June for the U.C. Folk Festival. Unfortunately he had prior commitments and couldn't make the Monterey Folk Festival week after next.

[*San Francisco Chronicle*, May 7, 1963]

Odetta the Incomparable

olk music may attract you by the message of the lyric, but in the hands of a performer such as Odetta even the best of the folk lyrics are secondary to the power and the substance of the performer herself.

Saturday night's concert at the Berkeley Community Theater was one of the most successful concerts Odetta has ever given in this area, a grand evening of work songs, blues, folk songs and bits of humorous nonsense, handled with the special deftness that comes only from supreme confidence.

Odetta brings many qualities to her performances, not the least of which is dramatic presence. When she came back and sang "This Little Light of Mine" as an encore, she abandoned her own guitar and sang with only the accompaniment of the bassist, Les Grinage, and her guitarist, Bruce Langhorn, and when she had finished, even during the last bars, she stood there proud, erect and haughty with a hint of a smile on her great, expressive face.

It was a moving moment in a concert of many moving moments. It came, I am sure, as a surprise to most of the audience that she sang "Cool, Clear, Water" and I, for one, had never expected to hear that Sons of the Pioneers song assume its rightful place as a part of American folk music. But it did.

What Odetta has, of course, is a magnificent voice with the power to expand and produce a swelling sound rivaled only by Mahalia Jackson and some few gospel singers.

In addition to that, she has the ability to swing, something which is not too often found in folk circles. Odetta has a nearly perfect sense of rhythm in her phrasing and in the control of her voice. When she strikes the perfect groove for the song (and groove is the only suitable word) as she did in "Walkin' and Talkin' With My Heart Set on Freedom" she swings like mad, in a deep irresistible fashion.

No one in my experience in listening to folk singing has the ability that she has to handle songs of humor with the right touch. Singing "Sweet Potatoes" and "Move Over," she, herself, becomes a great child in the singing and the net result is perfectly charming.

On the deeply felt and emotionally tense songs like "Another Man Done Gone" and "He Had a Long Chain On," she brings all the intensity of the blues performer to her work and makes each line searing in its conviction.

Odetta, more than any contemporary folk performer on the scene now, has been able to identify herself so strongly with her material that she sings a slave song as though she were truly a slave. It is a great tribute to her versatility as a performer.

Her concert Saturday night had the blessing of Bruce Langhorn's guitar accompaniment. He is a remarkable instrumentalist. He plays the Spanish guitar, unamplified and without picks, and he makes it sing and ring and talk and swing.

For any other performer on the same stage simultaneously with Odetta to reach out to the audience on his own is no small feat and Langhorn does this. He is especially effective on numbers like "Rocks For My Pillow" and the chain gang songs like "Another Man Done Gone." On the numbers like "Walkin' and Talkin'," he sets up an irresistible beat interspersed with cries and moans extracted from the guitar in an impressive fashion. Odetta's smiles when she finished each song made her look something like a huge Cheshire cat. It was an indication of her own contentment with how she had sung. The audience—and this reporter—loved all of it.

[*San Francisco Chronicle*, December 2, 1963]

A Folk-Singing Social Critic

■

The first law of mass media is to demean the artistic product. That is why poets can't write for newspapers and *Time* magazine's stories are never about reality but about some never-never Luceland in the sky.

Thus Saturday night's concert at the Berkeley Community Theater by Bob Dylan was especially notable. The pressures of mass media and mass culture have not yet forced Dylan to be anything but himself and Dylan himself is a lean, economical, astringent of reality in a stage world that's mainly pretense.

A packed house heard him sing his songs of vision and warning, heard him grind the emotions in direct confrontations with hypocrisy and heard him celebrate his belief in life with the flashing signs of poetry. And it was nonetheless poetry for being delivered in a nasal voice by a slim youth with uncombed hair wearing a chamois jacket, blue jeans and boots.

And the effect of his concert was not diminished by the appearance midway through the last half of Joan Baez, who joined Dylan for a series of deeply moving duets in which the crystal purity of her voice strangely complemented the rough tones of Dylan.

Together the two sang a group of songs including "With God on Our Side" and "Blowin' in the Wind" and for the first time the true message of the latter song came through to this listener.

Genius makes its own rules and Dylan is a genius, a singing conscience and moral referee as well as a preacher. It's not without significance that a young man remarked Saturday night that, for him, going to church meant going to a Dylan concert.

Dylan's special gift lies in the creation of poetic images that clearly pose the moral dilemmas of our society. In his song about the death of boxer Davey Moore, Dylan says "this is a true story, only the words have been changed." And he sings the refrain "don't say murder, don't say kill. It was destiny. It was God's will." As any rational citizen knows, Davey Moore was victim of the insatiable American crowd-lust for blood. If we were a truly moral people, there would be no professional boxing.

Dylan's songs are carved from the reality of the American dream contrasted to the unreality of how it is. And Dylan sings them out of his own experience, has been made wise by a poetic vision that truth is what's important. "The dirt of gossip blows into my face and the dust of rumor covers me . . ."

Folk music is so much big business success today that it is a major part of show business. We have folk singers sprouting like weeds—some good singers and some good performers. What Dylan has is the poet's ability to transmit a message. His is the personal honesty of a Lenny Bruce. He makes you think; it gets inside you and you can't turn it off when you leave the hall. His anti-performance pose symbolizes the distrust of his generation for the conventions we have lived by and in favor of truth.

Joan Baez is musically more orthodox but emotionally in the same bag. Together they gave one of the most deeply moving performances I have witnessed in many years. It is a moral crime that they have not been recorded together in concert.

The usual words do not fit Dylan. Exciting is not right; disturbing is more accurate. He is a charismatic social symbol to his generation, the voice protesting the compromises of the adult world they never made. It has always been thus, but Dylan's generation, it strikes me, has more strengths and more moral right going for it.

He is a magnificent songwriter (his repertoire is all his own, like Ellington and Monk) and he sang a great new song, "Chimes of Freedom," Saturday night.

He is gradually forming his voice into an effective instrument for the subtleties of his songs. His harmonica playing I find more and more impressive on further hearing and his guitar accompaniment is adequate for his performance.

When I first heard Bob Dylan at Monterey I did not like him. I was deaf. He is truly a great artist and to judge him by the standards of others is a total mistake. He is sui generis, a true loner. But not a misogynist. On stage with Joan Baez he is a charming, small boy full of a delight that belies the seriousness of his message.

Together they were magnificent Saturday night and Dylan alone is one of the great warning voices of our time. In his small boy's, anti-formal manner, he is advocating a moral and social revolution that is long past due.

[*San Francisco Chronicle*, February 24, 1964]

The Beatles' Mersey Sound

■

A spectre is haunting Europe. Four young men called The Beatles, who wear medieval haircuts and leather jackets and sing with a wild, roaring sound, are threatening to dominate the popular music lists in the Common Market, the Outer Six, the Benelux countries and points east. England succumbed months ago and even the United States is now in the throes of what is called "Beatlemania."

So far only Belgium seems immune. Even Finland has a Beatles record in its top-five best sellers.

In the U.S. at the present moment, four Beatles discs on three record labels (Capitol, Swan and VeeJay) are among the top 70 best-selling single discs.

A fourth disc, "My Bonnie," on M-G-M, is just below what Billboard calls "the Hot 100" in the category known as "bubbling under." It is 107. The Beatles, incidentally hate it; it's the first disc they cut, in Germany in 1960 backing up singer Tony Sheridan when the group was called the Beat Boys.

John Lennon, leader of the Beatles, says succinctly, "It's terrible. I wouldn't buy it."

In addition to the records already cut, The Beatles will record two concerts this month, one in Washington D.C., and one at Carnegie Hall, for Capitol. A film score for United Artists will be out at the end of the year.

The Beatles arrive in New York Friday for a live appearance on the Ed Sullivan show Sunday night. Then they go to Washington for a concert February 11, then back to New York to Carnegie Hall February 12 and then for a vacation in Florida which they will interrupt for another live show for Sullivan and a videotaped appearance to be shown later.

The Beatles' first Capitol disc, "I Want to Hold Your Hand," is number one in the U.S. right now, the fastest selling single in Capitol's history and one of the fastest in the history of the record business. When the number was released in England last year, it was the first disc in British history to have sold a million before it was issued!

All of The Beatles sing, and three of them play guitars. The fourth is a drummer. Their rise has been meteoric, to say the least. Within one year, they have come to dominate the popular music field in England and to inspire a whole new wave of "Mersey Sound" groups that are beginning to give them competition in England. Their concerts and personal appearances in England and in France have been definitions of mass hysteria and the madness of crowds.

At a recent provincial concert in England, the group had to be disguised as policemen to evade hysterical fans. Nearly 5000 fans packed outside the Queens Theatre in Blackpool last August forced the Beatles to enter the building by being lowered through the roof after climbing up on builder's scaffolds.

Their appearance at the Royal Variety Show at the Prince of Wales Theatre in London stopped the show for the first time in critics' memories. The Queen Mother is reported to have remarked, after meeting the Beatles backstage, "The Beatles are most intriguing." When told they would next appear in a concert at Slough, she added, "Ah, that's near us."

The Beatles' "Mersey Sound" (Mersey is a river in Liverpool, the city where the group comes from) has divided England into competitive camps (Liverpool vs. London vs. Manchester) in a fashion not seen since the War of the Roses split the country into York and Lancaster.

The Beatles in their present form evolved from several groups. First they were the Quarrymen (from Liverpool's Quarrybank Grammar School), then Johnny and the Moon Dogs, then The Rainbows and then The Silver Beetles. This last was because they admired the sound of The Crickets, an American rock 'n roll group of a few years back.

In 1960 they left Liverpool for a job at the Star Club in Hamburg, dropped the "Silver" from their name, became The Beat Boys and finally the Beatles. Rock 'n roll has long been known in England, incidentally as "beat music" or "the big beat."

George Harrison, the lead guitarist, recalls "We've spent so much of our time in Germany nobody knew us when we came back to Liverpool. We were billed as 'direct from Hamburg' and everybody thought we were German. One girl came up to me and said, 'Aye, don't you speak good English!'"

What do they play? "Well, we don't play rhythm and blues," says John Lennon, the leader. "We just play rock 'n roll as far as I'm concerned, in our own way."

"None of us can read," adds solo guitarist George Harrison, and drummer Ringo Starr says, "This isn't just a job, it's a dedication." Paul McCartney, the bass guitarist, says, "in the early days back at the pool, we didn't give a damn about making the big time. It never entered our heads."

More tomorrow.

[*San Francisco Chronicle*, February 5, 1964]

Who REALLY Is Bob Dylan?

■

The approach of Bob Dylan to the Bay Area—he'll appear in four concerts in Northern California beginning November 25 (San Jose) and including San Francisco (November 27), Sacramento (November 29) and San Mateo (December 1)—heightens interest in one of the great mysteries of our time.

Who is Bob Dylan? The recent *New Yorker* profile by Nat Hentoff, while a fascinating document, ducks this issue completely, and Dylan's own reply is simply: "My name it means nothing; my age it means less, and the country I come from is called the Midwest"—a line from one of his songs.

However, a young lady named Eileen Strong, in a letter to the folk music magazine *Sing Out!*, proposes a fantastic idea but supports it with considerable circumstantial evidence.

Can Bob Dylan be John Lennon of the Beatles? Miss Strong asks.

The idea is intriguing as well as insidious. As Miss Strong points out, both are poets and harmonica players. Dylan's harmonica is in evidence all through his albums and Lennon's can be heard on that great Liverpool folk song, "Love Me Do."

Of course, both play the guitar. Miss Strong points out another similarity, the stance while singing: legs apart and bouncing motions.

As further evidence of her historic theory, Miss Strong has analyzed the compositional similarities of the two singers. Both have high school educations but insist on grammatical "errors."

As Miss Strong points out, in "Money Can't Buy You Love," Lennon writes, "I don't need no diamond rings." In one of his songs, "Playboys and Playgirls," Dylan writes, "Not now or no other time." In addition, while both young men have made a great deal of money, they make a point in their songs at least, of not caring about the world's luxuries.

Although Miss Strong admits that none of her evidence is conclusive, she continues to amass it. Both young men have a sense of humor with definite Chaplinesque overtones. "Fair Thee Well," one of Dylan's songs, is sung to a tune that traces back to an old English ballad, "Farewell To Liverpool." (Of all places!)

And the habit both singers have of wearing the Huck Finn cap.

It was this that struck me as the hardest evidence in favor of the Strong Theory. I have been amazed by the similarity between the cover picture of Dylan on his first Columbia album and the picture of Lennon on the jacket of his book, "In His Own Write."

Add the striking physical resemblance to the similarities Miss Strong has pointed out and my mind went to work and I couldn't sleep.

Do we know of any published photos of Dylan and Lennon together? Ah, ha! Have you thought of the curious fact that when the Beatles were in this country, Dylan was off the scene? In fact, Dylan's 1964 tour of England was reported as taking place JUST BEFORE THE BEATLES CAME TO THE U.S.A.

On Dylan's most recent Columbia disc, "Another Side of Bob Dylan," at one point he obviously looks at or touches something visible to the studio audience and then remarks, "it's something I picked up in England." Curious indeed.

The only person I know who is acquainted with both the Beatles and Bob Dylan is Joan Baez, and this is the strongest evidence I have at the moment that Lennon and Dylan are, in actuality, two different persons.

Last summer when the Beatles and Miss Baez were all in Denver, they met and spent the evening talking ABOUT Dylan. This seems hardly likely if Dylan is, in fact, Lennon and thus was present at the discussion about himself.

On the other hand, I am nagged by one thought—has anyone actually seen them both together? That's the clincher.

[*San Francisco Chronicle*, November 16, 1964]

Jefferson Airplane, *Takes Off*

■

"We like to put the music down like a big hand and grab you and shake you. We like the excitement of the rock."

"We" is Jefferson Airplane and the statement is from their leader and spokesman, Marty Balin.

Jefferson Airplane was the first of the new rock groups to emerge from San Francisco, the Liverpool of the U.S.A. Its fame spread, even before this LP and the first RCA Victor single, far enough so that Donovan, the British songwriter and singer, wrote a song about them, Ride Jefferson Airplane, in which he refers to "trans-love airlines."

It's no accident that Donovan links love and Jefferson Airplane. "All the material we do is about love," Marty Balin says. "A love affair or loving people. Songs about love. Our songs all have something to say, they all have an identification with an age group and, I think, an identification with love affairs, past, beginning or wanting . . . finding something in life . . . explaining who you are.

"When we play, we're involved and I think that really communicates to an audience . . . something, the power of creating, you can feel it. To anyone who is involved, who really believes in what he's doing, it really comes across. Everyone in our group is very involved with what we're doing, enjoys doing it and really believes in it. No matter how many times we do it, we've never, ever, once been on stage when we didn't become one person."

"We're terrific fans of everything that happens and we experiment.

Sometimes the tune is completely finished and I give it to the rest of the guys . . . they start working on it and have ideas . . . it starts happening differently and we completely change the tune . . ."

"I never have to explain my songs to my age group," Marty said when we talked about this LP. There's an instant communication that goes on once you are familiar with Jefferson Airplane's language. It's loud like the world we live in and it's strong, too. But it is also romantic and lyrical. When Marty sings, he says, "I feel like I'm talking. It's the greatest way to communicate."

Listening to rock bands has convinced me—and I'm old enough to have teenaged children of my own—that we are in the process of evolving a new kind of electronic music. The sound of Jefferson Airplane is a jet-age sound, but its music speaks for all time, once you open your ears to it. I played this LP one afternoon, heard three rock bands that night, Muddy Waters the next night, Ray Charles the next, the Clancy Brothers the next and I still had Come Up the Years sounding in my ears. That's my standard for good music, when it sticks in your mind.

[Liner notes, RCA Records, LPM-3584 RE, 1966]

A Warm and Groovy Affair

■

The first annual Monterey international Pop Festival this weekend was a beautiful, warm, groovy affair which showed the world a very great deal about the younger generation.

In the first place, the music was fine, the staging was excellent and the shows were good. You know they are when audiences stay until well after 1 a.m.

But beyond that, it showed something else very important—you can have 35,000 long-haired, buckskin and beaded hippies in one place without a hassle.

"I've never seen a crowd like it. These people are polite and patient and gentle," Festival ticket director Arthur Samuel said yesterday. "You don't need cops when you don't have robbers," one of the staff added. "I've had more trouble at a PTA meeting," a Sheriff's squad member remarked and an assistant police chief of Monterey, Bob Trenner, put on a wig, decked it with flowers and reported to police chief Frank Marinello, saying "I'm joining 'em!"

It was like that. The pervading sound was bells, jingling on the arms, the moccasins, the earrings and in the hair of the audience. Thousands of orchid blossoms flown from Hawaii were thrown among the audience at the Saturday night show and showered on stage for various groups.

It was beautiful and even the hazy, then misty, Monterey weather didn't dampen the spirit of love that was the dominant emotion of the weekend. They slept in cars and trucks, under billboards and trees, on the fairgrounds, in tents and wigwams, in trailers and campers and anywhere they could.

Saturday night was the biggest crowd in the arena in the history of the fairground, according to George Rise, manager of the Monterey County Fairgrounds. At least 8500 people and again no trouble. While the show went on there were thousands—Chief Marinello estimated at 35,000—of people out on the fairground itself, wandering around, buying food at the booths, from the Arab Club of Monterey Peninsula to the Congregation Beth Israel, and clustering around the exhibits, the group of tambourine and guitar players and the singers. A free festival, which included the Jefferson Airplane, the Grateful Dead and other groups, went on Saturday afternoon through Sunday at the Monterey Peninsula College football field with free food and entertainment. Hundreds stayed there all night.

So much for an inadequate description of one of the most remarkable scenes in contemporary American history, a gigantic musical love-in which set a standard of peacefulness and sobriety for the entire country.

It was the greatest assembly of contemporary musical talent in history. The surprise hit of the Friday and Saturday night shows was the startling light show by Head Lights which, since it was new to the majority of the audience was doubly impressive, the swirling liquid colors projected on a huge plastic screen behind the performers.

Friday night's show began only a few minutes late and ran until almost 1:30, with the outstanding moment being the concluding one with Simon and Garfunkel's lovely choir boy set of "Sounds of Silence," "Homeward Bound," and several groovy new songs. Lou Rawls, whose nightclub act is really a little out of place on a festival stage, has a fine voice and is a good singer even if one could wish that his secular sermons were a little shorter.

Eric Burdon and The Animals were a surprise addition and they were good but eclectic. John Wheeler, the guitarist who doubles on violin, was the most interesting. The Association, despite their good material are entirely too set and routined and their humor is high school silly. Johnny Rivers is an anachronism, the last of the early rock 'n roll singers now turned Hollywood hippie. His best number onstage as well as on record was "Poor Side of Town." Beverly, the British girl, hardly had a chance, the band did not work well with her, and The Paupers are potentially a good rock group but lack much stage individuality.

The Saturday afternoon and evening shows were musically a gas. Steve Miller's Blues Band, Paul Butterfield and the new Mike Bloomfield Electric Flag knocked everybody out. Miller's driving blues, Bloomfield's interesting instrumentation and exciting solos and the great appearance of Big Brother and The Holding Company (with Janis Joplin's fine performance) highlighted the afternoon. Country Joe and The Fish were a disappointment, it was one of their off days, and Canned Heat was terrible. Al Kooper did a nice set, especially "Wake Me, Shake Me" and the Quicksilver Messenger Service was very good.

The Saturday night show had two unbelievable climactic moments; the magnificent performance by the Jefferson Airplane, which brought the crowd to its feet, and the wild, stomping, swinging, shouting Otis Redding's closing moments, which did it up all over again.

Earlier, Hugh Masakela gave an object lesson in boredom. He is a tedious, long-winded soloist and a dull singer whose only place on the show was doing his one solo bit with The Byrds. Conga drummer Big Black, who is the real star of Masakela's group, was magnificent.

Singer Laura Nyro was a disappointment, too. She now is an affected and pretentious performer who is very badly advised. Her act is less interesting, though more formally staged, than when she played the hungry i.

The Byrds were excellent, singing their Dylan songs and "He Was a Friend of Mine." Moby Grape, who opened the Saturday night show, were good. Skip Spence was exciting as usual but there is something about this group which seems to be pointed in the wrong direction for me. They just don't have the right feeling somehow.

Masters of Ceremonies for the first three shows were Peter Tork, Andrew Oldham, Tom Smothers, Chet Helms, Jerry Garcia, David Crosby and Mike Bloomfield and, of course, festival director John Phillips.

Even in the threat of rain yesterday morning, the Sergeant Pepper buttons set the theme: The splendid time guaranteed for all was taking place.

More Wednesday.

[*San Francisco Chronicle*, June 19, 1967]

Dawn of True Sexual Hysteria

Elvis Presley didn't have on blue suede shoes when I saw him. He wore black pumps instead and when he went on stage he removed his cream-colored striped jacket with the black velvet collar and put on a blood-red one.

Now that his TV special showed he still had the drawing power, Elvis and the Colonel are discussing his going out on tour and actually making personal appearances. Live concert appearances have been rare in the Presley career. He made a half-dozen or so in the beginning and then the TV shows and the hit records spun him right off into the flicks and he was gone.

Back in June of 1956 when Jim Morrison was 11 years old, Elvis Presley came to the Oakland Auditorium Arena across the Bay from San Francisco. It's been renovated since then but it was at the time a really raunchy, old hall with a huge stage, U-shaped balcony and a flat floor with movable seats. Elvis didn't sell it out.

That was most surprising. He did two shows, which may have been the problem, but he certainly came in with all the press and radio in the world going for him. Full coverage at the airport and the rest. It was a Sunday night but that shouldn't have stopped anyone. After all, it was Elvis. Right?

Before the show he hung around the dressing room, poking his head out the door occasionally to yell at the chickies hanging over the railing above him and talking with friends and people he'd gone to school with. He was afraid of the crowd even though he said he loved them. When he went to the head, he took along a police escort.

The crowd was overwhelmingly female and young. They screamed like their descendants did for the Beatles. The sound, echoing off those walls which had seen Ringling Brothers and the Harlem Globetrotters and so many old, tired prize fights, was deafening. He signed some programs (one chick fainted just before she got to him).

I asked him about the audience and he said, in a sick drawl, "Ah thunk they'yuh wonderful. It makes muh wont tuh live up tuh they-yuh opinion uv muh." Or something like that. The show left him sweating and he stayed in the dressing room for half an hour afterwards until a squad of Oakland cops could arrange an exit to his Caddy. Dozens of girls charged the police escort and almost got him as he climbed into the car (like Dylan in Don't Look Back) and as he drove away they stood there screaming and waving.

Before he made the run to the car, an occasional chick would get past the cops and bust all the way through to the dressing room door. He was sweet to them as earlier he had baited them as they hung over the railing or, when he was onstage, they ran up to the line of cops. He'd slap his crotch and give a couple of bumps and grinds and half grin at the insane reaction it produced each time.

He actually kissed a couple of them on the cheek after signing their programs and it was a clean, kind gesture that seemed quite removed from the hysteria that surrounded the rest of the show.

His Oakland appearance was the week he was on the Milton Berle program with Les Baxter, Deborah Paget and a wild looking chick named Irish McCalla. On stage in Oakland he sang his songs and he held the guitar (though he never played it, using it really as a prop). The group with him, described by one of the promoters as high school friends, did all the playing. Elvis just sang and did a kind of prehistoric Twist.

It was the first show I'd seen that had the true element of sexual hysteria in it. There'd been appearances by all kinds of other music stars, back to Fats Domino and Chuck Berry and including the Everly Brothers and Paul Anka, but never anything like what Elvis produced. Even Hank Williams at the zenith of his fame didn't arouse the kind of teen age thing Elvis did.

It wasn't the response The Beatles produced. Then it was love and adulation and the joy of recognition as if they were themselves an extension of the audience. It was somehow different with Elvis and I've puzzled about it in the years since then.

By the time The Beatles hit the U.S., they knew who they were, for one thing. And I don't think Elvis quite had it settled in his head then. Even though he got a lot of radio promotion for the event, the Colonel and the rest of the show's producers thought he was basically a Country and Western performer. Cowboy deejays sponsored the show and emceed it. Not rock 'n roll people.

Then again Elvis didn't represent at the time, no matter how much he may represent it in retrospect, any dawn of a new youth era. He was just another instant teenage success and the quality that he had, which as I said I think he was unclear about himself, was certainly not clear to his organization.

Johnny Ray had been big by virtue of imitating the rhythm and blues singers from Little Miss Cornshucks on. He came right out of R&B but Elvis came out of R&B and Country and Western and he sang the blues much better than Ray ever could have. After all, the blues had been around in the mouths of white performers before but there was a world of difference between Elvis' approach to it and the approach of Frankie Laine and Peggy Lee. And Elvis may have been a hillbilly but he didn't sound like a hillbilly. He sounded much more relaxed than that and he didn't have the hillbilly whine.

Nobody really suspected what was about to happen. It's a cinch that Milton Berle didn't. After all, he let him get away and the general public and mass media thought of him only as the kid who did the pelvic (remember Elvis the Pelvis?) grinds and made those awful sounds.

Whatever he had that turned them on was not anything that came over to the post-teen set either. Fats Domino reached an older age bracket and so did Chuck Berry and Chuck even reached a lot of white kids that Fats didn't. When Fats and Chuck made their first West Coast tours, the audience was black for Fats and white for Chuck Berry and the promoters, those hard-nosed, deaf-eared realists, immediately classified them accordingly.

The Colonel was a patent medicine hustler, a real-life W.C. Fields circus barker who had the quick reactions necessary in the carney circuit and when he latched onto Elvis he didn't see where it was going but he let it move a little and then he dug the course it might take.

Elvis was simple and direct and uncomplicated. He did the visual thing Jim Morrison does but he did it with less sophistication and without the pure cynicism of Morrison or Mick Jagger. He did it straight and seemed mildly surprised at the reaction and like a good showman, once he knew what they wanted he socked it to them. In later years a man associated with Harry Belafonte wrote a novel about a black sex symbol performer who wore skin tight pants with a jockstrap stuffed with Kotex. That was too contrived for the Presley of 1956. He was just a kid from the town where Nathan Bedford Forrest fought a battle and he sang what he had learned where he grew up.

It was as simple as that, I suspect.

The Oakland Auditorium had five or six thousand kids for those two shows of Presley's. I often wonder what music they listen to now and if they belong to the Playboy Club and live in the stucco and plastic suburban developments and if they ever happened to see Jim Morrison, what they think of it. Elvis's songs were songs of alienation, too, and of young love. None of us knew it then but a whole New World was opening up. I wonder what it will be like when he goes out on concerts now. And will those original fans return?

[*Rolling Stone*, February 1, 1969]

Hank Williams, Roy Acuff and Then God!!

∎

Hank Williams came out of the bathroom carrying a glass of water. He was lean, slightly stooped over and long-jawed. He shook hands quickly, then went over to the top of the bureau, swept off a handful of pills and deftly dropped them, one at a time, with short, expert slugs from the glass.

I didn't really know doodley-britt about country-western music except that I dug Ernest Tubbs and T. Texas Tyler and thought that "You Two-Timed Me One Time Too Often" was a great song. But I was writing about popular music for the *San Francisco Chronicle* and Hank Williams was by God popular and a fattish man with big glasses named Wally Elliott, who doubled as a country-western disc-jockey under the *nom du disque* of Longhorn Joe, was presenting Williams in several one nighters. So I went to see Williams and visit him at his hotel after one of the one nighters. So I went to talk to him.

The room was in the Leamington Hotel which is the biggest hotel in Oakland and could have been any one of the standard Muhlebach or old Statler hotels anywhere in the U.S., the salesman's shelter.

All I knew about Hank Williams was that he made records as Luke the Drifter and under his own name and had sold millions and he sure wrote good songs.

I was a little surprised by the pills, but then he looked pale and thin and had deep-set eyes and might've been hung over for all I knew. It was June, 1952, six months before he died in that car's backseat on New Year's Day, with everybody denying the first report that it was from an overdose.

So he threw the pillboxes into his suitcase, and we went down to the coffee shop. Hank Williams talked and ate an egg breakfast and I wrote it down.

"I've been singing ever since I can remember," he said. He was 29 then, doing 200 one-nighters a year and grossing over $400,000, he said. "My mother was an organist at Mount Olive, Alabama, and my earliest memory is sittin' on that organ stool by her and hollerin'. I must've been five, six years old and louder than anybody else.

I learned to play the git-tar from an old colored man in the streets of Montgomery. He was named Tetot and he played in a colored street band. They had a washtub bass. You ever seen one of them? Well, it had a hole in the middle with a broom handle stuck in it and a rope for the strings.

I was shinin' shoes and sellin' newspapers and followin' this old Nigrah around to get him to teach me to play the git-tar. I'd give him $.15 or whatever I could get a hold of for a lesson. When I was about eight years old, I got my first git-tar. A secondhand $3.50 git-tar my mother bought me. Then I got a jazz horn and played both of them at dances and had a band when I was 14 or 15."

Hank went on the air on WSFA in Montgomery when he was still in school and, after he met Fred Rose, he cut his first records for Sterling. "One session, $90 for four sides including 'Never Again Will I Knock on Your Door.'"

That started it all. MGM signed him. He started with the C & W radio programs for years and had an incredible string of hit records in the days of the 78 RPM disc and his songs were recorded by many other performers, too.

"A good song is a good song," Hank said as he ate. "And if I'm lucky enough to write it, well . . . ! I get more kick out of writing than I do singing. I reckon I've written 1000 songs and had over 300 published."

Hank surprised me by referring to his music as "folk music." "Folk music is sincere. There ain't nuthin' phony about it. When a folk singer sings a sad song, he's sad. He means it. The tunes are simple and easy to remember and the singers, they're sincere about them."

I don't say I ever write for popularity. I check a song by its lyrics. A song ain't nothing in the world but a story just wrote with music to it. I can't sing 'Rag Mop' or 'Mairzy Dotes.' But the best way for me to get a hit is to do something I don't like. I've been offered some of the biggest songs to sing and turned them down. There ain't *nobody* can pick songs. Because I say it's good, don't mean it'll sell.

I like Johnny Ray. He is sincere and shows he is sincere. That's the reason he's popular. He sounds to me like he means it. What I mean by sincerity, Roy Acuff is the best example. He's the biggest singer this music ever knew. You book him and you didn't worry about crowds. For drawing power in the South, it was Roy Acuff and then God!! He done it with 'Wabash Cannonball' and with 'Great Speckled Bird.' He'd stand up there singin', tears runnin' down his cheeks.

Acuff was his idol and Fred Rose his inspiration. "Fred Rose, it was my good fortune to be associated with him. He came to Nashville to laugh and he heard Acuff and said 'By God, he means it!'"

Sipping coffee and talking, Hank went on about now forgotten singers like Bill Darnell, about Roy Acuff and Fred Rose and Ernest Tubbs and Bing Crosby, about "Wheel of Fortune" and "I Love You So Much It Hurts Me."

Pretty soon Wally Elliott looked at his watch and said he had to take Hank off somewhere to plug that night's show. Hank was looking a little better now, the paleness under the close shaven jaws had been replaced with some color and he didn't look quite so peaked.

So they split and I split and later that night I drove out to San Pablo Hall which is 'way out past El Cerrito and Richmond and almost to Vallejo. San Pablo Ave., possibly the longest main street in the world, runs for almost 20 miles from downtown Oakland on out there and in 1952 there were no freeways. When you got to San Pablo, it looked like everyplace else only a little raunchier and San Pablo Hall was a one-story white building on a lot a block off the Avenue. You parked in the mud and walked past a tree up to the door and inside there was a long room with a bandstand at one end and a bar in an annex at one side.

Wally Elliott, who had been wearing a business suit in the afternoon and looked like one of Ralph Williams' Ford salesmen, was a Western dude now, with full Grand Old Opry regalia, Stetson hat, hand made boots. The whole bit. The band was terrible. I only remember that about them and shortly after I got there Hank Williams went on. He looked just like he looked at the hotel except that he now had a Western hat and a guitar. When he sang, he looked like he squeezed himself to get the notes out sometimes and he seemed shorter somehow than when we were talking in the coffee shop.

He did them all, all his hits. "Jambalaya," "Lovesick Blues," "Move It On Over." I don't remember him singing any of the Luke the Drifter religious songs. Not even "I Saw the Light." But he did the barrelhouse blues and the barroom ballads, "Cold, Cold Heart" and "Hey, Good Lookin'" and "Your Cheatin' Heart."

And he had that *thing*. He made them scream when he sang and that audience was shipped right up from Enid or Wichita Falls intact (like Elia Kazan shipped the bit players for *Baby Doll* up from the deep South to Long Island for a scene). There were lots of those blondes you see at C&W affairs, the kind of hair that mother never had and nature never grew and the tight skirts that won't quit and the guys looking barbershop neat but still with a touch of dust on them. "Shit-kicker dances" the outside world called them but then some great people came through to play for them and this time it was Hank Williams and the Drifting Cowboys, it said, but I believe now (as I suspected then) that the only Driftin' Cowboy was Hank.

At the intermission, it was impossible to talk to him. He was a little stoned and didn't seem to remember our conversation earlier in the day and the party was beginning to get a little rough. They were whiskey drinkers and so I gave them room, looked around a while and then went on back out.

Six months later when I read he had died I remembered him saying, in that Oakland hotel coffee shop, how much he loved his Tennessee ranch but how little time he got to spend there because he was on the road so much. "Last time I was there it rained," he said sourly and then he added that he was stocking the ranch with cattle and his ambition someday was to retire there and watch "them cattle work while I write songs and fish."

He never did, of course. I had no idea how tortured a man he was when I saw him. It came through more in his performance. He didn't cry but he could make *you* cry and when he sang "Lovesick Blues" you knew he meant it.

So he died in the backseat of a car en route from one gig to another, from one ratty dance hall to another ratty dance hall, while the world gradually came to sing his songs and his Hollywood-ized life was shown and re-shown on the late-night TV and the court fight for his estate went on for years. Still goes on, I think, that legal fight, like some ghost walking the Pine Hills for eternity.

[*Rolling Stone*, June 28, 1969]

Another Candle Blown Out

My candle burns at both ends;
It will not last the night;
But, ah, my foes, and, oh, my friends
It gives a lovely light.

—EDNA ST. VINCENT MILLAY

God knows, that blazing candle did cast a lovely light, even though from time to time when it flickered and the light dimmed, the looming face of tragedy appeared.

For Janis, gamin-faced, husky voiced little girl lost, seemed to me from the moment I first saw her to have that fatal streak of tragedy present. And what's more, to know it.

Laughin' just to keep from crying.

It was just paralyzing to hear the radio bulletin that she was dead. Inevitable but paralyzing still when it happened. How could it be? Why?

And it makes no difference, really, what any inquest finds. She's dead and that's it and the truth, which is sometimes much more difficult to see than the facts, ma'am, just the facts, is that she was driven to self-destruction by some demon deep within her from the moment she left that Texas high school where they had laughed at her.

She showed them, all right, she showed them plenty and the dues she paid to show them proved too much in the end.

Janis' effect on the San Francisco scene was like a time bomb or a depth charge. There was a long lag before it went off. She came up from Texas, a beatnik folksinger, and sang in the Coffee Gallery and the other crummy joints that were available at the end of the Beat era and just before the Haight blossomed so briefly only, like Janis, to self-destruct.

It wasn't until she came back from Texas with Chet and joined the band that she really hit, and what a hit it was. It took me a while to absorb it, but once that group got to you, they were a turn-on of magnificent proportions—much, much heavier than anything she ever got on record. That's why her own group, when she went out with it, was such a disappointment. Janis with Big Brother was magic, never mind that they played out of tune, never mind any of the criticisms, over in the corner on the stage at the Avalon when she screamed, our hearts screamed with her. And when she stomped on that stage at Winterland (and stomped is the word) and shook her head and hollered, it was just simply unbelievable.

For all the notoriety (what feature writer could overlook a girl who insisted on drinking like an F. Scott Fitzgerald legend?), Janis' greatest moments came at Monterey, really, which were perhaps the finest moments that movement of which she was so integral a part has ever seen.

Janice did it three times at Monterey. She broke it up in the afternoon show and was brought back in the evening. They couldn't believe what they had seen. The rock set from Hollywood and New York who had never heard of Janis Joplin nor of Big Brother & the Holding Co., got the hit of their lives that day. Her Monterey Pop appearance made her national news, the film made her national box office.

But the one I dug even more was three months later at the Monterey Jazz Festival (held in the same arena) when Janis came on at the afternoon blues show which featured B. B. King and T-Bone Walker, Clara Ward and Big Joe Turner.

There she was, this freaky-looking white kid from Texas on stage with all the hierarchy of the traditional blues world, facing an audience that was steeped in blues tradition, which was older than her ordinary audience and which had a built-in tendency to regard electric music as the enemy.

The first thing she did was to say "shit" and that endeared her right away. Then she stomped her foot and shook her hair and started to scream. They held still for a couple of seconds, but here and there in the great sunlit arena, longhairs started getting up and out into the aisles and stomping along with the band. By the end of the first number, the Monterey County Fairgrounds arena was packed with people writhing and twisting and snaking along in huge chains. It was an incredible sight. Nothing like it had ever happened before in the festival's 10 years and nothing like it has happened since.

It was Janis' day, no doubt about it. She turned them on like they had not been turned on in years. Old and young, long hair or short, black or white, they reacted like somebody had stuck a hot wire in their ass.

Janis had been scared silly before going on stage (I think she was scared silly every time she went on stage) and when she came off, she knew she had done it even though she was out of her mind with excitement. We had been filming for Educational Television that weekend and Janis' manager at the time, in a burst of paranoia still to be equaled, had refused to OK our filming Janis' performance. "Did you film it?" she asked, quivering, when she got off stage and I had to tell her "No." She was disappointed. She knew what it'd been. And God knows, the world has less than it might have because we couldn't film that incredible performance.

There were so many, though. Everywhere, but especially in the city she had adopted. At Winterland and California Hall and the old Fillmore and Fillmore West and the Avalon and all around Robin Hood's barn. But then Janis was really a part of the city when she was home. You'd see her anywhere, likely to pop up at a flick, in the park, at Enrico's. Anywhere. She dug it and the city, with its tradition of eccentrics back to Emperor Norton, dug her.

Janis was a phenomenon, no question about it. Nobody else ever came close to doing what she did. The whole stance of American popular music has been to sound black and generations of white girl singers, from Sophie Tucker to Dusty Springfield, have tried to do it. Some of them have been driven to as tragic an end as Janis in the attempt. But none of them, Peggy Lee, nobody, has ever made it in their own terms as a white girl singing black music to the degree Janis did.

It was only partly the voice and only partly the phrasing. It was, I am convinced, the concept. Janis was the very first white singer I ever saw who moved on stage with the music in a totally unselfconscious manner. She did not seem to *care* about anything but the music. And she conceived of it in different terms than did her predecessors, all of whom were trying to be blues singers of the Forties or Thirties or earlier. Janis was a blues singer of right now. And she took the blues, even the blues of ten or fifteen years ago, and made it immediate in its sound, by the way she propelled the words out of her mouth, by the way she shaped the sounds and by the volume she poured into it.

When she recorded that first time with Big Brother for Mainstream, she won my heart. I had said something about what an artistic crime it had been for Mainstream to make such a bad representation of what the band did. I met her a bit later in the dressing room at the Avalon. "Hey man, thanks for what you said about our shitty record," she said.

And her own albums on Columbia had their good and bad points, too. When I first heard "Little Girl Blue" I didn't dig it at all because I felt Janis lacked something that was necessary for that jazz-bent number. But it haunts me now as a symbol of her loneliness, her despair, little girl lost in the big, wicked world.

She was impulsive, generous, soft hearted, shy and determined. She had style and class and in a way she didn't believe it. What did she want? It was all there for her but something that she knew wasn't fated to happen. Many people loved her a very great deal, like many people loved Billie Holiday, but somehow that was not enough.

We'll never know and it doesn't matter, in a sense, because that brightly burning candle made an incredibly strong light in its brief life.

They heard Janis Joplin 'round the world, loud and clear and they will continue to hear her. I am only sorry for those who never had the flash of seeing her perform.

Janis and Big Brother sang hymns at Monterey. It never seemed to me to be just music. I hope now that she's freed herself of that ball and chain, that she is at rest. She gave us a little piece of her heart and all of her soul every time she went on stage.

Monterey, 1967. Otis, Jimi, Brian, Janis. Isn't that enough?

Little girl blue, with the floppy hats and the brave attempt to be one of the guys. She took a little piece of all of us with her when she went. She was beautiful. That's not corny. It's true.

[*Rolling Stone*, October 29, 1970]

Altamont Revisited on Film

I t was frightening to see *Gimme Shelter.* I could hardly talk after it and walked around for an hour and almost couldn't make the next meal.

What it is like for someone in, say, Indiana, to see, I can hardly imagine. I can't imagine. But to see the familiar faces, the people, the scene, and that we've re-created (no, not re-created, but reprised) that mad, frantic, unbelievable time is, at least for me, to concentrate all the bad vibes from Altamont all over again into an hour and a half.

The speculation and comment on this film will go on for years, I suspect. And it ought to, because it is an important record of a highly important event. A documented object lesson in what not to do. Visual education.

It has, of course, along with the leaden vibes, some incredible moments. Mick on stage prancing his way into his thing. Tina Turner copping the mike. The sound of the music and that beautiful half time sequence when Mick is singing "love in vain" and the movement is stopped down to form a ballet over the tempo of the music.

That was one of the most exquisite moments of film and music I have ever seen and it is only lamentable that the editors didn't have the courage to let it continue on through the entire number. The music can carry it but I do not believe they believed in the music. Or at least they didn't believe in it enough.

And God knows the entire affair would put you off music if you didn't have some feeling for it from before. Music brought those people together that day and the music provided the spark to set off the energies that went so sour so tragically. The Stones' music is great music, but it almost always hangs there on a thin edge of violence, usually resolving it and working it out, but on that day the stars and their puppets conspired to block off the resolution and the result was the chaos so vividly shown.

There are no specific guilty parties for Altamont. We were all guilty, myself included. To whatever degree we failed to take whatever steps we could have taken to assure that day would go down benignly, we share the guilt. But the Stones and the concept of a free day with them was such a powerful combination that everyone lost control. I believe that to be true and that Mick and the workers who put it together as well as the Angels who killed that man were all victims themselves. The ultimate victim was all of us. It was a miniature Vietnam, a machine out of control postulated on a mistaken assumption and evolving swiftly into the evil version of what could have been good.

It was a crime without a criminal, a free concert that will, in the end (as Woodstock went bankrupt to make millions), earn more money than any concert anybody ever paid for. In a way it typifies the alliance between greed and grace that is part of the whole presentation of music's magic in this society. The scenes in Mel Belli's office more than even the murder itself reek of a kind of evil we seldom see. Generally we see only what goes on out there on the stage. This time we saw the backstage greed of the manipulators just as plainly as we saw the magic of the performances.

It was wrong from the start somehow. We may never pinpoint exactly how. I suspect the first wrong was the alliance of the "free" concept with the profit—exploitation—greed of the film itself. But we have traditionally been able to bring off beautiful things from that tainted base. This time it didn't work because of one thing: the incredible magnetism and energy of the Stones blinded everyone, brought into the vortex of that day all the power lust and money lust surrounding the whole rock scene. It was a tribal ritual of evil and of death at the end. It is astonishing, as it unfolds on the screen, that there was only one death. There might well have been dozens. It teetered on the edge of that.

All the devices by which the Stones create excitement (in addition to their music) had been used over and over on this tour and on others without a fatal turn. But at all the other times there were controls that stopped the movement short of real danger. And part of the Stones' thrill is the feeling that there is real danger, just as there is in auto races and bullfights. The parallel to ancient warfare is striking. The excitement outweighed the danger — except for a few.

Mick still doesn't know where he was. He thought it was San Francisco, as Brooklyn is New York. But wherever Altamont was, it was a long way from San Francisco and those who set it up, the two bodies of thought, ran counter to each other throughout. One of them was straight out of the San Francisco Renaissance, the surviving elements of the Be-In. And the other was the money-changers.

The seeds of Altamont were present in Monterey, for that matter. There the conflict was between the styles of Hollywood and San Francisco, but the lines were not drawn so sharply and the jackpot was not so huge. In fact it was never really visualized. At Altamont, the idea inherited the momentum of all the other festivals and particularly of Woodstock, where it had become obvious that there were millions to be made at these things if they could be manipulated.

It was pitiful to see the reactions of Mick, and earlier, of Grace and the Airplane, to the violence. In those moments, the star trip came to worse and the human inadequacy was revealed. They were not prepared for such a thing as this. The dues were coming down and they were heavy; and response, to avert the danger, to turn the energy up rather than down, was not there.

By the time Mick exhorted the crowd to show the world that we are one, it was too late. The oneness had gone and it was, again, "us" and "them." Either/or. Power went to the wrong people but it went there unnecessarily and this documentary of how it happened (which is not at all what the filmmakers set out to do, I suspect) is very valuable and should be seen over and over for just what it is. An object lesson in danger.

There was a man standing on the stage near Mick at one point. As the music went on and Mick sang, the man just stood there, into the music all the way. Harmless. Eventually he was violently moved off the stage. The point, I think, is that once violence is used, it is like a lease from the devil himself. You have to pay the dues. Nobody harmed George Harrison when he walked through San Francisco and nobody harmed Mick or Keith at Altamont the night before. True, a nut ran up and hit Mick on arrival that afternoon, but by then it was obvious that there was fear in the wind.

We all know better than Altamont. Even the Angels. Actually the Angels most of all. But by our own weakness we were thrust into that thing and then pulled along by the momentum it generated.

As a people, we are not used to gathering in huge crowds such as this without visible lines of demarcation. The football games, especially the professional ones, bring the audiences to a frenzy of drunken violence many times. So even do the college and high school games. We confuse the music with the music maker to a truly demoniac degree, crediting the doctor with the power of the medicine and trampling others to get close to him like the cripples at a religious rite fighting for the cure.

When the whole turbulent mass is whipped into a frenzy by the media, most especially radio and in this specific instance FM radio and top 40 radio, a kind of override of energy is released which sets up a volatile and wildly dangerous situation in which almost all the frustrations and angers of life get involved.

Although I believe the Stones were victims as well as the rest of us and guilty as we all are guilty, they have made it easy for the load to be dumped on them (as have the Angels). But we expect too much and we expect it because we have made them into superhuman species, the mirror opposite of the subhumans we are licensed to kill.

Gimme Shelter preserves it all like a bad dream. And like a bad dream, it has reality and it also has beauty. But it is still a bad dream and if we can think about it and learn from it, it may not ever have to happen again. We ought to work on that.

[*Rolling Stone*, April 1, 1971]

Simon and Garfunkel,
Parsley, Sage, Rosemary and Thyme

■

T he New Youth of the Rock Generation has done something in American popular song that has begged to be
done for generations.

It has taken the creation of the lyrics and the music out
of the hands of the hacks and given it over to the poets.

This seems to me to be the true meaning of the remarkable achievement of Simon and Garfunkel. They have clearly demonstrated by the
ultimate logic of this materialistic society—sales dollar volume—that
there is not only a market for intellectuality, but that America's New
Youth, the Rock Generation, bred on rock 'n roll, rhythm and blues,
folk-rock and television shows, wants its music to deal with the meaning of life itself and not be just a mumbling collection of dream-world
images (half motion-picture and half slick-magazine fiction) hung up
on romance as opposed to love, speaking in a Bijou Theater vernacular
no one ever used in real life, and dealing not with truth or beauty, but
with least-common-denominator juvenile trivia.

That Simon and Garfunkel—and the other representatives of the
new generations songwriters, an elite which includes Bob Dylan, Phil
Ochs, John Sebastian, Marty Balin, Dino Valenti, Tim Hardin, Al
Kooper, Smokey Robinson, Mick Jagger, John Lennon, Paul McCartney, John Phillips and others—have succeeded in putting beauty and
truth and meaning into popular song, fractures the stereotyped adult
view that the music of youth is at best only trivial rhymes and silly teenage noise, and at worst offensive.

This generation is producing poets who write songs, and never before in the sixty-year history of American popular music has this been true.

The music of Simon and Garfunkel shows evidence of other virtues, too, besides the poetry of the lyrics. There's a delicate musical design of almost lapidarian detail. It has vitality but it is controlled, the sounds being made deliberately for the artist's conscious purpose. Take the second line in "Scarborough Fair/Canticle" (a delicate interweaving of two songs). The anti-war message that is implied and sometimes explicit in this is always signaled by the electric bass.

Take the glorious kaleidoscope of rushing feelings, blowing winds, shifting colors, bursting moods of joy and exultation in "Cloudy." The song is effervescent, one is refreshed hearing it. The references to Tolstoy and to Tinker Bell, and the great line, "Why don't you show your face and bend my mind," all assume a common experience and a common language, the international language of youth.

Take the way Art Garfunkel has arranged the voices—not only on "Cloudy" with its background, but also on "Scarborough Fair/Canticle" and his own featured number, "For Emily, Whenever I May Find Her." The voices blend, separate, interweave and sing counter to one another with the delicacy of a clear glass etching.

The range of expression of Simon's lyrics and melodies is impressive. In this album, there is the probing, almost enigmatic "A Poem on the Underground Wall," which has deep psychological implications; grave, murky images and mysterious, furtive figures. Yet it is a clearly seen episode with suggestions of religious, almost prayerful links to the subconscious ("he holds his crayon rosary").

Then there is the straight-ahead satire of "The Dangling Conversation" and "The Bright Green Pleasure Machine" (again the rhetoric of use: "Do the figures of authority just shut you down . . .") with their open shafting of the cocktail hour conversation and the mad, mad, mad world of television and radio commercials. "A Simple Desultory Philippic" carries this still further, snipping away at certain figures on the contemporary youth scene.

But even when the thrust is toward the New Generation, the moral, the implication and the message (these are not message songs in any heavy sense, each of them being so beautifully lyric and melodic) reach beyond the whole world, which may be why they are so effective. Only in Artie Shaw's fascinating autobiography, "The Trouble With Cinderella," has the very special loneliness of the performing artist in our society been so well expressed as it is in Paul Simon's "Homeward Bound": ("each town seems the same to me, the movies and the factory").

And then there is "7 O'Clock News/Silent Night." I will not tell you in advance what goes on here. My first hearing of it brought chills to my spine and tears to my eyes. It is one of the most effective statements about the world today that I have heard.

The pristine beauty of the voices, the delicate inevitability of the structure of the songs (both the lyrics and the music), the range from deepening seriousness to joyous exuberance (the "59th St. Bridge Song" is such a happy song) is overwhelmingly impressive.

There are songs of alienation but there are songs of love, too, and they touch closely the prevailing philosophical current of the New Youth which is that of creativity AGAINST the machine and, thus, FOR humanity.

It is no accident that this album is dedicated to Lenny Bruce. As is becoming evident, he was a secular saint. His torture, like that of youth and of the new music, at the hands of the Establishment (remember when Congressional hearings deplored the state of popular music?) links them together.

Today's popular music is in good shape indeed—at least the portion of it represented by this album. It has strength and it has beauty, it has lyricism, meaning and, above all, that quality of broad appeal that still retains form. And its music speaks for more than the moment. The songs in this album are songs for all time.

[Liner notes, Columbia Records—CS 9363, 1966]

Unreleased Bob Dylan Album

■

The poetry, the records and the performances of Bob Dylan puzzled the generation to which he is junior and produces in much of it the same sort of trauma felt by the saxophone section of the Freddie Martin band in the presence of Charlie Parker.

"Of course you cannot avoid the fact that he does say something to those under 30," one well-known popular folk musician said at a topical song panel during the Berkeley Folk Festival at the University of California in the summer of 1964. The reluctance implicit in the way that remark was phrased, indicates the difficulty which his poetry—and it is his poetry rather than his music in the strictest sense with which they have trouble—presents for his elders.

The difficulty is apparent on many levels and entangles Dylan's detractors in many legalistically styled evasions. Some object to his hair, some to his clothes, some to the sound of his voice, some to his rhymes and some to his images! And with the burning intensity bordering on the messianic.

But genius makes its own rules and it is a fact of life in 1965 that Bob Dylan speaks to a section of the youth of America as no one else does. The only others who are even granted honorary membership by the Dylan audience are Joan Baez and the Beatles! The inclusion of the latter is an indication that the Dylan audience which began with the folk fans, then embraced the atomic bomb generation of the disaffiliated, is now spreading out to the real mass of the teenage youth which is knowingly or unknowingly involved in a revision of the priorities of the society. The reality of the Beatles and their irreverence strikes a responsive chord in the audience that idolizes Bob Dylan for his reality and his concern with those things which the older generation regards as trite, those clichés which are really the substance of the new morality—love and truth and beauty in the original, uncomplicated and unsophisticated meaning of those terms.

For Bob Dylan articulates the thoughts and feelings of great numbers of youth. "He says the things I feel but I can't say" a 14-year-old girl wrote me. "Going to a Dylan concert is like going to church," another teenager told me and a woman old enough to be Dylan's grandmother said "he's so young and he knows so much."

There is a great malaise in our society, a giant absurdity, a cosmic distortion, which makes Catch-22 all too real. When the students at the University of California had their mass demonstrations in the winter of 1964–65, it was no coincidence that one of their badges of membership was an IBM card punched with the letters of their organization.

Nor was it any coincidence that, along with the anthem of the civil rights movement, "We Shall Overcome," the students were led into their now famous Sit-in by Joan Baez singing Bob Dylan's "The Times They Are A Changin'."

For it is perfectly obvious to any reasonably objective onlooker that the times indeed are a-changing and that Dylan's poems and Dylan's songs are among the more dramatic articulations of that change.

Bob Dylan in his Midwest come Woody Guthrie accent and his almost classically homely rhetoric, is giving voice to the fears and the beliefs and the truths of life in our anti-humanitarian society as seen by his generation. Dylan is a product of the post-Sputnik age for whom the bomb has been ever present. His songs are chains of flashing images strung together to get out past political rhetoric and pretense and to discuss things as they are in moral terms. As Malvina Reynolds has remarked, the youth of today has been betrayed by the slick voices and the well-dressed performers who tell them all will be well. They are disillusioned with what we have done with the world and they look to themselves, and not to us, to fix it. And on their terms—not ours. Bob Dylan speaks for them of their disillusionment and of their determination, and, above all, he speaks of their hope.

Dylan speaks of their belief, too; their great abiding belief in the basic truths of humanity. It is only natural in the course of the rise of such a charismatic figure, such an anti-authoritarian personality, that there would be dissent. His poems and his songs will not please all people—nor even his people all of the time. But they are all, from the storming, outraged cries against inhumanity, to the oblique introverted examinations of himself, part of the same delineation of the creed of anti-hypocrisy, anti-authority, anti-mechanization, anti-alienation and pro-humanity.

Dylan is, it seems to me, the first poet of the phonograph record. His series of albums represents chronology of his development as a poet and as a singer. Early versions of his songs have changed through performance in numerous slight ways so that the final version—which he now sings when one of his songs remains in his concert repertory—has a dimension not present in the original.

Dylan's concert manner is, like everything else about him, an amalgam of informality and conscious manner, with a citrus tang of humor. It is not that he isn't serious about his work. Like a jazz musician, there is no one more serious. But he doesn't take himself seriously and he shares his own joy and kicks and humor with his audience.

There is also something highly effective, even if it defeats description, in the way this slight, wispy figure can stand there alone on a huge stage and hold the attention of thousands. And then, in almost an awkward motion, throw back his head and cry forth those exhortations and roar out defiance to the Goliaths who still inhabit the world.

"Everything passes, everything changes, just do what you think you should do" Dylan wrote in "To Ramona." Nothing is more certain than that he, too, will change; it is in the nature of the artist. But it is also in the nature of the artist that each change will carry with it its own fascination for his audience. Lawrence Ferlinghetti calls Dylan "the poet of the Sixties." He is that, and more. He is the conscience, too.

[Liner notes, Columbia Records—CL 2302, January 1965;
album cancelled before release]

San Francisco—The American Liverpool

■

San Francisco—When Eric Burdon and The Animals were on their American tour this spring they played several concerts in the San Francisco area. Then, on a Sunday night, the English group asked if they might play—without fee—at the Avalon Ballroom, home of the Family Dog dances.

Last winter, The Yardbirds informed their booking agency that they wanted to play the Fillmore Ballroom in San Francisco. Two of the Yardbirds had visited the hole and thought the San Francisco scene was out of sight.

What is going on in San Francisco is the most important rock scene in America today!

It is making San Francisco the Liverpool of the United States, with a roster of important bands and singers that is making a very strong bid to leave a lasting mark on the national music scene.

Names to Drop

The Jefferson Airplane, The Grateful Dead, The Sopwith Camel, The Family Tree, Moby Grape, Blackburn & Snow, The Sons of Champlin, The Charlatans, Big Brother and the Holding Co., The Quicksilver Messenger Service—these are some of the San Francisco bands that have already recorded and whose discs are beginning to be heard nationally.

The key to the San Francisco Scene is the existence of two ballrooms, the Fillmore and the Avalon, relics of the dance era of 50 years ago. They have been presenting two and three nights of dancing each week for more than a year. Three, sometimes four, bands play each of these ballrooms for thousands of young dancers weekly. The music is pure rock.

The integration of light shows (projections on the walls, floor and ceilings of multicolored, liquid lights, filmstrips and cutouts) with the music has intrigued people from all over the world. The "Bell Telephone Hour," to B.B.C.-TV shows and innumerable local and regional TV programs have shown the ballrooms and the bands.

James Brown phoned from his Staten Island home asking to play the Fillmore ballroom this spring. The Byrds asked to play the Fillmore and David Crosby and Jim McGuinn came up from Hollywood on numerous occasions to dig the scene in person.

More recently, John, Michelle and Cass of the Mamas and the Papas spent two weekends listening and observing at the Avalon and the Fillmore and are planning on taking out a light show on their next concert tour.

Cass Elliot was so impressed by the Quicksilver Messenger Service at the Avalon that she recommended them to Lou Adler for his new record company. Last fall, Joan Baez and her sister, Mimi Farina, sang with The Jefferson Airplane at the Fillmore. On closing night of Paul Butterfield's first engagement there, Muddy Waters, David Crosby, The Grateful Dead and The Airplane all got on stage for a night jam session on "Midnight Hour."

The same audiences that pack the Fillmore and the Avalon (posters from the halls are now world-famous, being shipped out each week all over the U.S. and Europe) for the rock bands frequently get a chance to dance to or listen to the major figures in rhythm & blues.

Dino Valenti (the guitarist and composer of "Let's Get Together," recorded by The Jefferson Airplane and The Youngbloods, among others) has been working in a non-dancing club, the Kuh Auditorium, for the past year and frequently appears at the ballrooms.

Visiting bands from New York and other cities, groups such as The Young Rascals, The Blues Project, Love, The Peanut Butter Conspiracy, The Mothers, The Doors, and the Jim Kweskin Jug Band have all made the San Francisco ballroom scene.

San Francisco has become, because of the weekly dances, the focal point of talent scouts from all the American record companies. At least six companies made bids for the contract with The Moby Grape, a new San Francisco group, this spring. The Haight-Ashbury district in San

Francisco, with its psychedelic shops, newspaper, coffeehouses and hippie citizens, provides a ready-made audience for the bands but their attraction goes far beyond that.

Guitarists like Jerry Garcia of The Grateful Dead and Jorma Kaukonen, of The Jefferson Airplane are considered among the finest young soloists in rock music. It is an indication of the importance of the total San Francisco environment that the new band Mike Bloomfield is forming will live and rehearse and play there all summer before making its first records or going out on the road.

"Playing for dancing all the time helps us get together," says Garcia. Add to that the light shows and the whole psychedelic atmosphere of the San Francisco dances and a unique youthful rock community emerges which is having an effect on America's contemporary music that may well turn out to be historic.

[*Hullabaloo*, Volume 2, No. 4, July–August]

COMEDY

Satire, Reality and Dick Gregory

To make laughter out of tears and heartache, to turn tragedy into comedy, is the terrifying job of people like Dick Gregory, who opens tonight at the hungry i. Gregory is a satirist and, as he said the other night from Washington D.C., where he was playing a benefit, "the job of the comic is to go in and see and then make it funny."

"This is," Gregory continued, "the hardest job in the world for the people who deal in satire. If I get a divorce, I have to make it funny. If the President gets a divorce, I have to make jokes about that."

"It's nothing new. People have been doing it for years," Gregory added. And this is, of course, true, but there is—at least in the context of American comedy—a difference in what Gregory is doing today and, say, a Will Rogers was doing yesterday.

Gregory has gone in and seen. He has been in Birmingham and the question now is, can he go on stage and tell his audience what actually happened to him in Birmingham?

"All I know about in Birmingham is the jails," he says. And in the Birmingham jail Gregory was beaten by officers with a baseball bat and a sawed-off pool cue. He stepped forward when he wasn't supposed to step forward. His right arm is in a sling, as a consequence, and his doctor wants it in a cast and him in the hospital.

"Not yet," Gregory says.

Gregory has added to his stature by deliberately not trying to commercialize on his experiences. But he can't keep it all out of his performance.

He is in the process of transformation as a satirist, in the course of which he has entered into a rather rare atmosphere. He is no longer just telling jokes and commenting on the daily papers. He is now telling the literal truths about what has been happening to him. And the greater the degree of frankness, the more effective the result. The more he levels with his audiences, the more exciting his performances become. His appeal—and this increases as the frankness increases—is like that of Lenny Bruce and James Baldwin and the jazz musicians who tell it like it is.

In a culture of evasion and euphemism—even the word *mother* has symbolically altered—telling the truth cannot help but shock. It doesn't have to be well told in ringing phrases, either. Today, truth all by itself, by definition, has beauty and great magnetism.

To a man like Dick Gregory, fresh from the cells of Birmingham jail, there can't be much, even on the stage of the hungry i, that is really funny except the hard way.

The people who put him in jail, Bull Connor and his anti-law enforcers, were there to take that action on the votes of those who voted—the extremists and the moderates and the men of reluctant goodwill. It's quite plain the Negroes didn't elect them.

Gregory comes to us direct from a world where the values we have learned and which we teach, from the Pledge of Allegiance to the Ten Commandments, are being tested. He should have lessons for us all. And if he makes us laugh at the same time, that is the mark of the artist.

[*San Francisco Chronicle*, May 20, 1963]

Jonathan Winters,
Another Day, Another World

■

San Jose, California, is a blossoming city, caught between the dynamic of an exploding population and the static of deep California history. One does not think of it ordinarily as a concert or show business town, but when Jonathan Winters appeared at the San Jose Civic Auditorium January 23, 1961, for the first of his concerts on the West Coast, it seemed a good idea to go down there to hear him.

It was more than a good idea. It resulted in one of the most marvelously entertaining evenings I have ever spent; one that made the long ride in the cold night air more than worthwhile.

It was not only that Winters was really "on," and pushing for his best performance to start the series, but the audience was with him. The other acts lingered in the wings to hear him and even in the intermission there was a crowd around Winters backstage as he talked with the show's producer, Enrico Banducci, the beret-wearing owner of the San Francisco nightclub, the hungry i, at which Winters had made his California debut.

Jonathan Winters is a clown, perhaps the greatest we have had in this country and like all great clowns in history, from Grimaldi to Grock to Emmett Kelly, he combines sadness and joy, laughing to keep from crying, laughter through tears.

Jonathan Winters is one of the great American humorists, the real heir to Will Rogers and totally unique. He is in a class all by himself, with almost no relationship to the other leaders of the New Wave of Comedy: Mort Sahl, Shelley Berman and Lenny Bruce.

He produces the same response from his audiences as the great clowns have done; pure unadulterated joy. Although he continually refers to himself as a child (and adds, "we're all children"), and speaks of a world peopled with clowns ("we're all clowns in different ways"), Jonathan Winters' permanent character is the Rube on Broadway, the Great American Boy. And that is what is so marvelous about him. The Great American Boy, simple, homespun, talking to the sophisticates and the would-be sophisticates and to those who are only once removed from the American Boy world themselves. This is his link to Will Rogers.

But even in his most simple role, Jonathan Winters is deeply complex. His vocal accent is that of the wheat field, his vocabulary comes from TV and "the people" and his frame of reference is the great area covered by the mass experience of America: the Army, the movies, cops, baseball, television, spacemen, etc.

His basic tools are an ear for American regional speech and idiom unequaled on the stage today, a sharp eye for the pompous and the fraudulent in manners and attitudes, a mobile face that must be the envy of all character actors and a mind whose stream-of-conscious rambling is like a wild space missile.

His ability to create illusion rests not only on that magnificently mobile face, but upon a variety of sound effects (all made by hand-clapping, finger-snapping, mouth sounds and exploitation of the microphone) which are incredible as well as incredibly funny. When he gives you the slap of a ball in a mitt or the whoossh of a rocket going into secondary orbit, it creates an illusion of frightening reality.

But though he is concerned with the paradoxes of modern life (and is himself a paradox), Jonathan Winters' view of human beings is humane and full of compassion, for all his wild talk.

He has the great comic posture going for him, too. He is funny as soon as he comes on stage, before he says a word. By his simple boy pose, he appeals directly to the audience and takes the audience with him as they both observe the madness of life.

His humor is anecdotal, full of bright images of American life (the clay class and the fruit pickers on this LP are two excellent examples) and really never vicious. He is as far from a "sick" comedian as one can get in today's culture and thus he stands in the mainstream of American humor, an oral reincarnation of the great Grant Wood American humor, classic in its applicability to whatever is going on right now.

Perhaps one of the reasons he is so appealing is that he speaks directly to the child in all of us, to the simple, uncomplicated human for whom all the impedimenta of the mass media and the space-age are a maze of puzzlement and make up a world where the real and the unreal are indistinguishably mixed.

His canvas is the broadest aspects of American life and because of this, there is a strong suspicion that his work, as preserved in these albums, may well have a longer life than that of his contemporaries. At the least, he is surely a great American humorist.

[Liner notes, Verve Records—V15032, 1962]

The Bill Cosby World of Youth

■

Saturday's appearances by Bill Cosby at the Opera House proved conclusively that he is the most popular comic in the country right now. He sold out both shows long before the opening curtain. No other comic since the heyday of Mort Sahl and Shelley Berman could possibly have done this.

It is attributable, however, in a considerable degree, to his television popularity which builds another audience for personal appearances. This is not to say that Cosby is any less effective than he was (I sat there laughing throughout the show and a comic is supposed to make you laugh) but only that television blows the thing up out of proportion, as it does everything else.

Cosby now has two things going for him. His records, which produce an audience intimately familiar with his routines and bits, and TV which produces another audience to whom his face is intimately familiar and who are predisposed to laugh at anything at all he does.

The concert was like a good show at the hungry i without the booze and in more comfortable seats but also without the intimacy the club produces. It opened with a 50-minute set by the Pair Extraordinaire, a singer (who plays tambourine) accompanied by a bassist. They are good, flashy entertainers, but both the vocalist and the bassist suffered from intonation troubles, in addition to microphone problems. Their material ranged from standard show tunes to "I'm A Believer," a recent Monkees hit.

Cosby introduced them and came out once midway in their act and again at the end to announce the intermission. He returned for his own show at 9 PM (there was an early 8 PM curtain because of the two shows) and did an hour by himself.

The Bill Cosby expert around my house is a slender, eerily effective mimic named Toby who has spent more time memorizing Bill Cosby than working at the New Math. He reports that Cosby was less effective Saturday than on previous concerts. "I don't know why," he said. But added that the variation from the album performances ("he changed lines and forgot other lines") was not an improvement. To the contrary, the albums were funnier.

However, he laughed, as I did, and that is a tribute to Cosby's wonderful projection of the world of youth with which most of his humor concerned itself (aside from his "Noah" routine, which was the encore). Cosby's neighborhood kids, "Weird Harold" and "Fat Albert" are well on their way to being classic comedy characters.

Cosby is a fascinating example of how the comic styles (even without the content) of Lord Buckley and Lenny Bruce can serve as influences and he is in the great American tradition of making humor out of the contrast between the world as seen by children and the world as seen by adults, which goes back to Huck Finn and Penrod and Sam.

Tomorrow night one of the greatest performers in the history of popular music, Chuck Berry (composer of innumerable hit songs of the past 15 years including "Maybelline," "Memphis," "Sweet Little 16," "Roll Over Beethoven" and "Rock 'n Roll Music") returns to the Fillmore Auditorium for a week. It should be an exciting show. On the bill with him will be Eric Burdon and The Animals, the British group, and the Steve Miller Blues Band, which was such a success at Monterey.

Berry is in the process of discovering an entirely new audience among the Love Generation which was raised on his music. When he was here in March, he said he had never before had a response like he had from the San Francisco audiences. "They really make you play."

Tomorrow night at the Jazz Workshop, Julian "Cannonball" Adderley returns with his Quintet. This is a jazz group which has had almost unprecedented commercial success with hit records. "Mercy, Mercy," a composition by their Austrian pianist Joe Zawinul, is already the theme of all the rhythm and blues concerts as well as a hit in several recorded versions. Adderley's newest single, a jazz version of the gospel song "Why Am I Treated So Bad," is also a huge success.

[*San Francisco Chronicle*, June 26, 1967]

Lenny Bruce, *The Real Lenny Bruce*

■

I t's weird. The first memory I have of seeing Lenny Bruce is not connected to something he said at all, but a purely visual thing he did.

Lenny was working at Ann's 440 Club on Broadway in San Francisco's North Beach, his first engagement in San Francisco and the beginning of his rise to fame. His show was similar in some ways to what he did later but quite different in others.

One of the ways in which it was different was that Lenny had not yet worked out enough long pieces to carry the show and he still utilized two standard devices of the ordinary comic: short bits with a quick punch line which were really only jokes, and impressions.

It was an impression that he did which remains my first memory of him. At the end of his act he would turn away from the audience, pick up a grey felt hat, roll it into a small sombrero, slap it on his head at a rakish angle, look back over his shoulder towards the audience, the lights would go down and a pin-spot light would concentrate on his head and he would be James Dean.

It was a frighteningly accurate likeness.

Lenny had opened at Ann's 440 on April 2nd of 1958. It was the phone call from his Alto saxophonist Paul Desmond of the Dave Brubeck Quartet, who was the first person to tell us in San Francisco about Lenny, and a year or so before he opened at Ann's 440, when I was in L.A. along with Sol Weiss (who then was one of the owners of Fantasy) and Saul Zaentz, I went out to some club on the outskirts of town to see him but he wasn't there. He'd been fired the night before for taking his clothes off onstage, something he never did again.

Actually, we had dismissed him from our minds and might not have gotten over to Ann's 440 to see him when he came up here if it had not been for the Number One Tape Freak in the world, Wally Heider.

Wally had just moved to Los Angeles from his native Sheridan, Oregon, where he was one of the leading attorneys in town by day and a tape nut by night. During his vacations, Wally went all over the world taping music in those days and finally decided to abandon his law practice, move to L.A., and become a professional recording engineer.

One of the bands of which Wally was inordinately fond was the Woody Herman big band and in January of 1958 the band was playing a couple of weeks at a long-gone Hollywood nightclub called Peacock Lane (it was at the corner of Hollywood Boulevard and Western and the original building has since been torn down and a taco stand is in its place). Wally went to Peacock Lane to record Woody "and someone named Lenny Bruce was the intermission act and he was so funny that I kept the tape rolling after Woody's band got off the stand each intermission."

Lenny was in great form at Peacock Lane. He was turned on by the fact that it was the first club he had worked in the L.A. area where there were no strippers. That made it more legit show biz. And he was also turned on by the audience. Not just by the rounders and show biz people who came in, but by the presence of the members of Woody's band who stayed in the club in the intermissions to listen to him, and by the other musicians and jazz fans who came to hear the band and stayed to hear Lenny.

A couple of days after the Peacock Lane date, I got a frantic letter from Wally Heider saying he was sending me a tape by this unknown and hysterically funny comedian named Lenny Bruce.

I got the tape and didn't even listen to it right away. I don't know why, but I didn't. Then I heard that he was coming to San Francisco, so I played the tape. I fell out. No other way to describe it. I could not believe what I heard. It is hard now to appreciate how wildly exciting his original things were because in the sixteen years since, so many taboos have been lifted and so many comedians, from George Carlin on up to Richard Pryor (and that's a long way up) have rushed through the doors Lenny opened and utterly changed the world of comedy.

In those days it was absolutely sensational when Lenny, in his Fat

Boy routine about the used car hustler, used the word "shit" divided into two syllables and drawn out in a Southern molasses drawl. It was so sensational when he satirized organized religion in Religions, Inc. (this simply was not done) and related it to show business that people, the first time they heard him do it, might even glance apprehensively over their shoulders as if expecting a bolt of lightning. And Lenny himself took notice of this when he first did the piece by adding as a kind of tag, a line about a bolt of lightning and, making a little noise on the microphone that sounded like the crackle of lightning, he would throw his arms up in front of his face and back away in mock fear.

Like all really great creative talents, Lenny emerged fully formed from obscurity. What I mean is that everything he was later to become was present and even some of his things were totally together already when he first broke through to the public. His Religions, Inc. was on that first tape I got from Wally as well as Fat Boy and The Sound (both of which are used in this album) and a lot of other shorter things including the famous screech of his Aunt Mema which Lenny said sounded like a Jewish seagull and, of course, his famous Dracula imitation. Once I had played the tape, I could hardly stop playing it over and over. It became part of the ordinary life in my house and my kids went off to school happily chanting "schmuck! Schmuck!" or screeching "eeeeeych! Eeeeeych!" without the faintest idea of what it was all about.

I sent the tape on to New York to Ira Gitler who was a critic and free-lance writer about jazz. I knew Ira would dig it, not just because of the jazz references in it, but because Ira was himself a student of humor, especially of Yiddish humor, and if there was one thing Lenny was steeped in, aside from jazz and the jazz musician culture, it was Yiddish expressions. Lenny subscribed to the belief that all good humor is Jewish and all great comedians Jewish. Sometimes he would use Yiddish expressions that would baffle Sol and Max Weiss and they would have to check them out with their aged father, an Oakland tailor who still refused to make sports coats for them, the owners of a successful small record company, because his prices were too high.

Ira Gitler played that tape for everybody in New York. There was a command performance of Ira and the tape at the home of Dorothy Kilgallen, then a leading columnist, and Ira even played it for prospective employers, nightclub owners, one of whom said, "He's very clever but he's got no point of view."

At that time I was not only writing for *Down Beat* and the *San Francisco Chronicle*, but also was the local "mugg" for *Variety*, the show business magazine, so I went to see Lenny right away. Lou Gottlieb, who later formed the Limeliters and then became the celebrated guru of Morningstar Ranch and appeared in *I Love You, Alice B. Toklas* with Peter Sellers, was working at that time at the Purple Onion in San Francisco (the club that spawned the Smothers Brothers, the Kingston Trio and Phyllis Diller). Lou was desperately trying to put together a solo act after the collapse of the Gateway Singers, his first folk group, and had worked as a musician for many years in Los Angeles and San Francisco. Lou had heard a lot about Lenny from Sandy Barton, a remarkable entertainer of the Fifties, and insisted we go together on Lou's first off-night early in April 1958.

Like the tape, the effect of Lenny in person was devastating. His shows at Ann's 440 not only included Religions, Inc. and Fat Boy, but also bits on Eisenhower (the Ike, Sherm and Nixon routine), imitations of Lawrence Welk (which he eventually knitted together with his satire on the history of jazz into the full-length The Sound), a bit about Hitler, satires on commercials, the Non Skeddo Flies Again routine, and comments on the news of the day.

The first thing I did was write a review for *Variety* (signed "rafe," the pseudonym with which my *Variety* reviews were always signed). Sharing the bill with Lenny were Gloria Padilla, a shake dancer, the Belasco Four (I have no idea what they did), and a jazz trio led by a fine pianist, Johnny Price. Bruce, I said in *Variety*, was "farther out than Mort Sahl and devastating in [his] attacks on the pompous, the pious, and the phony in American culture . . . a good bet for any jazz club in the country . . . his humor is right out of a road band sideman's perspective and delivered in a hetero-geneous mixture of underworld argot, hipster's slang, and show business patter . . ." The next week I did a column in the *Chronicle* about him.

Later that year when Lenny opened in Chicago, the *Variety* review echoed what I had written. It was not until he appeared in New York and was reviewed by the then-editor of *Variety*, Abel Green, that Lenny was attacked for his "scatological references" in an issue of *Variety* that included a laudatory review of a Lamb's Club frolic in which all the humor was scatological!

In San Francisco, Lenny rapidly became a hit. Herb Caen, the leading columnist in the city, plugged him frequently and the word-of-mouth plus the plugs on radio shows, all combined to fill the club. Hugh Hefner, if my memory is accurate, came out to see him and later that spring had a hand in getting him a date in Chicago and a subsequent profile in *Playboy*.

Ira Gitler, already a confirmed Bruce fan, even used to sign himself "Mayor of Bruceville" and his address as Lenny Bruce Fan Club #2 (in deference to my claiming of #1). Ira came out to San Francisco during Lenny's engagement at Ann's 440 and we walked in, as Ira recalls, "right in the middle of Hitler. I was gassed instantaneously." I later pointed out to him it was probably because he was Jewish.

Lenny's Hitler bit, while having some funny things in it, never actually came together and, although he recorded one version of it for Fantasy later on, eventually he dropped it. It was an old bit of his, dating back to when he first went on the Arthur Godfrey show, but somehow he couldn't sustain it as he was able to later sustain other ideas into long pieces that sometimes ran 20 minutes.

In the intermission, Ira met Lenny on the sidewalk in front of the club. In those days, Lenny wore dark blue or black suits, white shirts and a black tie and his hair was short in the style of the times. He looked very show biz himself. But he blew Ira right out of his mind by knowing about jazz essays and liner notes Ira had written, including one famous at the time in which Ira said, "Dave Brubeck doesn't swing."

Inside the club, Lenny did his usual bits but in his second show dropped into them references to me and to Ira, a habit of his when he had friends in the audience. One little bit of New York in-group knowledge was a reference to Stauch's Baths on Stillwell Avenue in Coney Island. Ira almost fell to the floor when Lenny dropped that name.

Lenny also had another bit then that was a surefire hit with jazz musicians and/or hard-core jazz fans since it contained the names of two well-known Hollywood musicians, bassist Leroy Vinnegar and drummer Larry Bunker. It was a parody of the jazz and poetry fad of the time in which Lenny would have the house piano player improvise while he recited some lines, sprinkling Latin double talk with phrases such as "cop the joint of Leroy Vinnegar" and "Larry Bunker, mother funker."

At that point in time (if I may recycle that phrase), record companies had discovered that there was money to be made with albums by comics. Mort Sahl and Shelley Berman had both had tremendous success as recording artists, simply putting on albums the material they did in nightclubs. Another development was the combination of jazz and comedy in concert, a creation, I believe, of Irving Granz (younger brother of Norman Granz who produced Jazz at the Philharmonic). Irving had presented several comedians in concert tours with jazz groups sharing the bill, thus breaking comedy away from the nightclub scene completely. He was later to present a tour by Lenny.

So it was an obvious thing to think of making records with Lenny and it was something he was thinking about himself. The only record company in San Francisco was (and still is) Fantasy and, as I noted earlier, the people who ran Fantasy were already aware of Lenny and had heard the Wally Heider tape and had been to see him.

Lenny was very worried about making records. He didn't want to be censored but he was willing to compromise. That really was a characteristic of his. He was almost always, until the final hassles with the law, willing to compromise. And he had rather unusual ideas about what he wanted to do. For instance, he wanted to sing! And eventually he recorded four numbers aimed, at least in his mind, right at Top 40 radio.

Fantasy was already in the comedy-satire business with their hit disc of "Two Interviews." This was the famous satire on the jazz musician, Shorty Pedderstein, with ultra-hip talk and the takeoff of the pompous musicologist Dr. Sholem Stein.

The two tracks, which were the work of Woody Leafer and Henry Jacobs (an early experimenter in tape techniques) had been leased from Folkways Records and issued as an Extended Play disc, a 33-1/3 rpm disc the size of a present-day 45 rpm disc. It was a big hit, but the recording business was then turning to the 12-inch Long Playing record and Fantasy wanted to flesh out the "Two Interviews" with enough material to make a 12-inch album.

So Lenny agreed to record some short bits and to let them be used on the *Two Interviews of Our Time* 12-inch album (the one with the *Pigs Ate My Roses* book in the cover photograph). He did not, however, want his name to be used, since he didn't want to be coupled with any other comics and wanted his own album. Fantasy did use his name, though, in the liner notes but X'd it out on many copies after Lenny complained.

Later, Fantasy ran a cover line using Lenny's name that further confused the issue and thus led to the situation in which critics always credit Lenny with all the bits on that album. There's really no resemblance in voices, though, but maybe they didn't listen.

After they made a deal with Lenny, Fantasy attempted to tape his shows at Ann's 440 and did succeed in getting some good material there, but Lenny was a difficult performer to record and remained so throughout his career. The problem was that he was bursting with energy and leaped around the stage all the time. If the microphone remained on a stand, he would lose the volume of sound by being too far away. And when he worked with a hand held mike, he was always shoving it too close to his mouth or waving it around. The result was a continually changing recording level.

And there was another thing. Lenny was his own best fan (aside from his mother, Sally Marr, who used to sit by the cash register taking the money at the door and whose high-pitched laugh can sometimes be heard on his records). He had a marvelously innocent delight in the things he created and sometimes would get so carried away by what he was doing that he would forget to keep the right accent in the voice he was using for some character and revert to his own normal voice.

So, they tried to record him in the loft over the old Fantasy offices on Natoma Street, a narrow alley south of Mission Street in the heart of San Francisco.

While it was never literally true that the Three Stooges or the Marx Brothers ran Fantasy, the Weiss Brothers gave as good an imitation as they could of that kind of operation. The loft was leased (to help pay the rent) to a woman who had a wholesale distributorship for toilet brushes and was known as "the toilet brush lady" and to a man who stored containers of a liquid that put out fires. He even mixed it there and sold it to ships docking in San Francisco. It was called, so help me, Firewater! Downstairs, the Weiss Brothers, Edwin Chune (still with Fantasy), and a philosophical black man named Nolan, operated a couple of record presses, wrapped and shipped the Dave Brubeck discs and indulged in all manner of nonsense. Every Monday morning, for instance, Sol Weiss was late because he had to go by the Hall of Justice and spring Nolan from the drunk tank where he spent his Saturday nights and Sundays.

So Lenny attempted to record upstairs in the loft surrounded by the paraphernalia of the toilet brush lady and the fire-fighting liquid business.

It didn't work. Or at least, it didn't work very well, though I think some of the early bits that were on the *Two Interviews* album actually were done there. But Lenny quickly established the fact that he worked and sounded better, regardless of the problems, when he had an audience in a club so that was how he was recorded for the rest of his career.

Another problem with location recording was the fact that he rarely did one of his pieces the same way twice. Like a jazz musician, an analogy that was obvious, Lenny worked from a framework of a routine into which he dropped all kinds of spur-of-the-moment references. Sometimes he would even stop the logical development of one piece to launch on off into another that had occurred to him for one reason or another.

In one early performance I remember, he was doing either the Lawrence Welk bit about hiring the jazz trumpet player (The Sound) or his Tarzan routine. In any case, he stopped and asked the audience if they had ever noticed the similarity in the sound of the voices of Tarzan and Lawrence Welk, and then went off into the other piece, coming back to his original number only when he finished what might be called an extensive insert.

It took quite a while to put together the early Lenny Bruce pieces, especially the long ones. Saul Zaentz and Lenny would work for hours snipping bits from various performances and splicing them together to make the whole thing include as many of his goodies as possible. But inevitably there were things that were lost, which is why so many people who heard him do, say, Religions, Inc., remember something that is not on the final recorded version. He may only have done it once.

There was really no final version. I think he kept changing things right up to the last time he appeared in performance.

Towards the end of Lenny's engagement at Ann's 440, I produced a pilot for a jazz program called *Jam Session,* which featured the Dave Brubeck Quartet and the Modern Jazz Quartet and was financed by Jay Ward, a Berkeley real estate salesman who later became the producer of numerous Hollywood TV cartoon shows. I wanted Lenny to be the emcee for the show, but Jay Ward and his associates were afraid and we settled for Mort Sahl. We filmed the show at the Black Hawk one weekday afternoon and Lenny, a confirmed fan of Mort's, was there all the time giving us advice and comment—before the show, during it, and afterwards when we all went to dinner at New Joe's.

After Lenny closed out of Ann's 440, he went to Chicago for his debut there at The Cloisters in July of 1958. In Chicago, Lenny had much the same effect he had had in San Francisco. Studs Terkel interviewed him on WFMT. He was profiled in *Playboy.* Dorothy Kilgallen saw him and wrote him up in the *New York Journal-American.*

Local critics either hated him or loved him. There was no middle ground.

When he returned to San Francisco he came to Fack's. Fack's II was the actual name of the club because the owner, a dedicated horse player and bon vivant named George Andros, already had another club on Market Street called Fack's.

Fack's II was beautiful (it was in the building that now houses the Boarding House and for a while later on was a recording studio and a jazz club called The Neve). Originally it had been a Hungarian restaurant called The Balalaika, a huge room that was very comfortable. The stage was against the wall on one side of the room and the bar was at the opposite end from the entrance, and the dressing rooms were behind the bar.

Andros loved comics as well as music and horses and he stood at the door taking the admissions while his brother, Nicky, tended bar. They were not hoods, as some uninformed writers have claimed, nor was it a "hood" joint. It was a straight-life club and the Andros brothers were simply a couple of native San Franciscans trying to make a living. The club, incidentally, was the launching pad for a number of careers, including those of Jack Jones and Johnny Mathis, and numerous top attractions such as Duke Ellington played there.

I will never forget the night Lenny opened. George Andros was at the door and Nicky behind the bar and Lenny came onstage, walked up to the microphone, paused for a moment, and then said he'd forgotten something he wanted to show us and raced offstage back to the dressing room.

The two Andros brothers panicked. Never had a performer done such a thing! They raced toward each other desperately seeking aid and advice, George from the door and Nicky from the bar, and collided right in the middle of the room! It was that kind of a club.

For most of Lenny's stay there the other attraction on the bill was the present conductor of the London Philharmonic Orchestra, then a struggling young film music composer and would be jazz pianist named André Previn. I would go to the club night after night and sit through Previn's lukewarm jazz set talking to Bruce, but then a problem arose. Previn always thought I came there to see him, and he'd talk to me, or rather tried to talk to me, since I didn't listen, throughout Lenny's set.

During Lenny's engagement at Fack's II, I had a fascinating glimpse of how he worked. Sometimes he would write out the original idea for a piece on scraps of paper, eventually typing it out painfully himself. And then he would use it as the framework for what he would do on stage, keeping some of the things in all performances. But sometimes he would work out a piece in his head and then try it out before his friends.

One night I had dinner with Lenny and several people at the Leopard, in San Francisco's financial district. Throughout the meal, Lenny regaled us with an account of his relations with Gene Norman, the owner of the Hollywood nightclubs, The Interlude and The Crescendo. Lenny had just that day met Kaye Ballard, the comedienne who was working at the hungry i, and they were both opening later in the month for Gene Norman, one of them in The Crescendo and the other upstairs in The Interlude.

Lenny told us a long story about how, when he had once worked for Norman, he had told the audience that Gene had a dog named Boris that he balled in the parking lot. After he left the stage, Lenny told us,

Gene Norman came up to him and told him not to do that again. "Nobody knows who Boris is, Lenny," he quoted Norman as saying. Lenny was really unkind to Gene Norman, even though it was a devastatingly funny story as he told it, because, though the two of them argued and battled over money, Gene Norman was one of the first and most fervent Lenny Bruce fans in Hollywood.

Later that night at Fack's II, I was surprised to hear Lenny go into the whole thing all over again as part of his show. He kept much of what he had told us at dinner, but actually embellished it with all kinds of little goodies, keeping in the parts we had laughed at and dropping others that had not gained any reaction. Lenny never made too much out of that particular piece, since it really had nowhere to go, but it did illustrate how he worked.

Although Lenny was a success at Fack's II, and dug the nutty Greek owners, George and Nick Andros, he detested the condition of the men's room and used to talk about it, to George Andros' horror, on stage. One night he came out carrying a sopping wet, dripping rag, walked over to the microphone and said, "My agent didn't want me to work any more of those jazz joints, those toilets, so he put me in here." The Andros brothers fainted.

Billy Graham ran one of his crusades at the Cow Palace during that time and the night before Graham opened, there was a prizefight at the Cow Palace. Lenny took out an advertisement in the local papers pointing out that the seats the Christian Crusaders occupied that night had been occupied the night before by the prizefight fans who came to see blood. Once again, Lenny posed the paradox.

Lenny recorded frequently during his Fack's II engagement, including his How to Relax Your Colored Friends at Parties, on which the background piano was played by the present conductor of the London Philharmonic who asked not to be credited.

Then he went back to Chicago and in April of 1959 opened in New York at The Den of the Duane Hotel in Greenwich Village.

All the crowd that Ira Gitler had been playing the tape for were there, plus a lot of other celebrities including Martha Raye. When he opened his act saying, "A lot of my friends are here tonight. Ira Gitler, the great jazz writer, he really knocks me out. There's Martha Raye who he's been balling lately." Philly Joe Jones, the great jazz drummer whose imitation of Dracula was the original inspiration of Lenny's Enchanting Transylvania bit was there with Orrin Keepnews and Bill Grauer of Riverside Records, and even Miles Davis made it the second night.

By that time Lenny had worked out much of his famous Comic at the Palladium routine and the New York audiences, especially the show biz crowd, really loved it.

After that first New York date, Lenny went back to Chicago, this time to Mister Kelly's, and then to the hungry i in San Francisco. Jonathan Winters had flipped out while working there that year and when Lenny opened he started right in with references to that episode. *Time* was then doing its cover story on so-called sick comics and Lenny even had a series of bits about that. Lenny worked out a whole fantasy about it including how he had bribed Hugh Hefner to run the article in *Playboy*, leaving the money in a phonebook in a booth. Like many other random excursions that were really stream of consciousness improvisations on what was going on with him at the particular moment, he didn't keep this bit. It was cued into the *Time* cover story and then its timeliness was over and he dropped it.

While he was at The Den of the Duane in New York, Lenny did several TV shows including the Steve Allen show (a kinescope of that is frequently shown these days along with his other Steve Allen appearance on double bills and art houses) and even taped his own program for WNTA, a New York station no longer active. On it he presented Philly Joe Jones and himself doing Dracula bits, "trading four" on Dracula, as musicians would call it, in which each took a few lines alternately. Cannonball Adderley and several friends of Lenny's from Times Square sideshows were also on the program. It was never shown, to the best of my knowledge, and has long since been lost.

For the next couple of years Lenny made real money. He was very successful and his records sold well, too. He worked clubs like the Crystal Palace in St. Louis, Mister Kelly's in Chicago, Freddie's in Minneapolis, the Celebrity Room in Philadelphia, the Blue Angel in New York, the Trade Winds in Chicago, the Racquet Club in Dayton, the Town House and the Fallen Angel in Pittsburgh, and Basin St., East in New York. He toured with several jazz groups for Irving Granz, appeared at Carnegie Hall and the Academy of Music and in other clubs in the East.

Finally, he was busted in Philadelphia for possession of drugs for which he had a prescription (case dropped) and that began the arrest and legal hassle turmoil that dominated the rest of his life. The story of that and of the San Francisco arrest is told in detail in his Curran Theater album on Fantasy.

Jobs began to be scarce. Many clubs would not book him and several cities would not let him perform.

He went back to Chicago, was arrested there (the guilty verdict was thrown out eventually), and in New York (again the verdict was overthrown). He appeared in London where Sioban McKenna walked out on him, and tried to perform in Australia but was evicted from the country before he could appear. He tried to get back into England, but was ejected. In 1963 he was even invited to the Edinburgh International Drama Festival but the British government refused to let him enter the country.

His life became horribly complicated, what with court cases, arrests, and the constant struggle for employment. He had some engagements in New York, Los Angeles, and San Francisco in 1964, but his 1965 booking in Chicago was canceled and eventually all he could do was an occasional concert, though he could always get club work in San Francisco.

He kept trying to put on stage shows, a kind of vaudeville review, and even persuaded Phil Spector to help him with this in Los Angeles. But nothing seemed to work right. Police harassment continued every time he appeared in public and his celebrated fall from a hotel window in San Francisco made headlines all over.

Lenny had told me when he came back to San Francisco once that he expected it. He knew they would go for him when he attacked the church and the rest of society's sacred conventions. And they did, even if they were unaware, really, of what he was doing.

He desperately tried to get the various courts to allow him to do his routine for the judge so that he could be judged for what he actually did and not for what some cop on the beat thought he did, but the courts would never permit him. The Lenny Bruce live film, that extraordinary document made at Basin St., West in San Francisco by John Magnuson, was designed originally to be a substitute for an in person performance in court. Lenny wanted to enter the film of his show as evidence in his own defense but he could never get that accepted either.

So on August 3, 1966 he was found dead in his Hollywood home from an overdose of morphine. The following February, his New York obscenity conviction was voided, thus only his narcotics conviction in Los Angeles held up under first appeal and no one knows how that appeal eventually would've gone, since one of the arresting officers was eventually himself convicted of smuggling drugs. There was even a hassle over Lenny's burial. The cemetery wouldn't let a public service be held.

Lenny died fighting. He never gave up. And I don't think for a minute that he OD'd on purpose. He was convinced he was right and was being misjudged. But the whole stance of the American court system went against him and in the end the truest verdict was what Phil Spector said: "Lenny died of an overdose of police."

Since that first night when I saw Lenny Bruce at Ann's 440, it has been one of the aims of my life to turn the entire world on to his humor. In the first place because I found him so devastatingly funny that I wanted everyone to share that experience, but also because I found the vision implicit in his work so very useful as a tool with which to examine this insane society in which we live.

Lenny, despite his public reputation then and the reputation his biographers (consciously?) have saddled him with was, in the words of my friend Irwin Kaiser, "a primitive Christian preaching a moral message." He believed in basic things while at the same time understanding (and being amused and outraged by) the inconsistencies, paradoxes, and hypocrisy of the world around him. There is no good and no bad, only what is, he would say. And if he were alive today, I'm convinced he would be attacking Ford and Kissinger for preaching the virtues of capitalism and free enterprise on the one hand and threatening the Arab oil states with military force when they practice it.

Lenny's audience in the beginning—and it is important to understand this—were those people he found in the crummy bars and strip joints where he worked, the rounders, the night people, the bartenders, strippers, waitresses, and musicians.

They belong to an American substrata which early on in life learns the true realities of the system and Lenny talked to them out of their common experience and in the framework of the American myths as seen in films and heard on radio and TV.

Lenny was a child in the 30s, a volunteer in the Navy in World War II (he used to point out a case where a veteran had been awarded a medal for killing 22 Italians in combat and arrested for killing one in a Manhattan gunfight). The frames of reference in which he worked were the films of the 30s and 40s and the characters from those films populate his routines and bits along with the characters from the world of show business in which he found himself in Hollywood later.

Lenny understood instinctively that the myths of American culture are reflected on the screen and not in indigenous religious texts and he set his pieces, or most of them, in that framework. Others he constructed as events, using as characters typical real-life names, each of whom represented the thing he was describing.

His first converts (and they were converts, in a religious sense) were members of that first audience. Next he brought in those people who, while themselves outside the world of nightlife and show business, were involved in it tangentially. People such as Artie Samuels, the box office manager in San Francisco, and Saul Zaentz, who was sales manager of Fantasy when Lenny first came to San Francisco, memorized literally hours of Lenny's routines.

Lenny, as he deepened the scope of his attack on the system, appealed to the alienated, the cultural dropouts represented by the beats and the new generation of pop music artists. Bob Dylan dug Lenny and even wrote me thanking me for defending Lenny at a time when I did not dig Dylan myself. Paul Simon and Art Garfunkel were Lenny Bruce fans, even incorporating a news broadcast about his death into their *Parsley, Sage, Rosemary and Thyme* album. Grace Slick wrote a song, "Father Bruce," about him. Lenny loved Frank Zappa as much as he loved the jazz musicians and Zappa eventually issued Lenny's classic *Berkeley Concert* album (one of the last things he did) on Zappa's own Bizarre label. John Mayall devoted years to acquiring an extensive collection of Lenny Bruce tapes and the Beatles, particularly John Lennon, were devotees. Phil Spector, of course, became his patron saint at the end.

And Lenny bits entered into the common language just as Bob Dylan lines have entered. It is not only that you hear them on comedy shows on TV out of the mouths of people who did not stand up for him when he was in trouble, but they crop up everywhere. I was startled right in the middle of the documentary on Bob Dylan, *Don't Look Back*, where Dylan is listening to his road manager, Bob Neuwirth, describe some lady, to hear Neuwirth say she was wearing a dress, "the kind you can see through, but don't wanna." That's a direct quote from Lenny's Lima, Ohio skit.

Traditional show business people, naturally, abhorred him because he violated all their taboos and in many instances made them face their own hypocrisy. But there were those among them, such as Prof. Irwin Corey, Steve Allen, Shecky Green, and even Milton Berle, who loved him. Many, of course, simply did not understand what he was doing or what he was. Jerry Lewis was astounded that Lenny turned down an offer of $10,000, when he was out of work, to write comedy material for him.

Lenny could not do that. He had passed the point where he could write for others. He had to write for himself alone.

At the end, Lenny had also passed the point where he was interested in doing set pieces, no matter how much he might change them from performance to performance. Like Miles Davis and the other modern jazz musicians (most of whom considered him one of their own) who had stopped playing songs in order to create totally everything they did, Lenny wanted to just stand up and improvise. "Free associate," he called it. But his trials kept him from that even though they provided him with the transcripts, subject for endless commentary that brought him a whole new audience of lawyers.

Because Lenny was, in a real sense, especially in his original work, the child of his own frames of reference, and because some of those references need explanation now for full understanding, I am going to run down here some aids for listening to the tracks on this collection.

Thank You Masked Man is Lenny's fantasy of the Great American myth of the solitary stranger, The Lone Ranger, who unselfishly aided all who needed him. He had worked it out during the time between his Jazz Workshop arrest and his Curran Theater concert and intended to give it its first presentation there but became so enraptured with his ability to free associate that night that he never got around to it.

"Here's a bit," he would say in introducing it, "about a man who was better than Christ and Moses."

The celebrated animated cartoon, Thank You Masked Man by John Magnuson, uses as a soundtrack a special performance of the bit that Lenny did for the film. (Here, however, we use the original.) He takes all the parts. Sometimes in his longer pieces he would do as many as 40 voices for different characters and sometimes would get carried away and forget to change accents when he changed characters! This was why he considered these pieces as dramas and himself as an actor and tried unsuccessfully to get that concept into his legal defense.

It was when this concept first occurred to Lenny and he had the routines transcribed and typed up as a drama script, that the idea of a play about him first cropped up.

Like in many of his pieces, Lenny dropped into Masked Man references to films (Dr. Ehrlich and His Magic Bullet, for instance) and he always brought in Jonas Salk, Lenny Bruce and J. Edgar Hoover, saying, "these men thrive upon the cultivation of violence and disease" and adding that "without polio, Salk is a putz." The Lone Ranger becomes addicted to "thank you's" after he accepts a few, and then says, "I'll make trouble, I must have a 'thank you, Masked Man!'" Also in this piece, Lenny uses several Yiddish expressions. When one of the witnesses says, "the masked man is a Jew!" Lenny precedes it with the Yiddish word, zugnisht, which means, loosely, "don't tell." And in another place, expressing his delight, he says, "g'zint in dein pippick," which translates, again loosely, as "a health on your belly button," or simply, "I love you."

Non Skeddo Flies Again is an adaptation of a Will Jordan piece that Lenny simply took over and made his own by his brilliance in creating a different set of characters and language. In those days—the 50s—there was a cheap kind of commuter air flight between cities such as San Francisco and Los Angeles, which was not available on any set schedule. You bought your ticket and you waited for the plane to be full before takeoff. They were propeller planes (jets were in the future then for most commercial flights). A man named John Graham had been arrested, in Denver, I recall, for blowing up a plane on which his mother was traveling, for the insurance payment on her life, and Lenny incorporated that into the piece. The airline stewardesses would go through the plane in those days offering Chiclets to the passengers so they could chew them and help the ear-popping which always occurred in the non-pressurized cabins. There are lovely little bits in this: the reference to Smiling Jack, the comic strip character, the whistling in the background which is the theme from The High and the Mighty, a film about an airplane that has to turn back because of trouble, and the delightful dialogue between the juiced out pilot and copilot. I was startled recently to read in the paper the transcript of the tape found after an air crash in which one of the pilots said, "now all we have to do is find the airport!" Shades of Lenny Bruce!, I thought. He again uses Yiddish words, starcher, meaning a real heavy guy, and potzlah, a term of affection. And again he brings in names of actors from the old movies, Otto Krueger and Gene Lockhart.

Religions, Inc., is, of course his most famous long routine (along with Comic at the Palladium) and it is a classic satire on the concept that religion has become big business. Lenny sometimes made note of the fact that there were more ads in the weekend papers for church services and revivals than for nightclubs. The laugh in the background, incidentally, is Lenny's mother, Sally Marr.

The whole piece is replete with references to the Forties and Fifties and even the Thirties. In the beginning, where he has the fantasy introduction of the religious leaders (he used real names, too, here: Oral Roberts, H. O. Allen, Billy Graham, and Rabbi Wise), Lenny talks about the "old days" when they were hustling Gideon Bibles (shades of Paper Moon!) and were into shingles and siding, another sales racket in which hustlers traveled all over the South selling unsuspecting farmers nonexistent repairs.

When he has the preacher ask, "Where is the heavenly land?" And the answer is "Chavez Ravine! And the sons of bitches are stealing it from us!," the reference is to the city of Los Angeles expropriating the land in Chavez Ravine in L.A. on which to build the new Dodgers Stadium. In his line about the napkins with "Another martini for Mother Cabrini" printed on them is a reference to a newly canonized saint. When Lenny first did this routine, Pope Pius had just died and the new pope was Pope John. Hence, "Johnny, baby." The puff of smoke was a reference to the Vatican custom of releasing a puff of smoke when a new pope has been chosen. And Lenny tied it into the cigarette ad of the smoker with the tattoo on his hand.

He also touched on the civil rights protests then in the news and used two black stereotypes, Stepin Fetchit and Scatman Crothers (later to be seen in *Lady Sings the Blues*). His conversation with the Pope in terms of his Holiness coming to the coast for an appearance on the Ed Sullivan show ("Wave and wear the big ring") precedes his question "Did you dig Spellman (the late Cardinal Spellman, a familiar figure on TV) on *Stars of Jazz* (a jazz series then being shown in Los Angeles)?" Lenny ends it after saying "Philly Joe says 'hello,'" referring to the jazz drummer Philly Joe Jones, with a bow to superstition and the line "Look out for the lightning!"

Side 2 begins with Enchanting Transylvania, the routine that grew out of Lenny's admiration for the way drummer Philly Joe Jones imitated Dracula. The concept of setting up the vampire, Dracula (Bela Lugosi), as a junkie jazz musician trying to make a living and explaining his failure to his wife, was bizarre and funny at the same time. She calls him a "bebopper" as many dance band leaders used the term to describe young musicians they hated. "We can work Vegas, the lounges, better than The Goofers," Dracula says, referring to the standard fallback position of jazz groups, working the miserable jobs in the Las Vegas hotel lounges. The Goofers was a novelty musical act of the Fifties, incidentally. And when he says, "that fink, Russ Morgan, took all my good men," he was speaking to a standard caper in the music business of raiding another's band. Russ Morgan, of course, was a sweet dance band leader of the Thirties, Forties and Fifties.

Incidentally, when Bella Lugosi died and it was revealed that he had been a morphine addict, the phones of Lenny's friends in Hollywood buzzed into the night as they once again found his fantasy come true.

How to Relax Your Colored Friends at Parties, Lenny's shafting of the white liberal, has Eric Miller, the black guitarist and longtime Bruce friend and associate, as the other voice, and the piano of André Previn in the background. All the clichés of black-white relations of the time were there.

White Collar Drunk is the total barroom satire, an extension of the drunk sequence, "Guzzler's Gin," which Red Skelton used to do. It is one of his few bits with no show business or music references, just the scene itself.

The Sound, in its original form incorporating the Lawrence Welk bit, is Lenny's classic satire on the history of jazz in which he drops the names of many jazz musicians. Buck Clayton Oliver, the old musician, is a combination of trumpet players (King Oliver and Buck Clayton), and the mythical film, the Vinnegar-Cannonball Story, refers to the bassist, Leroy Vinnegar, and the saxophonist, Julian "Cannonball" Adderley.

The last time I listened to this, I flashed again at the universality of Lenny's work. When Buck asks the aspiring young musician where he lives, he replies, "in a paper box at the Ranch Market (a familiar shopping center in Hollywood)." I had just that very day read a review of a book written by an Oriental novelist, the central character of which lived in a paper box!

Lenny's concept of his satire is rooted in the incongruity of Lawrence Welk, the personification of middle Western, straight-life America, hiring a junkie jazz musician for his band. He drops in many music business references—Charlie's Tavern in Manhattan, the Roseland building, Al McIntyre (the saxophonist from the Glenn Miller band who later led his own orchestra), and Earl Bostic, the black rhythm-and-blues saxophonist, "balling the Lennon Sisters," then closely associated with the Lawrence Welk show.

The junkie jazz musician character fits so many people in the jazz scene of that time that it is not fair to single out one of them, but the line "the agency, Mr. Glaser, sent me" refers to Joe Glaser, manager of Louis Armstrong and many other jazz musicians, who operated a huge booking agency. And the line about "I knew Basie before he could count" is the perfect in-group quote from a hippie jazz musician of that time.

Tarzan requires no special knowledge to appreciate, even though

Lenny occasionally drops in the names of Hollywood clubs. The idea is all that counts here.

My Werewolf Mama is Lenny's bid for top 40 radio and has never before been available on LP. The lyric is Lenny's, the musical arrangement the product of bassist Jack Weeks.

Comic at the Palladium, also known simply as the Palladium, is for many people Lenny's finest piece. It is certainly, like Religions, Inc., a transcendentally inspired and complete satire on an important segment of American culture and something which will never be improved upon. It was recorded at the hungry i in San Francisco and begins right away with references to such people as Bullets Durgom (manager of Trini Lopez and other stars), Helen Noga (manager of Johnny Mathis), Bobby Breen (a boy tenor of the Forties and early Fifties), Bob Burns and his bazooka (a comic from radio shows of the Thirties and Forties whose daughter, Barbara Burns, had just been busted when we first did this piece), and Attorney Liebowitz and his clients, the celebrated Scottsboro Boys, a famous civil rights case of the Thirties.

The "comic" is Frankie Dell, "dean of satire and mimicry," a real-life comic who never really made it. He was a friend of Lenny's mother, Sally. His account of getting his booking at the London Palladium (then considered the best job in show business) includes the note that he can work "to the eggheads, that Stevenson stuff," referring to Adlai Stevenson and his reputation for being an intellectual. The "gang at Lindy's" refers to Lindy's Restaurant, for many years the favorite lunch and late-night hangout in Manhattan for show business people, especially comics.

The Rehearsal, with the accompanying music, is almost a literal recap of vaudeville shows of the early Fifties with The Dunhills, Nick Lucas (a ukulele player famous for his version of "Tiptoe Through the Tulips"), and Bronco and his Dog—I'm not sure of the spelling of this but their theme was "Doggie in the Window," that vapid record by Patti Page. Ron with his Swiss Bells was another standard vaudeville act, as was Wanda and her Birds.

Georgia Gibbs was the vocal star of the radio show, *The Hit Parade*, and later a recording star of considerable magnitude if slight talent. Her "tribute to Sir Harry Lauder" is a reference to the Scottish entertainer who was one of the biggest stars of London for many years. Val Parnell and Jack Durant were familiar names to London show business audiences and Parnell was the booker at the Palladium. At the end of his first conversation with the comic, there is a lovely little drop in line: "See if Ms. Toklas is in with a bit of candy for me." That was Alice B. Toklas whose cookbook's goodies were just beginning to be appreciated.

In the second half of this piece, Lenny refers to Martha Raye, the actress and entertainer, to actor Will Fyffe, to Art Baker's TV show, *You Asked for It*, and to the mau mau, the African nationalist terrorist group, and Robert Ruark. Ruark was an American newspaper columnist of the Forties and Fifties who wrote a book, famous at the time, on the mau mau. In the hysterical bit of "Screw the Irish," Lenny drops in the line, "They stole the grail!," which refers to a classic religious argument over the Holy Grail. And at the end, when Val Parnell is canceling out Frankie Dell and sending him home in disguise, he says, "Julian Eltinge left a wig in a closet." Eltinge, the great female impersonator of the years before World War I, had theaters named after him all over the world. Lenny could stretch this whole piece out, sometimes prolonging the Georgia Gibbs part almost indefinitely and it made for some of the most hysterically funny shows he ever did.

Djinni in the Candy Store is one of Lenny's early excursions with his imitation of Sabu, the Indian actor, and includes a reference to Sol Weiss of Fantasy. It was one of his most successful short bits.

Lima, Ohio is, like Middletown, USA and Winesburg, Ohio, an examination of the social structure of the typical American Midwestern town. "'Peyton Place' is a lie," Lenny would say, contradicting the implication, from the novel, the TV show, and film, that Small Town, USA was packed with action of all kinds. This is where his "crinkly dresses you can see through and you don't wanna" line comes from, as well as a detailed listing of all the things he hated about the small towns, as well as the types he saw, from the man who sold Capezio shoes to the girl's gym teacher with a butch haircut. It is a vicious satire, one of Lenny's most savage pieces even though funny, and frighteningly sharp.

Black Boys satirizes a Hollywood TV show, *Rocket to Stardom*, and its commercials for used cars. Lenny is at his best here doing the exaggerated red-neck accent of the used-car salesman with his references to having out to his car lot "Jack Johnson [the old black prizefighter] and busting his head with a baseball bat." Believe it or not, this refers to a practice in the Twenties and even in the Thirties, at fairs, of throwing baseballs at the head of a black man in a sideshow, the myth being that his head was so thick he couldn't get hurt. Incredible! The salesman, telling the audience that "we're all good pee-pul" in his area, points out that they haven't shown a Charlie Chaplin picture in 15 years. Chaplin's films were barred from many U.S. communities because he was too left-wing politically. Then, in naming the visitors the used-car lot has had, consistent with the above-noted prejudices, the salesman lists the names of two of the best-known bigots of the Thirties and Forties, Father Coughlin, the Catholic priest eventually silenced by the Vatican, and Fritz Kuhn, the head of the German-American bund, the pro-Hitler German organization in the late Thirties and early Forties. Lenny then, possibly unconsciously, reverts to Religions, Inc. and has the salesman, the used-car pitch man, shift into a preacher role selling his cars and he does a fine job with the accents and the speech rhythms as well as the lines themselves.

Father Flotski's Triumph (unexpurgated) is Lenny's satire on all the prison riot pictures he has seen. Listening to it now, I can't help but think of Attica. In it he drops the names of a long list of character actors including Frankie Darrow, Charles Bickford, Warren Heymer, Barton MacLane, Nat Pendleton, Ann Dvorak, Iris Adrian, Glenda Farrell, Hume Cronyn, H. B. Warner, and Arthur Shields, the brother of Barry Fitzgerald of the Abbey Theatre in Dublin. Shields was famous in the late 50s for a TV commercial in which he said, in his broad Irish brogue, "This is Arthur Shields for Swiss Colony Wine."

This piece had elements of several others in it in its final form. Lenny long had done a satire on the "last mile," "death march" scenes in prison pictures and he includes it here, as well as a line from a commercial, "more people are using natural gas than ever before." The concept of one of the leaders of the rioting convicts being overtly gay and asking, as part of the settlement terms, for a "gay bar in the West Wing," was incredible in those days. A naftka, incidentally (as in Kinky, you naftka, you), is a hooker, a whore. And when Kinky says, "I feel just like Wally Simpson," the reference is to the woman for whom the King of England (later the Duke of Windsor) gave up his throne.

The warden's heartless instructions to shoot the prisoners is particularly haunting today. Satire cutting close to the bone.

Towards the end of his active performance career, Lenny used to close his shows saying, "And so, because I love you, fuck you and good night," after setting it up clearly to show that what he meant was love. Some time I hope to find one of those lines on tape to include in a future album of his work. For now, I'll just quote it.

[Fantasy Records—F-79003, 1975]

POLITICS AND CULTURE

The Casualties of Mass Society

■

The first casualty of the mass society seems to be the artist, whose basic declaration in favor of beauty and of truth apparently sets off conditioned reflexes that turn the society against him.

Many artists achieve success in the reward system of the society only in terms of something other than the reality of their art.

Thus a Miles Davis is treated as a controversial figure and as an irritant; thus a Thelonious Monk is treated as an exotic; thus a Duke Ellington is treated as an entertainer. And all rewarded for that, if not for their music.

This structures curious personalities for, as Nelson Algren says, when you deny someone the reality of the world, he builds himself another world.

Algren on art and the artist is fascinating. There's a very great deal of it in "Conversations With Nelson Algren" by H.E.F. Donohue (Hill & Wang; 333 pps.; $6.50). This is the new book composed of taped conversations that Donohue conducted with Algren. It ranks with any in-depth interview I have ever read, as fascinating as "Conversations With Casals" and a bitter indictment of the whole American culture system.

Algren has been made this bitter by his experience with his novels, "Never Come Morning," "The Man With The Golden Arm" and "A Walk On The Wild Side" and he feels cheated by his own time for the lack of reward he has had. He doesn't want money really, what he wants is for people to follow him in the streets the way they followed Dickens.

He seems to feel that he has achieved little reward and that the effort it would take to write another major book now is not worthwhile.

Algren seems to me to underrate himself. The most important new writers in American letters in recent years have been Ken Kesey, Joe Heller, Bruce J. Friedman and Terry Southern and all of them are deeply indebted to Algren.

Algren has a vivid way of putting things in conversation (he really talks like a character out of "A Walk On The Wild Side"). "Conversations" is replete with examples of this. On Dwight MacDonald's essay on Hemingway, Algren says, "MacDonald's piece is completely true. There is no way of denying any of it. And it's totally false. He's got a way of falsifying a thing and making it appear absolutely invulnerable logic."

On "selling out": "What I mean by selling out is: How long are you going to keep on doing what other people want?" On writers: "I have never heard of anybody being great at anything—fighters or writers— who did not go all out."

Algren's philosophy is really the jazz philosophy. "The important thing is: keep your life for yourself" he says. And for specific program, he adds, "I would like a country that is more interested in preserving life, in improving life than in destroying. I'm very limited that way . . . I'd put the ninety-nine billion dollars—whatever it is—that's being appropriated for the Air Force and the Navy and I'd put it into schools."

"To swing is to affirm," Father Kennard once wrote, and Algren, like the jazz artists, is involved constantly in an affirmation of life which is why he has been at loggerheads with Hollywood and with the Madison Avenue stream of American literature.

He is an artist, one of the most important men of American letters of this century, and if people literally do not follow him in the streets as they did Dickens, some do follow him intellectually and poetically wherever he goes, a bigger achievement than he realizes.

[*San Francisco Chronicle*, November 13, 1964]

The Tragedy at the Greek Theatre

"I agree with you that this may seem to be a rather theatrical performance today," President Kerr said at the tragedy presented by the University of California Monday in the Greek Theatre. And then he added "thanks to the audience, not to those of us up here."

And what he said had the sad ring of truth greater than he knew because, as it has since the beginning, the dynamic of the whole tragi-comedy, the whole farce, the whole incredible sequence of events has, indeed, come from the students and not from their elders.

"indeed I live in the dark age," Berthold Brecht wrote 30 years ago, ". . . A smooth forehead betokes a hard heart . . ." And it is obvious that the students and the student leaders are not the smooth-forehead IBM products their elders want them to be (and in so wanting have become themselves). It is, really, a continuing contrast in styles.

There is a time when the operation of the machine becomes so odious, makes you so sick at heart that you can't take part; you can't even tacitly take part, and you've got to put your bodies upon the gears and upon the wheels. upon the levers, upon all the apparatus and you've got to make it stop. And you've got to indicate to the people who run it, to the people who own it, that unless you are free, the machines will be prevented from working at all.

Those were the classic words of Mario Savio as he led the sit-in at Sproul Hall last week, later heard on the magnificent KPFA documentary.

And then the next morning—Berkeley's Black Thursday—the armed, booted and helmeted police infested the building and dragged the students down the stairs, carefully covering the windows of the stairwell with newspaper so they could operate unseen.

"Don't drag 'em down so fast," one cop said to another. "Take 'em down a little slower, they bounce more that way."

It has been a contrast and a confrontation in styles all along; a struggle between a C. Wright Mills-Paul Goodman-Catch-22 generation for whom the bomb dropped before they were born and a generation where cleanliness is next to godliness and you don't make waves, just ride on them.

And the ultimate tragedy is that the older generation will never see how wrong it is, how deeply it has misjudged these youngsters, how sadly it has maligned them and how deviously it has taken refuge in rhetoric and in legalities when the youth has been speaking in plain moral terms.

"We have been betrayed by articulate intellectuals, we have been betrayed by men who know better," the Graduate Student cries in Lawrence Ferlinghetti's playlet, "Servants of the People" in his new book, "Routines" (New Directions). "We have no media, we have no person of prominence in our country who will lead us in any sort of campaign. There is no dialogue," and, he adds, "this is the true sadness of our position."

But on the bright side, the redeeming feature of the adult tragedy whose most macabre moment came when the policeman slammed his arm across Mario Savio's throat, not only to remove him from the stage but to keep him from speaking (and what was it all about but the right to speak?) is what these students have done.

In the face of a university which abandoned its nerve center to armed police, on the first university campus outside Mississippi to be taken over by the cops, dragged to jail by cops who removed their badges so as not to be identified, in the face of a torrent of apoplectic outrage from the elders of the tribe who felt their positions threatened, this generation has stood up and continued to speak plainly of truth.

"When you go in, go with love in your hearts," Joan Baez said. Those words, and Mario's eloquent speech, remain the only rhetoric of these 10 weeks that history will remember. Literature, poetry and history are not made by a smooth jowl and a blue suit. They are made with sweat and passion and dedication to truth and honor.

[*San Francisco Chronicle*, December 9, 1964]

The Times They Are A-Changin'

■

The slender girl with the glowing eyes and the long dark hair stood before the microphone and sang, "Come mothers and fathers throughout the land." Joan Baez' voice carried out the words soft but clear with their plea for understanding. "And don't criticize what you can't understand." The crowd of over 5000 stood motionless. "Your old road is rapidly aging. Please get out of the new one if you can't lend a hand/ for the times they are a changin'!"

The song was Bob Dylan's testament of youth, "The Times They Are A Changin'," and it symbolized the confrontation of the generations. So did her words as she spoke and urged the audience to "muster up as much love as you can."

Later, to the almost mesmerizing repetitions of "We Shall Overcome," the anthem of the Civil Rights movement etched in the hearts of every Freedom picket line North or South, she led the University of California Free Speech Movement demonstrators into Sproul Hall for their now famous sit-in.

It was no coincidence that this wise child should lead the student demonstrators, nor was it a coincidence that she should lead them with a song, especially the two songs she chose.

It is, in fact, quite logical. Because the revision of morality and the priorities of our society that are evolving—and which the Berkeley FSM movement represents—first broke through the surface of social apathy in the form of folk singers like Joan Baez and topical songs like "The Times They Are A Changin'."

Topical songs are at the picket point of folk music, and are made, one might suggest, upon any occasion when the pressures of our restrictive society become so unbearable that a conscience in touch with truth must burst forth in song.

The singers of these songs—and most of the singers today, with the exception of Joan Baez, are also the writers—occupy a unique position in our society. While they are the poets and the troubadours heralding a revolution, they are at the same time highly rewarded by the very society against which their revolution is aimed.

It is difficult to see this from within the United States, perhaps, but it is quite plain from abroad. When a Brazilian jazz musician first heard a recording of Bob Dylan, one of the leading composers and singers in the topical song field, he said, "Do the authorities let him sing that? He's a saboteur!" and the French poet Luis Aragon included a quotation from "Ballad of Oxford, Mississippi," a song by the young writer-singer Phil Ochs, in his most recent book on poetry.

Joan Baez and Bob Dylan are the two leading figures in this crusade for a New Morality. Both of them are immensely successful by all the standards of the American entertainment world. Their albums rank among the best sellers in the music trade sales reports, fully the equal and sometimes the superior in sales volume to the recordings by Frank Sinatra, Elvis Presley or even the Twist star, Chubby Checker. *Variety*, the show business trade paper, regularly reports box office grosses of their concerts and it is obvious that they rate high in the echelons of entertainment concert attractions.

Dylan, in addition, is one of the most prolific and successful composers of songs to appear in the past decade. His own and other artists' recordings of his compositions such as "Don't Think Twice, It's All Right," "Blowin' In The Wind," "With God On Our Side," "It Ain't Me, Babe," and "It's a Hard Rain" may earn him as much as his concerts.

"Give me the making of the songs of a nation and I care not who makes its laws" wrote Andrew Fletcher of Saltoun, a salty seventeenth-century Scot, and it may be that the power he concedes to song will, when added to that of the pen, be mightier than nuclear fission.

Because something is going on here of which we catch glimpses now and then. We see it in Joan Baez' speaking out directly to Lyndon Johnson at the White House in an unprecedented act when she was invited there to sing. We see it again in the similar occasion when she sang at a United Nations affair and bluntly asked Stevenson why, if we really wanted to dis-engage in Vietnam, didn't we just leave. We see it again in Bob Dylan's rejection of the attitudes of the liberal Emergency Civil Liberties Committee in New York, who had chosen him for its Tom Paine Award. He spoke to them of Lee Oswald and how "I saw a lot of myself in Oswald and I saw in him a lot of the times we're all livin' in." Naturally, they booed him.

We see it again when the young folk singers, like scagnozzi, wander across the country from the coffee houses in Cambridge and Green-wich Village to those in Los Angeles and Berkeley, trying out their songs against The Bomb, against capital punishment, against hypocrisy, and death and deceit and in favor of love and truth and beauty, unashamed in the face of the centuries of misuse which has worn those words thin.

The youth of 1965, the college students who stood on the steps of Sproul Hall to hear Joan Baez tell them to have love in their hearts, have lived with the Bomb all of their lives. It has been a part of their consciousness ever since they were aware of anything at all outside of the home. They are the true fallout from the blast that changed the world, the real "Bomb Babies."

Ten years ago they heard Elvis Presley and his "Houn' Dog." Then they heard or read about the Beatniks and their rejection of the world they never made. Four years ago the youngsters who will vote this year for the first time, made an eloquent poem of peace, a deeply anti-war song called "Where Have All The Flowers Gone," into a national juke box hit. True, it was in a version by the Kingston Trio, the popular singing group that is a sort of Madison Avenue glossed up version of authentic folk. But "Where Have All The Flowers Gone" (which was written by Pete Seeger to a Ukrainian folk song he found in Sholokov's "And Quiet Flows the Dawn") made a tremendous impression. Mar-lene Dietrich recorded it for the European market and made it into a hit there. Seeger himself, as well as several other singers and singing groups, recorded it in this country. And the sentiment it expressed was so unusual and so openly anti-war (and thus opposed to the Cold War position of the U.S. as well as the U.S.S.R.) that the *New York Times* considered its success news fit to print.

Later in the same year, the vocal trio of Peter, Paul and Mary, which is more fakelore than folklore, but which possesses a beautiful long-haired ash blonde as one of its members, made another message song into a hit. This was "If I Had A Hammer," a declaration for brotherhood and for freedom written in the '40s by Pete Seeger and Lee Hays when both were members of The Almanac Singers. The Almanac Singers, it should be noted, were the parent group for The Weavers, who in turn set the style which later made an oil-gusher success for the Kingston Trio, the Limeliters, the Rooftop Singers and other folk groups.

The Weavers themselves were on the verge of being really huge show business successes with hit records ("Goodnight Irene" was theirs) and concert tours, when they were wiped overnight by the vicious blacklist of the McCarthy era, their records banned from the air, bookings cancelled and record companies unwilling to record them at all.

Then, in 1963, Peter, Paul and Mary hit again with "Blowin' in the Wind." This was a Bob Dylan song with repetitious questions like "how many roads must a man walk down before he's called a man?" and "how many times must a man turn his head and pretend that he just doesn't see?" all answered by the refrain "the answer, my friend, is blowin' in the wind."

High school children the country over sang that song, and while it would be optimistic beyond the limits of reason to maintain that they grasped the full significance of the lines, some of it rubbed off.

Dylan wrote the song as a direct protest against the monstrosity of the world as he saw it. "Some of the biggest criminals are those that turn their heads away when they see wrong and know it's wrong," he told the bimonthly magazine *Sing Out!* ($3 a year; N.Y., N.Y.), one of the most important communications links in the folk song network. "The answer . . . ain't in no book or movie or T.V. show or discussion group, man, it's in the wind . . . and just like a restless piece of paper it's got to come down sometime . . . I'm only 21 years old and I know that there's been too many wars . . . You people over 21 should know better, 'cause after all, you're older and smarter."

And concurrently with the smash hit of "Blowin' in the Wind" (it's now a standard and has been recorded by jazz saxophonist Stan Getz as well as orchestra leader Duke Ellington), Trini Lopez, a Texas border-land Latin, put "If I Had a Hammer" back on the top rung of the hit lists again. A short time later, Pete Seeger, for the first time a hit-maker on his own, though he was a major figure in folk music for over a decade, sang "Little Boxes," that wry satire on the organization man's Exurbia and made it a contemporary classic.

Deeper still in the country's subconscious ring the charges of "We Shall Overcome," the reprised and renovated old Baptist hymn that has become the symbol of the Freedom Movement and the Southern sit-ins. Countless thousands of Americans vicariously experiencing the Negro revolution in their living rooms, heard that song on television program after television program, heard it drilled into the fibres of the bones from the Washington march and Martin Luther King's appearances. Those hundreds of students who last summer went to Mississippi in the Summer Project grew to know it as intimately as the beat of their own hearts.

All of this experience has prepared the youth of 1965, dissatisfied with the world they came into, convinced that the answers are blowing in the wind, to find expression of their feelings in topical songs.

What is a topical song? A topical song is a folk song, but one with an immediate and topical point—usually political or social—rather than the love ballad or the murder ballad that is free of specific time, generally, and not pinned to an issue.

Blues songs through the years were topical songs many times, though for a particular audience. Woody Guthrie who is with Leadbelly (Huddie Ledbetter), one of the father images in the folk movement, wrote dozens of topical songs.

The radical tradition in America, all the way back to the revolution and on through the Wobblies and the union songs of the 30's, laid the groundwork for the folk song revival of the past few years. The Weavers, the Almanac Singers and others in the late 30's were consciously trying to preserve folk songs and to apply the topical song method ("Talkin' Union Blues," "This Land Is My Land," "The Sinking of the Reuben James") to communicate to the mass audience.

But only after World War II did the record buying public become a mass audience, actually, and then the political repression of the McCarthy era, the hot war of the American Right, stifled the burgeoning folk song movement.

Not until the music broke through the political barriers by going outside it to be sung by purely commercial pop artists did it really hit the masses. The pure pop artists were commercial figures free of any political taint, and anyway the recording business is a mass operation guided only by the principle of profit and caring for nothing but that profit.

Thus the message spread out. Why did these singers prove attractive to youth? Why did Bob Dylan, for instance, with his unkempt hair, his baggy clothes and his cowboy cum beatnik look emerge as a hero figure?

Malvina Reynolds, the greyhaired grandmother who wrote "Little Boxes," ties it all together. "He is saying something and saying it effectively and the fact that he has no voice and looks like nowhere is incidental," she says. "These kids have been betrayed by the good voices all their lives, have been told lies by the good voices, I mean social lies— that love is all, y'know, and if you're good everything will be wonderful. These are the things the good voices have told youth," Mrs. Reynolds points out and youth has rejected them in favor of Dylan's lyrics, his anti-slick image clothes and his Charlie Chaplin put-on style.

The other mass media latched on to the folk music boom the moment the money glittered. The American Broadcasting Company started a weekly TV show, "Hootenanny," and it immediately demonstrated that the mass media is frightened by poets. All the singers sang his songs, but Pete Seeger was too hot politically to be allowed on a national TV show. The same was true for the Weavers and then, in a move that should have been but wasn't obvious to the producers, both Joan Baez and Bob Dylan refused to have anything to do with "Hootenanny" ("money doesn't talk, it swears" is a line in one of Dylan's songs).

The new songs, like the old radical songs, had a fatal flaw. They said things and thus frightened people. It was a rare song in the 30's, 40's or even the 50's, that ever really came out and said anything and still was a popular hit. One of the few that comes to mind is "Sixteen Tons," the classic protest against the company store and the miner's exploited life. It was a big jukebox hit, but that was a decade ago.

The rock and roll, rhythm, and rhythm and blues songs of the past few years have had implications of a social nature. The Drifters' "Up

On The Roof," for instance—with its lines about the teenager's rooftop hideout "right smack dab in the middle of town, I found a paradise that's trouble proof" is certainly a song of alienation and the lonely urban crowd.

And there's the hit country and western song of a few years back, "Hey Oakie" ("if you see Arkie, tell him I got a job for him, out in Californy"), a sentiment straight from a migrant worker's knapsack.

Malvina Reynolds' "The Concrete Octopus" protested the freeway rape of parks and timberland but was never a hit. One juke box song a couple of years ago told of a girl who was ashamed to bring her boyfriend home because her neighborhood looked so bad and she had to meet him where the surroundings were nicer—a sort of plea for urban renewal.

But it took Pete Seeger, Joan Baez and Bob Dylan to get the topical song, hard-hitting at specific issues, really going. It's spread out now so that a pop-folk (the music trade's category for the non-authentic but commercially successful) group like the Chad Mitchell Trio can record "The John Birch Society" or a satire on Goldwater, "Barry's Boys," and even the usually tepid Kingston Trio can go deeply into protest songs for an entire album.

Of course the subjects of the topical folk songs from "Who Killed Davey Moore" (death in the boxing ring) by Bob Dylan to "As Long As The Grass Shall Grow" by Peter La Farge (a protest against the treatment of the American Indian) are not new. Nor are they unknown. But it is unusual for them to reach the mass audiences that the topical folk songs now do. And it is the fact that a good deal of the attitudes and opinions presented in the works of Dylan, Paxton, Ochs and the other writers, are not reflected in the mass communication media that has given added thrust to their concentration on topical songs. In essence the topical song writers have consciously or unconsciously transformed the medium of the phonograph record from pure entertainment to that of the communication of ideas and made the concert hall a political platform.

When Bob Dylan finished a concert at the Berkeley Community Theater to which a capacity house of over 3000 had paid upwards of $4 each, one of the audience said, "Do they know he's a revolutionary?

Do they realize they have paid $4 to hear him attack the whole social structure?"

Joan Baez, whose stepping stones to the top rank in the concert field were the old English and Kentucky ballads, has for some time now sprinkled in among them the direct message of the topical songs. Before an audience of 7000 in the gymnasium on a rainy Homecoming Day at the University of California, she paused in her program of "Copper Kettle," "Silver Dagger," and "Koom-bayou" to sing Malvina Reynolds' "What Have They Done to the Rain?" And before a similar crowd outdoors in the Greek Theater, she sang Richard Farina's memorial to the school children massacred in Alabama, "Birmingham Sunday." And I have witnessed uniformed officers of the U.S. Army and Marine Corps applaud her for singing "With God on Our Side," Dylan's classic antiwar song.

Sometimes the audience objects and customers call out "don't give us messages." But this doesn't have any effect. Miss Baez, like the others in this movement, is determined to have her say. Last year in a concert at Baltimore, Md., where the Negro maid, Hattie Carroll, was beaten to death by a cane-wielding farmer who got off with a light sentence and probation, she sang Dylan's "The Lonesome Death of Hattie Carroll." "I felt the audience stirring," she says, "and I couldn't think why until I finished and remembered it was Baltimore."

There is a deep thing at work in all of this. The Reality behind the American dream and the truth behind its mythology is being attacked relentlessly by a generation that takes nothing for granted from its elders. The have added the weight of words to the anti-establishment humanitarian position the jazz musicians have wordlessly occupied for years. "There's a saying in the movement that you can't trust anyone over 30," Jack Weinberg, one of the University of California Free Speech Movement leaders, has said, and it is manifestly obvious that, with the exception of Pete Seeger, all the leaders in the field of topical song singing are well under 30, some barely out of their teens.

This is their audience, too. This post-beatnik group of Atom Bomb babies has produced some wildly devout Bob Dylan fans who have even, maintaining that he is, above all, a poet, insisted on bringing Dylan lyrics to English classes in high school and junior high school.

And as the Negro revolution is being played out and documented on that great equalizer, television, this generation has seen the history of the black man revised. Not only the history of the black man in America, but the history of Africa as well has undergone a great revision. It turns out that what it says in the textbooks is not the way it is, and it doesn't take a particularly perceptive youth to recognize it.

And not only to recognize it, but to apply it to other things as well. To the history of the American Indians, for instance, and why stop there? Why not apply it to China and Vietnam and encourage the inevitable sneaking suspicions that the rest of history could bear a similar revision?

At the University of California, the FSM rebels sang parodies of Christmas carols like "Joy to the World" or irreverent lyrics to the theme of Beethoven's Ninth—"Make the students safe for knowledge, keep them loyal, keep them clean. This is why we have a college/Hail to the IBM Machine!"

"For all people laugh in the same tongue and cry in the same tongue," Dylan says, expressing the universality of what he believes. "There's no right wing or left wing . . . there's only up wing and down wing."

Dylan's lyrics are being collected in book form as poems and "A Hard Rain" has already been included in an anthology of contemporary poetry. America's youth seems to have found a voice. Is there something symbolic in the fact that it belongs to a young Minnesotan who changed his name from admiration of a Welsh poet? But "my name means nothing, my age it means less" Dylan wrote in "With God on My Side" as if to answer the critics. Perhaps it symbolizes his rebirth in a new world.

In any case, denied the orthodox channels of communication—as the graduate student says in Lawrence Ferlinghetti's "Routines," "we have no media, we have no person of prominence in our country who will lead us in any sort of campaign"—they have gone directly to the people with broadsides and with topical songs.

The traditional apolitical attitude of the American entertainment world, the pattern since Bogart apologized, is no more. These artists speak out. "Indeed I live in the dark ages," Brecht wrote 39 years ago, "a smooth forehead betokes a hard heart and he who laughs has not yet heard the sad tidings."

There are overtones of Brecht in Dylan, to be sure. "I saw ten thousand talkers whose tongues were all broken/I saw guns and sharp swords in the hands of young children." And there is tragedy in Peter La Farge's "Coyote." "They strychnined the mountains, they strychnined the plains/my little brothers, the coyote, won't come back again." But there is, too, a dedication to joy and to life, as if the promises of the New World have not yet been lost entirely, but just expressed differently.

"Bob Dylan says all the things I feel but can't say myself" a fourteen year old girl wrote. And among the things that he and Joan Baez and the other conscience singers are saying is that the Emperor has no clothes. "We have believed too long that he has," they tell us. And they add, "we want to love, not to be blown up, and we want to live free."

This is the New Morality and these are the New Moralists who are revising the priorities of the entire society. They are simplistic and evangelical and military visionaries. They say the virtues are Love and Truth and Beauty and the ultimate sins are to hurt another human, to break trust and not to love.

They have rejected so thoroughly all the language and attitudes and the concepts of their elders that a fragment of Dylan's verses seems like a summary of it all:

Shoot craps
in the alley garbage pot
You say "nothin's perfect"
An' I tell you again
There are no politics.

Folk music began its revival with Leadbelly and Woody Guthrie and union songs, and is topical now and confronts Bull Connor as well as Vietnam. The times, indeed, are a-changin' and these young artists are among the reasons why and they have served notice on their elders to get out of the way.

[*Ramparts Magazine*, April 1965]

The Flower Children

■

Sometimes you see them standing beside the highway, their long hair blowing in the wind, army surplus jackets hanging sloppily from their shoulders, rumpled sleeping bags at their feet, hitchhiking to New York, to San Francisco, to Chicago. Sometimes you glimpse them packed into an old bus, a Volkswagen camper, or even an ancient hearse painted with flowers, paisley designs, or other exotic markings—a long-haired driver and a sad eyed, long-haired girl and generally a dog and a guitar. Sometimes you hear them first, walking along a pass in a park somewhere. The sound of bells precedes them—light, soft, tinkling, elfin noises.

Sometimes you know they are there even when you can't see or hear them. Driving along a city street at night you come on a brightly lit open window, shapeless, giving you a glimpse of a room with a huge, blown-up picture of Lenny Bruce or Joan Baez or the multicolored dance-hall posters from the Fillmore and Avalon Ballrooms in San Francisco. Or you ride down a country lane and there, miles from any town, is a mailbox on a fence post where the lane leaves the highway and disappears over the hill. A typical country scene, except that the mailbox is carefully covered with multicolored flower designs.

These first generation American gypsies are called hippies. They call themselves by that name and, in turn, they are called that by "the straight world," as they describe the non-hippie majority. "Hippie" is a curious word, deriving from the jazz term "hip" meaning aware, sharp, in tune with all that's going on. In the jazz world those who were hip were called hipsters and those who pretended to be hip, or who were so unbearably hip that their very hipness was unhip, were called "hippies." In what one might consider a significant departure from the jazz-hip-beatnik generation of the late '40s and '50s, the new Bohemians took the pejorative word and made it their badge of honor.

Who are these people?

The hippies, says Lou Gottlieb, the Dr. of Music who formerly led the folk singing trio called The Limeliters, are "the first wave of an approaching ocean of technologically unemployable people created by snowballing cybernation in American industry."

Peter Cohan, a hippie and a member of the Diggers, the unorganized group of hippies who run the Free Store (in which everything is free for the taking) and hand out free food every afternoon in the park adjacent to San Francisco's Haight-Ashbury district, says that the hippies are "the fruit of the middle class and they are telling the middle class they don't like what has been given them."

Only in the conditions of affluence could the hippie rebellion occur, according to Bryan Wilson, an Oxford fellow doing research at Berkeley. "The hippies are escapists from the affluent society that produces and sustains them. They are opposed to the everyday middle-aged values of affluent America—its commercialism, mechanism and bureaucracy; its car culture, hygiene and unquestioned acceptance of the work ethic and the quick buck." Poet Allen Ginsberg, the most important literary figure to emerge from the beat movement and one of the very few from that era whom the hippies accept as their own, says "I think of these people as young seekers." Allen Cohen, poet and editor of a Haight-Ashbury newspaper called *The Oracle*, refers to them as "the prophetic community."

"This is not a rebellion," University of California sociologist Mark Messer quotes a hippie as saying. "We are not necessarily fashioning ourselves as a sort of anti-image to our parents. It's just that we have grown up in an environment that was very, very different from the Depression, and we're entirely different people. . . ."

THE NEW MENDICANTS

Hippies are first of all young people. Generally they are young people in their teens or early 20s living out a rejection of material wealth and the Puritan ethic. The hippies believe hard work by itself is not a virtue, though they are willing to work long and strenuously (contrary to common belief) on anything they are interested in. A penny saved is not a penny earned to them; they live for now. Cleanliness is not next to godliness, for though they bathe (again contrary to popular myth), at no time do they manifest the maniacal drive to constant sanitary perfection that marks Americans off from the rest of the world.

In contrast to the Elders of the Tribe, the hippies regard fun and enjoyment as laudable, even as a goal. Dancing has returned with the hippie and dance halls, which all but vanished from the American scene after World War II, have reappeared. In San Francisco, where the hippie movement began and which is still the capital of hippiedom, hundreds and sometimes thousands of hippies dance each week at the various ballrooms or at outdoor functions.

Almost all hippies are white and this is significant. They are the children of the "haves" who are rejecting the values and rewards of the society—the same values and rewards that Negroes are struggling to obtain. In the course of their rejection, they have created a new way of looking at things and a new context in which to live.

Dedication to the work ethic has produced the alienation that the hippies see all around them in the "nine-to-fives." They will work hard at a task for the delight and/or fulfillment it gives them. The only other full-time work they will accept, apparently, is with the U.S. Post Office, currently the largest employer of hippies. There, by conforming to the minimal requirements of dress and procedure, the hippie may work without scorn, without rejection, without criticism. In the San Francisco Bay area, it has become commonplace to have one's mail delivered by a long-haired blonde—male or female—in blue jeans.

In the late spring of 1967, British historian Arnold Toynbee toured the hippie enclave in the Haight-Ashbury district and concluded that "the hippies repudiate the affluent way of life in which making money is the object of life and work. They reject their parent's way of life as uncompromisingly as St. Francis rejected the rich cloth merchants way of life of his father in Assisi . . . The question is whether the hippies are going to transfigure, like St. Francis, a defiant voluntary poverty into something positive and redeeming."

Beatle George Harrison, a fellow member of today's British ruling classes, toured the Haight-Ashbury later in the summer and, while applauding the manifestations of love that characterize the hippie movement, adamantly refused to approve the panhandling. (Mr. Harrison believes in hard work.) Toynbee was reminded of Gautama, the king's son, and Francis, the merchant's son, holding out the begging bowl. Harrison was outraged. "There were people just sitting around the pavement begging, saying 'give us some money for a blanket.' These are hypocrites," he said. "They are making fun of tourists and . . . At the same time they are holding their hands out begging off them. That's what I don't like."

Toynbee and Harrison were only two of the dozens of sociologists, anthropologists, journalists, TV filmmakers, and other students of mankind who jammed the Haight-Ashbury in the summer of 1967 examining the natives. Few movements in this century have inspired the intense interest the hippie movement has created. This attests, at least in one way, to its importance. It would appear to strike deeply into something in the American character to have caused such a fuss.

ANATOMY OF A SUBCULTURE

At the University of California in Berkeley, where the off-campus community evolved into a hippie culture after a few years of radical politics, assistant professor of sociology Benjamin Zablocky predicted that within five years the hippie movement would become the dominant teenage subculture.

Across the Bay, where the San Francisco State College sociology department was equally fascinated by the hippies, H. Taylor Buckner ran an intensive, in-depth study of 50 residents of the Haight-Ashbury "scene" chosen because of their costume and manner. Only 14% live alone, 25% shared quarters with 10 or more people; 2% were above the age of 30, 60% between 16 and 21, 36% between 22 and 30 and 2% under 16; 69% were employed; 70% were from outside California, 60% from cities; 68% had some college education; 44% had a father who went to college and 46% a mother who went to college; 96% stated that they some time had smoked marijuana, 90% that they had taken LSD, but "very few" had ever tried any of the addictive drugs, such as heroine.

When the beat generation faded in importance and its living area in San Francisco's North Beach was overrun by tourists, some of the beatniks fled to the Haight-Ashbury, a little over two miles away. The Haight-Ashbury district was one of two- and three-story Victorian homes that had seen better days, four- and five-story apartment houses, and a generally free atmosphere. Many students and some writers (Kay Boyle was one) lived there because of its proximity to Golden Gate Park, its excellent transportation system, and the permissive atmosphere that came with the students and the racially integrated population.

As the transistor generation evidenced its interest in music, rock 'n roll bands sprang up. Folk musicians, jazz musicians, and others banded together to prove they, like Bob Dylan and the Beatles, could produce a meaningful and artistic music from rock. They began living in communal flats and houses, and the Haight-Ashbury district was one where houses could be rented, amplified guitars and drums played night and day, and, since this was above all a drug culture and a man's home is his castle, groups could be relatively secure against police raids.

The drug culture needs a few special words. As the first preliminary surveys have shown (and all empirical observation supports), the hippie community, like the youth of the nation at large, is deeply committed to the proposition that marijuana is less dangerous than alcohol, non-habit-forming, and mistakenly classified as an illegal and harmful drug. LSD is regarded in much the same way. As the *New Statesman* pointed out in discussing the arrest on narcotics charges of Mick Jagger and Keith Richards of the Rolling Stones, young people today "not only do not agree that marijuana is wrong—they deny the right of their elders to pronounce on the matter . . . They challenge the morality of a society that accepts the excesses of alcohol and makes both governmental and private profit from nicotine."

One of the remarkable aspects of the hippie movement—in contrast to the beatniks—is its tremendous surge of energy. Early in 1967, a group of hippies, including former political science students, actors, and dancers, leased an abandoned movie house on Haight Street, raised about $60,000, and spent it to transform the rococo interior into a marvelously utilitarian "environmental theater" with a dance floor, a super high fidelity sound system, 120° screen for light projection shows, motion picture projection room, a dance school, rooms for drama classes and a children's art class, and rehearsal halls. Other groups of hippies have organized day camps, schools, and communes in the adjacent suburban countryside, living in groups of 10 or 20 on farms and, in one case, operating a huge ranch in the Valley of the Moon as a six-day school with a volunteer faculty.

When the city of San Francisco's Board of Supervisors refused to come to the aid of the Flower Children who had flocked into the city during the summer school recess, the hippies organized themselves into work details, swept the streets, expanded the Digger free food and free store operations, started a hip switchboard telephone exchange to locate runaways and lost friends and to put people in contact with needed services.

The question remains, of course, what does all this really mean and how will it affect the future? Will the hippies, like the beats, simply disappear, their revolution a natural casualty of time?

Since the student activist movement first began to emerge, the visionary students have learned the truth of disillusionment and angrily accepted the reality that on certain basic issues the society simply does not give way. This is what shunted them off into the rock bands and the hippie movement. John Kenneth Galbraith once admonished a critic of the technological society: "He must not ask that jet aircraft, nuclear power plants, or even the modern automobile in its modern volume be produced by firms that are subject to unfixed prices and unmanaged demand. He must ask instead that they not be produced." The hippies are asking that many things not be produced, that our whole way of looking at the reasons for production be re-examined, together with all the standards of our behavior.

Thus, the very base of the American Society is being attacked by an important segment of the hippie movement. Money is not sacred to them. In Bob Dylan's words, "money doesn't talk, it swears." Even the names of their business organizations—the Family Dog, Faithful Virtue Music, the Grateful Dead—imply a refusal to treat a business organization, and hence money, as sacred.

The hippies believe in love, simplistic though it may be. In an article on the Ideology of Failure, which the Diggers present as their basic creed, they say: "To show love is to fail. To love to fail is the ideology of failure. Show Love. Do your thing. Do it for FREE. Do it for Love. We can't fail. . . ."

No matter how these youngsters end up, no matter what their roles are a decade from now, they will have reaffirmed the basic religiosity of their lives sufficiently by doing their thing for free, for love, to have received love in return.

If the hippies have done nothing else—and if they do nothing else—they have made the rest of us re-examine our lives, look again at what we are doing and why we are doing it. In the process they have challenged all the paradoxes and hypocrisies—as Bill Resner of the Straight Theater put it, "The dichotomy between what we've been taught and what's going on." This alone is a valuable service to humanity.

[*Encyclopedia Britannica Yearbook*, 1968]

Like a Rolling Stone

■

Forms and rhythms in music are never changed without producing changes in the most important political forms and ways.
Plato said that.

There's something happenin' here. What it is ain't exactly
clear. There's a man with a gun over there tellin' me I've
got to beware. I think it's time we stop, children, what's that
sound? Everybody look what's goin' down.
The Buffalo Springfield said that.

For the reality of politics, we must go to the poets, not the
politicians.
Norman O. Brown said that.

For the reality of what's happening today in America, we must
go to rock 'n roll, to popular music.
I said that.

For almost forty years in this country, which has prided itself
on individualism, freedom and non-conformity, all popular
songs were written alike. They had an eight-bar opening
statement, an eight-bar repeat, an eight-bar middle section
or bridge, and an eight-bar reprise. Anything that did not fit
into that framework was, appropriately enough, called a novelty.

Clothes were basically the same whether a suit was double-breasted
or single-breasted, and the only people who wore beards were absent-
minded professors and Bolshevik bomb throwers. Long hair, which was
equated with a lack of masculinity—in some sort of subconscious reference to Samson, I suspect—was restricted to painters and poets and
classical musicians, hence the term "longhair music" to mean classical.

Four years ago a specter was haunting Europe, one whose fundamental influence, my intuition tells me, may be just as important, if in another way, as the original of that line. The Beatles, four long-haired Liverpool teenagers, were busy changing the image of popular music. In less than a year, they invaded the United States and almost totally wiped out the standard Broadway show/Ed Sullivan TV program popular song. No more were we "flying to the moon on gossamer wings," we were now articulating such interesting and, in this mechanistic society, unusual concepts as "Money can't buy me love" and "I want to hold your hand."

"Societies, like individuals, have their moral crises and their spiritual revolutions," R. H. Tawney says in *Religion And The Rise Of Capitalism*. And then the Beatles appeared ("a great figure rose up from the sea and pointed at me and said 'you're a Beatle with an "a"'"—Genesis, according to John Lennon). They came at the proper moment of a spiritual cusp—as the Martian in Robert Heinlein's *Stranger In A Strange Land* calls a crisis.

Instantly, on those small and sometimes doll-like figures was focused all the rebellion against hypocrisy, all the impudence and irreverence that the youth of that moment was feeling vis-à-vis his elders.

Automation, affluence, the totality of instant communication, the technology of the phonograph record, the transistor radio, had revolutionized life for youth in this society. The population age was lowering. Popular music, the jukebox and the radio were becoming the means of communication. Huntley and Brinkley were for mom and dad. People now sang songs they wrote themselves, not songs written for them by hacks in grimy Tin Pan Alley offices.

The folk music boom paved the way. Bob Dylan's poetic polemics, "Blowin' In The Wind" and "The Times They Are A-Changin'," had helped the breakthrough. "Top 40" radio made Negro music available everywhere to a greater degree than ever before in our history.

This was, truly, a new generation—the first in America to be raised with music constantly in its ear, weaned on a transistor radio, involved with songs from its earliest moment of memory.

Music means more to this generation than it did even to its dancing parents in the big-band swing era of Benny Goodman. It's natural, then, that self-expression should find popular music so attractive.

The dance of the swing era, of the big bands, was the fox trot. It was a really formal dance extended in variation only by experts. The swing era's parents had danced the waltz. The fox trot was a ritual with only a little more room for self-expression. Rock 'n roll brought with it not only the voices of youth singing their protests, their hopes and their expectations (along with their pathos and their sentimentality and their personal affairs from drag racing to romance), it brought their dances.

"Every period which abounded in folk songs has, by the same token, been deeply stirred by Dionysiac currents," Nietzsche points out in *The Birth Of Tragedy*. And Dionysiac is the word to describe the dances of the past ten years, call them by whatever name from bop to the Twist to the Frug, from the Hully Gully to the Philly Dog.

In general, adult society left the youth alone, prey to the corruption the adults suspected was forthcoming from the song lyrics ("All of me, why not take all of me," from that hit of the thirties, of course, didn't mean all of me, it meant, well . . . er . . .) or from the payola-influenced disc jockeys. (Who ever remembers about the General Electric scandals of the fifties, in which over a dozen officials went to jail for industrial illegalities?)

The TV shows were in the afternoon anyway and nobody could stand to watch those rock 'n roll singers; they were worse than Elvis Presley.

But all of a sudden the *New Yorker* joke about the married couple dreamily remarking, when the disc jockey played "Hound Dog" by Elvis, "they're playing our song," wasn't a joke any longer. It was real. That generation had suddenly grown up and married and Elvis was real memories of real romance and not just kid stuff.

All of a sudden, the world of music, which is big business in a very real way, took another look at the music of the ponytail and chewing gum set, as Mitch Miller once called the teenage market, and realized that there was one helluva lot of bread to be made there.

In a few short years, Columbia and R.C.A. Victor and the other companies that dominated the recording market, the huge publishing houses that copyrighted the music and collected the royalties, discovered that they no longer were "kings of the hill." Instead, a lot of small companies, like Atlantic and Chess and Imperial and others, had hits by people the major record companies didn't even know, singing songs written in Nashville and Detroit and Los Angeles and Chicago and sometimes, but no longer almost always, New York.

It's taken the big ones a few years to recoup from that. First they called the music trash and the lyrics dirty. When that didn't work, as the attempt more recently to inhibit songs with supposed psychedelic or marijuana references has failed, they capitulated. They joined up. R.C.A. Victor bought Elvis from the original company he recorded for—Sun Records ("Yaller Sun Records from Nashville" as John Sebastian sings it in "Nashville Cats")—and then bought Sam Cooke, and A.B.C. Paramount bought Ray Charles and then Fats Domino. And Columbia, thinking it had a baby folk singer capable of some more sales of "San Francisco Bay," turned out to have a tiny demon of a poet named Bob Dylan.

So the stage was set for the Beatles to take over—"with this ring I can—dare I say it?—rule the world!" And they did take over so thoroughly that they have become the biggest success in the history of show business, the first attraction ever to have a coast-to-coast tour in this country sold out before the first show even opened.

With the Beatles and Dylan running tandem, two things seem to me to have been happening. The early Beatles were at one and the same time a declaration in favor of love and of life, an exuberant paean to the sheer joy of living, and a validation of the importance of American Negro music.

Dylan, by his political, issue-oriented broadsides first and then by his Rimbaud-ish nightmare visions of the real state of the nation, his bittersweet love songs and his pure imagery, did what the jazz and the poetry people of the fifties had wanted to do—he took poetry out of the classroom and out of the hands of the professors and put it right out there in the streets for everyone.

I dare say that with the inspiration of the Beatles and Dylan we have more poetry being produced and more poets being made than ever before in the history of the world. Dr. Malvina Reynolds—the composer of "Little Boxes"—thinks nothing like this has happened since Elizabethan times. I suspect even that is too timid an assessment.

Let's go back to Plato, again. Speaking of the importance of new styles of music, he said, "The new style quietly insinuates itself into manners and customs and from there it issues a greater force . . . goes on to attack laws and constitutions, displaying the utmost impudence, until it ends by overthrowing everything, both in public and in private."

That seems to me to be a pretty good summation of the answer to the British rock singer Donovan's question, "What goes on? I really want to know."

The most immediate apparent change instituted by the new music is a new way of looking at things. We see it evidenced all around us. The old ways are going and a new set of assumptions is beginning to be worked out. I cannot even begin to codify them. Perhaps it's much too soon to do so. But I think there are some clues—the sacred importance of love and truth and beauty and interpersonal relationships.

When Bob Dylan sang recently at the Masonic Memorial Auditorium in San Francisco, at intermission there were a few very young people in the corridor backstage. One of them was a long-haired, poncho-wearing girl of about thirteen. Dylan's road manager, a slender, long-haired youth, wearing black jeans and Beatle boots, came out of the dressing room and said, "You kids have to leave! You can't be backstage here!"

"Who are you?" the long-haired girl asked.

"I'm a cop," Dylan's road manager said aggressively.

The girl looked at him for a long moment and then drawled, "Whaaaat? With those boots?"

Clothes really do not make the man. But sometimes . . .

I submit that was an important incident, something that could never have happened a year before, something that implies a very great deal about the effect of the new style, which has been quietly (or not so quietly, depending on your view of electric guitars) insinuating itself into manners and customs.

Among the effects of "what's goin' on" is the relinquishing of belief in the sacredness of logic. "I was a prisoner of logic and I still am," Malvina Reynolds admits, but then goes on to praise the new music. And the prisoners of logic are the ones who are really suffering most—unless they have Mrs. Reynolds' glorious gift of youthful vision.

The first manifestation of the importance of this outside the music —I think—came in the works of Ken Kesey and Joseph Heller. *One*

Flew Over The Cuckoo's Nest, with its dramatic view of the interchange-ability of reality and illusion, and *Catch-22*, with its delightful utiliza-tion of crackpot realism (to use C. Wright Mills' phrase) as an explana-tion of how things are, were works of seminal importance.

No one any longer really believes that the processes of international relations and world economics are rationally explicable. Absolutely the very best and clearest discussion of the entire thing is wrapped up in Milo Minderbinder's explanation, in *Catch-22*, of how you can buy eggs for seven cents apiece in Malta and sell them for five cents in Pianosa and make a profit. Youth understands the truth of this immediately, and no economics textbook is going to change it.

Just as—implying the importance of interpersonal relations and the beauty of being true to oneself—the under-thirty youth immediately understands the creed patiently explained by Yossarian in *Catch-22* that everybody's your enemy who's trying to get you killed, even if he's your own commanding officer.

This is an irrational world, despite the brilliant efforts of Walter Lippmann to make it rational, and we are living in a continuation of the formalized lunacy (Nelson Algren's phrase) of war, any war.

At this point in history, most of the organs of opinion, from the *New York Review of Books* through the *New Republic* to *Encounter* (whether or not they are subsidized by the C.I.A.), are in the control of the prison-ers of logic. They take a flick like *Morgan* and grapple with it. They take *Help!* and *A Hard Day's Night* and grapple with those two beautiful creations, and they fail utterly to understand what is going on because they try to deal with them logically. They complain because art doesn't make sense! Life on this planet in this time of history doesn't make sense, either—as an end result of immutable laws of economics and logic and philosophy.

Dylan sang, "You raise up your head and you ask 'is this where it is?' And somebody points to you and says 'it's his' and you say 'what's mine' and somebody else says 'well, what is' and you say 'oh my god am I here all alone?'"

Dylan wasn't the first. Orwell saw some of it, Heller saw more, and in a different way so did I. F. Stone, that remarkable journalist, who is really a poet, when he described a *Herald Tribune* reporter extracting from the Pentagon the admission that, once the first steps for the Santo Domingo episode were mounted, it was impossible to stop the machine.

Catch-22 said that in order to be sent home from flying missions you had to be crazy, and obviously anybody who wanted to be sent home was sane.

Kesey and Heller and Terry Southern, to a lesser degree in his novels but certainly in *Dr. Strangelove,* have hold of it. I suspect that they are not really a New Wave of writers but only a last wave of the past, just as is Norman Mailer, who said in his Berkeley Vietnam Day speech that "rational discussion of the United States' involvement in Viet Nam is illogical in the way surrealism is illogical and rational political discussion of Adolf Hitler's motives was illogical and then obscene." This is the end of the formal literature we have known and the beginning, possibly, of something else.

In almost every aspect of what is happening today, this turning away from the old patterns is making itself manifest. As the formal structure of the show business world of popular music and television has brought out into the open the Negro performer—whose incredibly beautiful folk poetry and music for decades has been the prime mover in American song—we find a curious thing happening.

The Negro performers, from James Brown to Aaron Neville to the Supremes and the Four Tops, are on an Ed Sullivan trip, striving as hard as they can to get on that stage and become part of the American success story, while the white rock performers are motivated to escape that stereotype. Whereas in years past the Negro performer offered style in performance and content in song—the messages from Leadbelly to Percy Mayfield to Ray Charles were important messages—today he is almost totally style with very little content. And when James Brown sings, "It's A Man's World," or Aaron Neville sings, "Tell It Like It Is," he takes a phrase and only a phrase with which to work, and the Supremes and the Four Tops are choreographed more and more like the Four Lads and the Ames Brothers and the McGuire Sisters.

I suggest that this bears a strong relationship to the condition of the civil rights movement today in which the only truly black position is that of Stokely Carmichael, and in which the N.A.A.C.P. and most of the other formal groups are, like the Four Tops and the Supremes, on an Ed Sullivan TV trip to middle-class America. And the only true American Negro music is that which abandons the concepts of European musical thought, abandons the systems of scales and keys and notes, for a music whose roots are in the culture of the colored people of the world.

The drive behind all American popular music performers, to a greater or lesser extent, from Sophie Tucker and Al Jolson, on down through Pat Boone and as recently as Roy Head and Charlie Rich, has been to sound like a Negro. The white jazz musician was the epitome of this.

Yet an outstanding characteristic of the new music of rock, certainly in its best artists, is something else altogether. This new generation of musicians is not interested in being Negro, since that is an absurdity.

The clarinetist Milton Mezzrow, who grew up with the Negro Chicago jazzmen in the twenties and thirties, even put "Negro" on his prison record and claimed to be more at home with his Negro friends than with his Jewish family and neighbors.

Today's new youth, beginning with the rock band musician but spreading out into the entire movement, into the Haight-Ashbury hippies, is not ashamed of being white.

He is remarkably free from prejudice, but he is not attempting to join the Negro culture or to become a part of it, like his musical predecessor, the jazzman, or like his social predecessor, the beatnik. I find this of considerable significance. For the very first time in decades, as far as I know, something important and new is happening artistically and musically in this society that is distinct from the Negro and to which the Negro will have to come, if he is interested in it at all, as in the past the white youth went uptown to Harlem or downtown or crosstown or to wherever the Negro community was centered because there was the locus of artistic creativity.

Today the new electronic music by the Beatles and others (and the Beatles' "Strawberry Fields" is, I suggest, a three-minute masterpiece, an electronic miniature symphony) exists somewhere else from and independent of the Negro.

This is only one of the more easily observed manifestations of this movement.

The professional craft union, the American Federation of Musicians, is now faced with something absolutely unforeseen—the cooperative band. Briefly—in the thirties—there were co-op bands. The original Casa Loma band was one and the original Woody Herman band was another. But the whole attitude of the union and the attitude of the musicians themselves worked against the idea, and co-op bands were discouraged. They were almost unknown until recently.

Today, almost all the rock groups are cooperative. Many live together, in tribal style, in houses or camps or sometimes in traveling tepees, but always together as a group; and the young girls who follow them are called "groupies," just as the girls who in the thirties and forties followed the bands (music does more than soothe the savage breast!) were called "band chicks."

The basic creed of the American Federation of Musicians is that musicians must not play unless paid. The new generation wants money, of course, but its basic motivation is to play anytime, anywhere, anyhow. Art is first, then finance, most of the time. And at least one rock band, the Loading Zone in Berkeley, has stepped outside the American Federation of Musicians entirely and does not play for money. You may give them money, but they won't set a price or solicit it.

This seems to me to extend the attitude that gave Pete Seeger, Joan Baez and Bob Dylan such status. They are not and never have been for sale in the sense that you can hire Sammy Davis to appear, as you can hire Dean Martin to appear, any time he's free, as long as you pay his price. You have not been able to do this with Seeger, Baez and Dylan any more than Allen Ginsberg has been for sale either to *Ramparts* or the C.I.A.

Naturally, this revolt against the assumptions of the adult world runs smack dab into the sanctimonious puritan morality of America, the schizophrenia that insists that money is serious business and the acquisition of wealth is a blessing in the eyes of the Lord, that what we do in private we must preach against in public. Don't do what I do, do what I say.

Implicit in the very names of the business organizations that these youths form is an attack on the traditional, serious attitude toward money. It is not only that the groups themselves are named with beautiful imagery; the Grateful Dead, the Loading Zone, Blue Cheer or the

Jefferson Airplane—all dating back to the Beatles with an A—it is the names of the nonmusical organizations: Frontage Road Productions (the music company of the Grateful Dead), Faithful Virtue Music (the Lovin' Spoonful's publishing company), Ashes and Sand (Bob Dylan's production firm—his music publishing company is Dwarf Music). A group who give light shows is known as the Love Conspiracy Commune, and there was a dance recently in Marin County, California, sponsored by the Northern California Psychedelic Cattlemen's Association, Ltd. And, of course, there is the Family Dog, which, despite *Ramparts*, was never a rock group, only a name under which four people who wanted to present rock 'n roll dances worked.

Attacking the conventional attitude toward money is considered immoral in the society of our fathers, because money is sacred. The reality of what Bob Dylan says—"money doesn't talk, it swears"—has yet to seep through.

A corollary of the money attack is the whole thing about long hair, bare feet and beards. "Nothing makes me sadder," a woman wrote me objecting to the Haight-Ashbury scene, "than to see beautiful young girls walking along the street in bare feet." My own daughter pointed out that your feet couldn't get any dirtier than your shoes.

Recently I spent an evening with a lawyer, a brilliant man who is engaged in a lifelong crusade to educate and reform lawyers. He is interested in the civil liberties issue of police harassment of hippies. But, he said, they wear those uniforms of buckskin and fringe and beads. Why don't they dress naturally? So I asked him if he was born in his three-button dacron suit. It's like the newspaper descriptions of Joan Baez's "long stringy hair." It may be long, but stringy? Come on!

To the eyes of many of the elder generation, all visible aspects of the new generation, its music, its lights, its clothes, are immoral. The City of San Francisco Commission on Juvenile Delinquency reported adversely on the sound level and the lights at the Fillmore Auditorium, as if those things of and by themselves were threats (they may be, but not in the way the Commission saw them). A young girl might have trouble maintaining her judgment in that environment, the Commission chairman said.

Now this all implies that dancing is the road to moral ruin, that young girls on the dance floor are mesmerized by talent scouts for South American brothels and enticed away from their happy (not hippie) homes to live a life of slavery and moral degradation. It ought to be noted, parenthetically, that a British writer, discussing the Beatles, claims that "the Cycladic fertility goddess from Amorgos dates the guitar as a sex symbol to 4800 years, B.C."

During the twenties and the thirties and the forties—in other words, during the prime years of the Old Ones of today—dancing, in the immortal words of Bob Scobey, the Dixieland trumpet player, "was an excuse to get next to a broad." The very least effect of the pill on American youth is that this is no longer true.

The assault on hypocrisy works on many levels. The adult society attempted to chastise Bob Dylan by economic sanction, calling the line in "Rainy Day Woman," "everybody must get stoned" (although there is a purely religious, even biblical, meaning to it, if you wish), an enticement to teen-agers to smoke marijuana. But no one has objected to Ray Charles's "Let's Go Get Stoned," which is about gin, or to any number of other songs, from the Kingston Trio's "Scotch and Soda" on through "One For My Baby and One More (ONE MORE!) For the Road." Those are about alcohol and alcohol is socially acceptable, as well as big business, even though I believe that everyone under thirty now knows that alcohol is worse for you than marijuana, that, in fact, the only thing wrong about marijuana is that it is illegal.

Cut to the California State Narcotics Bureau's chief enforcement officer, Matt O'Connor, in a TV interview recently insisting, á la Parkinson's Law, that he must have more agents to control the drug abuse problem. He appeared with a representative of the state attorney general's office, who predicted that the problem would continue, "as long as these people believe they are not doing anything wrong."

And that's exactly it. They do not think they are doing anything wrong, anymore than their grandparents were when they broke the prohibition laws. They do not want to go to jail, but a jail sentence or a bust no longer carries the social stigma it once did. The civil rights movement has made a jailing a badge of honor, if you go there for principle, and to a great many people today, the right to smoke marijuana is a principle worth risking jail for.

"Make Love, Not War" is one of the most important slogans of modern times, a statement of life against death, as the Beatles have said over and over—"say the word and be like me, say the word and you'll be free."

I don't think that wearing that slogan on a bumper or on the back of a windbreaker is going to end the bombing tomorrow at noon, but it implies something. It is not conceivable that it could have existed in such proliferation thirty years ago, and in 1937 we were pacifists, too. It simply could not have happened.

There's another side to it, of course, or at least another aspect to it. The Rolling Stones, who came into existence really to fight jazz in the clubs of London, were against the jazz of the integrated world, the integrated world arrived at by rational processes. Their songs, from "Satisfaction" and "19th Nervous Breakdown" to "Get Off Of My Cloud" and "Mother's Little Helper," were antiestablishment songs in a nonpolitical sort of way, just as Dylan's first period was antiestablishment in a political way. The Stones are now moving, with "Ruby Tuesday" and "Let's Spend The Night Together," into a social radicalism of sorts; but in the beginning, and for their basic first-thrust appeal, they hit out in rage, almost in blind anger and certainly with overtones of destructiveness, against the adult world. It's no wonder the novel they were attracted to was David Wallis' *Only Lovers Left Alive*, that Hells Angels story of a teen-age, future jungle. And it is further interesting that their manager, Andrew Loog Oldham, writes the essays on their albums in the style of Anthony Burgess' violent *A Clockwork Orange*.

Nor is it any wonder that this attitude appealed to that section of the youth whose basic position was still in politics and economics (remember that the Rolling Stones' Mick Jagger was a London School of Economics student, whereas Lennon and McCartney were artists and writers). When the Stones first came to the West Coast, a group of young radicals issued the following proclamation of welcome:

> Greetings and welcome Rolling Stones, our comrades in the desperate battle against the maniacs who hold power. The revolutionary youth of the world hears your music and is inspired to even more deadly acts. We fight in guerilla bands against the invading imperialists in Asia and South America, we riot at rock 'n

roll concerts everywhere. We burned and pillaged in Los Angeles and the cops know our snipers will return.

They call us dropouts and delinquents and draft dodgers and heap tons of shit on our heads. In Viet Nam they drop bombs on us and in America they try to make us make war on our own comrades but the bastards hear us playing you on our little transistor radios and know that they will not escape the blood and fire of the anarchist revolution.

We will play your music in rock 'n roll marching bands as we tear down the jails and free the prisoners, as we tear down the State schools and free the students, as we tear down the military bases and arm the poor, as we tattoo BURN BABY BURN! on the bellies of the wardens and generals and create a new society from the ashes of our fires.

Comrades, you will return to this country when it is free from the tyranny of the State and you will play your music in factories run by the workers, in the domes of emptied city halls, on the rubble of police stations, under the hanging corpses of priests, under a million red flags waving over a million anarchist communities. In the words of Breton, THE ROLLING STONES ARE THAT WHICH SHALL BE! LYNDON JOHNSON—THE YOUTH OF CALIFORNIA DEDICATES ITSELF TO YOUR DESTRUCTION! ROLLING STONES—THE YOUTH OF CALIFORNIA HEARS YOUR MESSAGE! LONG LIVE THE REVOLUTION!!!

But rhetoric like that did not bring out last January to a Human Be-In on the polo grounds of San Francisco's Golden Gate Park twenty thousand people who were there, fundamentally, just to see the other members of the tribe, not to hear speeches—the speeches were all a drag from Leary to Rubin to Buddah*—but just to BE.

In the Haight-Ashbury district the Love Generation organizes itself into Jobs Co-ops and committees to clean the streets, and the monks of the neighborhood, the Diggers, talk about free dances in the park to put the Avalon Ballroom and the Fillmore out of business and about communizing the incomes of Bob Dylan and the Beatles.

The Diggers trace back spiritually to those British millenarians who took over land in 1649, just before Cromwell, and after the Civil War freed it, under the assumption that the land was for the people. They tilled it and gave the food away.

The Diggers give food away. Everything is Free. So is it with the Berkeley Provos and the new group in Cleveland—the Prunes—and the Provos in Los Angeles. More, if an extreme, assault against the money culture. Are they driving the money changers out of the temple? Perhaps. The Diggers say they believe it is just as futile to fight the system as to join it and they are dropping out in a way that differs from Leary's.

The Square Left wrestles with the problem. They want a Yellow Submarine community because that is where the strength so obviously is. But even *Ramparts*, which is the white hope of the Square Left, if you follow me, misunderstands. They think that the Family Dog is a rock group and that political activity is the only hope, and Bob Dylan says, "There's no left wing and no right wing, only up wing and down wing," and also, "I tell you there are no politics."

But the banding together to form Job Co-ops, to publish newspapers, to talk to the police (even to bring them flowers), aren't these political acts? I suppose so, but I think they are political acts of a different kind, a kind that results in the Hells Angels being the guardians of the lost children at the Be-In and the guarantors of peace at dances.

The New Youth is finding its prophets in strange places—in dance halls and on the jukebox. It is on, perhaps, a frontier buckskin trip after a decade of Matt Dillon and Bonanza and the other TV folk myths, in which the values are clear (as opposed to those in the world around us) and right is right and wrong is wrong. The Negro singers have brought the style and the manner of the Negro gospel preacher to popular music, just as they brought the rhythms and the feeling of the gospel music, and now the radio is the church and Everyman carries his own walkie-talkie to God in his transistor.

Examine the outcry against the Beatles for John Lennon's remark about being more popular than Jesus. No radio station that depended on rock 'n roll music for its audience banned Beatles records, and in the only instance where we had a precise measuring rod for the contest—the Beatles concert in Memphis where a revival meeting ran day and date with them—the Beatles won overwhelmingly. Something like eight to five over Jesus in attendance, even though the Beatles charged a stiff price and the Gospel according to the revival preacher was free. Was my friend so wrong who said that if Hitler were alive today, the German girls wouldn't allow him to bomb London if the Beatles were there?

"Nobody ever taught you how to live out in the streets," Bob Dylan sings in "Like A Rolling Stone." You may consider that directed at a specific person, or you may, as I do, consider it poetically aimed at plastic uptight America, to use a phrase from one of the Family Dog founders.

"Nowhere to run, nowhere to hide," Martha and the Vandellas sing, and Simon and Garfunkel say, "The words of the prophets are written on the subway walls, in tenement halls." And the Byrds sing, "A time for peace, I swear it's not too late," just as the Beatles sing, "Say the word." What has formal religion done in this century to get the youth of the world so well acquainted with a verse from the Bible?

Even in those artists of the second echelon who are not, like Dylan and the Beatles and the Stones, worldwide in their influence, we find it. "Don't You Want Somebody To Love," the Jefferson Airplane sings, and Bob Lind speaks of "the bright elusive butterfly of love."

These songs speak to us in our condition, just as Dylan did with, "look out kid, it's somethin' you did, god knows when, but you're doin' it again." And Dylan sings again a concept that finds immediate response in the tolerance and the anti-judgment stance of the new generation, when he says, "There are no trials inside the gates of Eden."

Youth is wise today. Lenny Bruce claimed that TV made even eight-year-old girls sophisticated. When Bob Dylan in "Desolation Row" sings, "At midnight all the agents and the superhuman crew come out and round up everyone that knows more than they do," he speaks true, as he did with "don't follow leaders." But sometimes it is, as John Sebastian of the Lovin' Spoonful says, "like trying to tell a stranger 'bout a rock 'n roll."

Let's go back again to Nietzsche.

Orgiastic movements of a society leave their traces in music (he wrote). Dionysiac stirrings arise through the influence of those narcotic potions of which all primitive races speak in their hymns (—dig that!—)

or through the powerful approach of spring, which penetrates with joy the whole frame of nature. So stirred, the individual forgets himself completely. It is the same Dionysiac power which in medieval Germany drove ever increasing crowds of people singing and dancing from place to place; we recognize in these St. John's and St. Vitus' dancers the bacchic choruses of the Greeks, who had their precursors in Asia Minor and as far back as Babylon and the orgiastic Sacea. There are people who, either from lack of experience or out of sheer stupidity, turn away from such phenomena, and strong, in the sense of their own sanity, label them either mockingly or pityingly "endemic diseases." These benighted souls have no idea how cadaverous and ghostly their "sanity" appears as the intense throng of Dionysiac revelers sweeps past them.

And Nietzsche never heard of the San Francisco Commission on Juvenile Delinquency or the Fillmore and the Avalon ballrooms.

"Believe in the magic, it will set you free," the Lovin' Spoonful sing. "This is an invitation across the nation," sing Martha and the Vandellas, and the Mamas and the Papas, "a chance for folks to meet, there'll be laughin, singin' and music swingin,' and dancin' in the street!"

Do I project too much? Again, to Nietzsche. "Man now expresses himself through song and dance as the member of a higher community; he has forgotten how to walk, how to speak and is on the brink of taking wing as he dances . . . no longer the artist, he has himself become a work of art."

"Hail, hail, rock 'n roll," as Chuck Berry sings. "Deliver me from the days of old!"

I think he's about to get his wish.

* The Be-In heard speeches by Timothy Leary, the psychedelic guru, Jerry Rubin, the leader of the Berkeley Vietnam Day movement, and Buddah, a bartender and minor figure in the San Francisco hippie movement who acted as master of ceremonies.

[*The American Scholar*, Autumn 1967]

Sound Is Without Color

■

Item: Otis Redding dethrones Elvis Presley as top male vocalist in the annual poll of the London Melody Maker.

Item: The British Broadcasting Corporation flies a TV documentary crew to Otis Redding's 300 acre "Big o" Ranch outside Macon, Georgia, to film Redding.

Item: A radio broadcast from the Memphis studios of Stax/Volt featuring Otis Redding, Carla Thomas, the Mar-Keys, Booker T. and the M.G.'s via satellite is carried on the national radio network of France.

Query: Why has there never been any similar broadcast on U.S. TV or radio of Otis Redding (or James Brown or Wilson Pickett or Jackie Wilson or Ray Charles or Chuck Berry or even Nat Cole or Sam Cooke)?

The answer is color.

They are black and in America in the echelons of power, which control these things, color is a handicap.

Sound is without color and if sound sells, it is broadcast on radio via recordings. But national TV in the U.S. has yet to grasp the point that Otis Redding sells more records than Frank Sinatra and Dean Martin and therefore his audience is greater.

The change will come in time, inevitably, but this is the reason it has not come already.

Racial prejudice is a drag but it is also a fact and the fact of prejudice is the reason why the great performers of the early era of rhythm and blues (Otis Redding is really something else, perhaps rock and soul) such as Muddy Waters, Howlin' Wolf, Chuck Berry and the rest never had the chance to become the star figures in the country in which they were born that they were immediately seen to be in, for instance, England.

"I had to come to you behind the Rolling Stones and the Beatles," Muddy Waters poignantly told the Stanford University students the first time he appeared at a major college concert. It was less than two years ago and Muddy's equipment was patched together with masking tape, thumb-tacks, toothpicks and glue. No expensive speakers and mikes.

Nobody wants to be hung up with race, but it is still there, showing in the shadows behind the movement. Ray Charles was a leading recording artist for years before he ever appeared in downtown San Francisco, the liberal city of the West.

Otis Redding (and before him Chuck Berry and the others) came through the major cities playing in the "chitlin' joints" Lou Rawls refers to, and were never greeted at the airport by photographers and reporters and TV cameras, because the media managers did not think people with black skin (except the Harry Belafontes who made it in the white style) were newsworthy.

Back during the years when Ivory Joe Hunter and La Vern Baker and Ruth Brown were making the real hits, watered-down versions by Pat Boone and Georgia Gibbs were the discs that attracted the media managers' attention and resulted in the publicity interviews and TV appearances. Joe Turner's "Shake, Rattle and Roll" was overlooked by them when Bill Haley and the Comets scored, and even Howlin' Wolf's booking agency did not know who he was until the Rolling Stones put him on TV in a position of reverence. They listed him on their talent roster as Chester Burnett.

Not that a Chuck Berry did not make money. He certainly did and does—from the hundreds of his songs on the hundreds of discs by other artists, as well as his own. But it is his royalty checks from Capitol Records (thanks to the Beatles) that have enabled him to retire from the chitlin' circuit.

It's changing. The contemporary pop scene is almost blind to color and the white musicians are past imitation in general (though it was shocking at the Pop Festival to hear Canned Heat sing "I'm going down to Central Avenue and get me a TV set, you know what I mean") and into their own thing, which has value and aesthetics in and of itself. But we still should remember that it was there in front and is still there, lurking in the shadows.

The reason why no network does an Otis Redding spectacular is because of the veto power of the Southern TV stations, which make up a substantial part of the network and hence of its revenue. Ella Fitzgerald was denied the use of her racially mixed band only a few years ago on the Telephone Hour because the Southern Bell Telephone Companies objected or it was presumed WOULD object. Her white guitarist either had to be replaced or hidden behind a screen.

The times they are a-changin' and we may make this into a better world, but there is a usefulness in memory and the past cannot be denied or forgotten without jeopardizing the present and the future.

[*Rolling Stone*, November 9, 1967]

Fighting Fire with Fire

An End to Logic

■

Some reflections on guidelines to sanity in a time of madness.
One of the results of the awakening knowledge of the reality behind the American dream has been the ineluctable
passage on the road to madness of those whose knowledge
has been awakened.

Lenny Bruce was, I believe, driven quite literally mad by the built-in
hypocrisy of the American Society. Lenny believed in the law and the
law won; but only by being illegal.

This is what is the basis for Catch-22's brilliant template, which is as
useful to thinking about planet Earth in 1970 as it was in 1965.

If you take the American society literally, and the American Society attempted a drive to universality in the late Sixties that was kin to
Coca-Cola, then you are going to short out. The intellectual overload
will do it every time. No rational explanation can possibly work for the
particular kind of Mad Hatter organization of our lives we have. Recognition of this basic fact seems to me to be the clue to the writhings
and twistings of all branches of radical politics and analysis and for the
ostensible calm of the radical right.

If you zip around the TV channels with UHF and the gift of several extra channels, you are bound to encounter Rev. Oral Roberts and
Dr. Fred Schwartz. It is startling (not to say frightening) how much
these men resemble Nixon and Agnew. Because Oral Roberts is a faith
healer, it has been possible for liberals, as an example, to look at him
with objectivity and to analyze him. Because Fred Schwartz surfaced at
the end of the McCarthy era (and spoke in an Australian accent as he

tied his kangaroo down, Jack) it was possible for them also to regard him with objectivity. Both are instantly seen as religious extremists hallucinating a Communist devil against which to conduct their holy crusade and without which their babblings would have no reference point at all.

But Nixon and Agnew came from what is ordinarily considered respectable America (as opposed to faith healing, holy rollers or snake cults) and it has simply been impossible to get even the brightest of the TV commentators, no matter how opposed he may be to the deadly duo, to see either of them in that light.

But Nixon and Agnew, like Welch and the rest of the right-wingers, make what they say sound rational and they say it in a rational tone of voice (i.e. with ostensible calm and quiet) simply because they do not in any real way deal with American society in a rational manner. They do it by hallucination, with a kind of surrealism and with a religious commitment to angels and devils.

It has been built into our society from the very beginning and is sanctified in the Constitution. That really remarkable document would be the basis of as free a society as is possible under a profit-making system were it only possible to exercise it. As it stands, and as it has stood from the beginning of the Union, the document is to be honored in the breach and not the observance. Even more, it is to be sworn to, testified to, appealed to and then perverted.

That is what does it. The perversion of the Constitution for private and personal profit, gain and power has become so commonplace and is embedded so deeply in our national character that appealing to the protection of the Constitution, as Lenny Bruce, the Black Panthers, the Chicago conspiracy, John Sinclair, and a growing army of other political prisoners have done covertly or unconsciously, is to run headlong into madness.

What I mean is—the system drives you insane unless you join the game and pervert it. It certainly drives you insane if you attempt to deal with it logically and with trust.

Even the guarantees of our "racist Constitution" (as the Black Panther said in New York) are not extended to those whom the society cuts loose.

Lenny survived as long as he did and to the extent that he did because he could break up and laugh at the totality of the madness. Abbie Hoffman has that same quality. I'm not sure about the others.

Goebbels' Big Lie caper was as cool as a freight train and as subtle as a crutch compared to the Catch-22 functioning of the American society. We are not invading Cambodia, Nixon/Agnew said as the troops marched in. We are not going to occupy Cambodia. In fact, we aren't even there! It's like Jimmy Durante in Jumbo, leading the elephant off the lot; when the cop yells "Where are you going with that elephant?" Durante asks "What elephant?"

The pure purveyors of the new religion—Nixon, Agnew, Reagan, the Sacred Trinity of their hagiography—simply turn it all inside out, twist logic around, deny everything and go straight ahead doing what they say they are not doing. So-called decent people are in general too decent to make the challenge to them more than a formality.

What has been as irritating as the TV news people with Daley and Agnew and Reagan? No one even gave Ronnie baby a bad time when he said of his own remark (that it made no difference where the bullet came from which killed the Santa Barbara student) that it was a "figure of speech."

Reagan was asked mildly didn't he think it contradictory for him to dismiss his own statement about the possible necessity of a bloodbath to quell the student disturbances as a "figure of speech" while condemning David Hilliard's dismissal of his statement about offing Nixon as a figure of speech.

No, Reagan didn't see the connection. And nobody pursued the point.

They never do. Because if you pursue the point, you get to be a nut like Lenny or a troublemaker like Cleaver or a conspirator or whatever it is that they want to label you as.

Now what all of this has meant to me for some time is the true bankruptcy of radical movements and politics, their utter inability to accomplish anything positive at all; because every time they are dealing with an insane situation and trying to deal with it logically. I do not think it can be dealt with by logic. History proves that, I believe. I do think that it can be dealt with—to what extent I don't know but to the extent it can be dealt with at all—by intuitive kinds of things. By poetry. By music. By art.

That is why Dylan seems to me to be more important than the Weathermen. They blow buildings in New York. He blew minds all over the world. Ginsberg's poems speak to more people than all the SDS pamphlets put together. And it does not change it to point out that the world is still too fucking much with us.

There is no effective way logically to react to the presidential horror show of Cambodia anymore than there was to the horror show of Vietnam. We send the telegrams and sign the petitions because we don't know what else to do. But the logical steps are useless and we know it.

The violence, while it may be understandable, is just as useless since it demonstrably brings down upon its head more of the same and they have the horses (actually I'm a CIA agent, sir).

If there is no way to change this world (always supposing we can live on it long enough to enjoy the change) without killing half of us, then fuck it. I'll do my best to have a ball and go out swinging. No violent revolution is worth it, no matter how you have to break eggs to make omelettes and no matter where power comes out of. It also comes out of the mouths of poets and musicians and babes. (Not the "it ain't me" kind.)

I know one thing only: It will take time and we don't have any to spare. But we have enough not to kill with it and it's just as wrong to kill someone we call "pig" as it is to kill someone they call "Gook."

[*Rolling Stone*, May 28, 1970]

We Need an Honest President

W hen Nixon made his surprise visit to the Lincoln Memorial in 1970 and spoke to the students there, some of them said they were from California so he asked them if they were interested in surfing!

And when American bombs blew up the French Embassy in Hanoi, Nixon's lapdog, Laird, suggested it was actually a North Vietnamese anti-aircraft missile that had fallen back down!

One suspects alternately that they are all made of Silly Putty or are ventriloquist's dummies operated by Dr. Strangelove in between his dates with glamour girls.

So they run the country. They set up a monster business deal with Russia (whose problem is a shortage of wheat) and sell the dirty Commie rats all the U.S. wheat that their friends, the wheat brokers, bought up cheap from the farmers earlier in the summer. Only now it ain't cheap. It's a huge profit deal. But not for the farmers. Just for the wheat brokers and those who will profit by the Russians agreeing to pay up the money owed the U.S. for World War II. That was part of the deal.

You getting turned off by politics? It's bullshit, true and true again, but you better watch out, some of this bullshit just might get you killed. Or if not killed outright, it just might kill an ever-increasing bit of your psyche as it encroaches on liberty on all fronts.

As it is now laid out in the carefully orchestrated propaganda mill that Washington operates, Nixon will win by a landslide because labor doesn't like McGovern (Meany doesn't, but most labor unions do), youth (which means you, babe) is for Nixon, the blacks dig him (Sammy Davis ever hug you on TV?), Democrats love him (Franklin Delano Roosevelt is spinning in his grave, but then his sons never did do the old man justice), business digs him (easy to see why), the Jewish vote is against McGovern because they are afraid he won't let the Air Force bomb Cairo, in case the fellaheen manage somehow to scrape up a fighting force and threaten Israel.

And what's more, the faithful chorus chants, Nixon actually deserves to win because after all (and you can see this any night on TV in the Nixon commercial) it was he alone who saw that we were being blind to the real China and then went to Peking and opened the door.

Now this is what in the Olden Days (Hitler's war) was known as the technique of the Big Lie. This theory, which was always attributed to Goebbels, Hitler's flack, was that you could get away with any lie if it was big enough. The Nazis practiced it rather successfully and even Lyndon Johnson picked up on it with his Tonkin Gulf resolution concerning the nonexistent North Vietnam naval attack.

So now, in 1972, Richard M. Nixon is presented as the leader who recognized the People's Republic of China and who went to Moscow and sat down with the Russians in the Kremlin. The TV commercial is one long parade of implicit endorsements from Mao, Chou and the Russian leaders.

Never in the history of this country has a man's open, public record been so perverted. Nixon ran as an avowed enemy of all that even touched "Red China" and Moscow all of his political life. He aided in the hunting down and political lynching of anybody in the State Department who even so much as hinted, 20 years ago, that Mao might have something going for him and that Chiang Kai-shek was a loser.

As Lenny Bruce said about Chicago, "it's so corrupt it's thrilling," Nixon's monumental chutzpah in allowing himself to be presented this way is really an insult to the American people. It says they are brainless idiots who can't remember what happened yesterday and who care less.

It may work. God knows it's a slick enough job and the other thing going for Nixon is the mushy-headed McGovern campaign. And that's why it's so important at this point to keep a clear head. It may be the only way to keep it.

It's like this when you get down to the bone:

Politics is a drag and bullshit but if you stay home and don't vote, you are voting for Nixon, who not only believes in and practices the Big

Lie, but who is the personification of the use of political power for the benefit of business.

What it could very easily mean to you—if Nixon is re-elected and gets to appoint the next justices to the Supreme Court as well as the other federal judges—is a series of opinions which will make life a lot harder.

These people are serious. They do not want long-hairs on welfare; they consider welfare an immoral act against the government. They do not want blacks independent of them, nor Chicanos nor anybody. They want to impose standards not only of dress but of language and custom which would make the obscenity laws of Boston tame by comparison. They want to alter the whole concept of the law, give the police even more powers than they have and inhibit and punish judges who function on the concept that one is innocent until proven guilty.

Elect McGovern and the priorities of the world will not be realigned, leading to social justice for all. But it will prevent Nixon from solidly nailing down the fascist formula he has begun to impose on this country. Just remember that the Chief Justice of the United States Supreme Court, when two reporters knocked on his door in the late evening, answered holding a gun in his hand. That, friends, is a Nixon court.

Do not be misled by Nixon and the draft. He is going to end it all right, and he has withdrawn almost all the US ground personnel from South Vietnam; but this is, as European military experts with no stake in the matters see it, making a political virtue out of military common sense. He has increased the bombing, increased the mechanization and electrification of the war (it is really a push button war, science fiction style in many ways) and the ground troops, with their cumbersome supply lines and other problems, are an embarrassment. Especially since, in the context of that particular war, they had a declining factor of usefulness. They were, it should be said, in the way. It's much easier to bomb now.

Back to the big lie. Last year, Nixon told Cyrus Sulzberger of the *New York Times* "I rate myself a deeply committed pacifist." God save us all from any more of those, if he's an example.

I have always been unable to make up my mind whether or not Nixon and his gang really believe the nonsense they spout. The temptation is to consider them so corrupt and dishonest that they speak cynically while knowing the real truth.

Actually, I don't think they do. I believe they are impervious to it. Nixon copped to this when he said "I understand that there has been and continues to be opposition to the war in Vietnam on the campuses and in the nation. As far as this activity is concerned, we expect it. However, under no circumstances will I be affected whatever by it." There it is. Don't bother to offer him facts, his mind is made up.

All right, there is really only one thing to do. Vote him out of office, not because we will be electing a Savior in his place, not because McGovern is the answer to our prayers, but because Nixon has completely and thoroughly violated his sacred duty to represent us for our best interests and, since we apparently can't try him as a criminal, we can at least replace him with an honest man.

[*Rolling Stone*, November 9, 1972]

We've Got to Get Rid of Nixon

This one was supposed to be about John and Yoko and how disgusting it is that the U.S. government is trying to throw them out of the country and how odd it is that so few of the people in and out of music who owe so much to the Beatles and hence to John have come to his aid.

But something got in the way. What it was, was Nixon. His speech, when he raised the ante to the Russians and the Vietnamese by mining the harbors, frightened me out of my wits. I saw him on TV and heard him on radio and then read it in the paper. No matter how I looked at it, it always came out the same way:

It is essential to get this man out of office before he kills us all.

I really believe that with all my heart and it is a terrible thing to say. I mean that I find it terrible to have to say it. I was raised to believe that even if one disagreed with the president he was, after all, the president. Make no mistake about that. And the office carried the respect one might not otherwise have given the man.

Now I find myself so far beyond that concept laid on me by my father, old free speech/tax reform Democrat/horse player that he was, that I can barely manage to remain coherent, much less reasonable, talking about Nixon's Imperial war.

I have thought about it for days now and considered it from every angle and I find only two possible explanations, both of which reduce me to disgust when I think of the man who occupies that honored post.

The first explanation is that Nixon, the Chinese and the Russians are all involved in a cynical power-play to allow the U.S. to make a lot of face-saving statements and rattle a lot of pompous sabres before accepting the inevitable and withdrawing from Vietnam and ending the war already lost.

Dishonorable though this may be, I certainly prefer it since it will, if this is the plan, get us the hell out of Vietnam and end this inhumane and inexcusable war. It is perfectly possible that it is, indeed, the scenario since I am forced to say that I can conceive of no act Richard Nixon would not commit in the name of re-election and if he does get us out of Vietnam, he certainly will make his strongest bid to adult America and re-election.

The Russians, if they see enough to gain from this, are perfectly willing to sacrifice the Vietnamese, based on past performance. In World War II the Poles and the Jews in the Warsaw ghetto rose against the Nazis as the Russian armies approached Warsaw only to be murdered as the Russians halted almost within eyesight of their lines and let the Germans finish their work. Pragmatists the Russians are. The end justifies the means every time, even if that means an alliance with Hitler.

As to the Chinese, there is more hope. Their record is cleaner but then again they are engaged now in a power game vis-à-vis Russia, not only for a struggle within the socialist world, but possibly for their own survival. And in such a game, the Vietnamese people are only a small factor.

So it is possible. We know it is possible for Nixon, of course, because in his every speech and act he shows us how incalculably cynical he is. Orwell's 1984 madmen with their instant rhetoric that changed as they needed it had nothing on Nixon. When the whole world knows the only salvation for America's honor is to stop the bombing and killing and withdraw, he turns it inside out and makes it a plea for honor to resume the bombing. He disclaims any responsibility for being in Vietnam in the first place, cynically ignoring his own role, not only as Eisenhower's Agnew, but as the personification of hawkishness both before and after.

The second explanation is that Nixon is just doing what he says he is doing. I hate to believe that because if it is true we are in greater trouble than even our nightmares tell us. Didn't you think you might drop nuclear bombs when he started that speech? Didn't you fear the worst? That's what Nixon is: the manifestation of the worst. If he meant what he said—literally—then we can only pray we will all live long enough to elect someone else president and by all my logic, that someone has to be McGovern. He is the only candidate who can win.

I know you are tired of politics. Can you know how tired I am? I cast my first vote for Roosevelt when we lived in an era when a man in public office could be trusted. We have not had his like until McGovern, I believe. Robert Kennedy was on his way there, he was much further advanced than JFK ever had a chance to be. But it was not to be. Maybe there is no hope. Yet I can't accept that because if I did then there would really be no choice but death and I opt for life and for love every time. I believe it is the only way. Maybe it's just my nature, but I don't care. I have to believe man has some control over his fate and I have to believe that man can be humane as well as human.

"I don't know if I can go for it one more time," a friend of mine said the morning after Nixon's speech. She meant go for the whole electoral process and in the end be betrayed again. I told her I see it, not as one more time, but as one last time. And I think it is.

If we do not extinguish ourselves before November, I am convinced we must make it to those voting booths and throw that man out of office. I know—we are all still alive—that it can be done. He only got in there by a photo finish against the silly putty personality of Humphrey. Against a real man, he can't make it.

If we do not elect McGovern, we will be at the mercy of the most cynical and ignorant chief executive any horror show could devise. We will be at the mercy of a man we cannot believe even when he may be telling the truth. We will be at the mercy of a man in whose hands are all the mechanisms of the space-age but in whose mind it is possible to conceive of a Third World war, who can ignore the obvious fact that we are, yard by yard, decimating the very country he professes to save, turning it into the biggest graveyard in the history of man with more high explosive bombing than World War II.

So I hope he is cynical beyond cynicism and that the answer is in the first concept. Even at that, we are ignoring the gallant Vietnamese who just might upset the whole coldly calculated caper and throw us out of Vietnam on their own. God knows what Nixon would do in that case.

We have one fail-safe factor. The Chinese and the Russians, for all their cynicism, are just as aware as you and I of the true dangers of an atomic war. The Russians saved our ass over Cuba by walking away from the confrontation. They may save our ass again by not picking up the gauntlet so callously thrown to them by Nixon now.

If they believe in our ability to throw him out of office they have as much to gain by it as we do. Nixon's defeat may be a victory for Peking and Moscow, but it will also be a victory for the human race. It is our one chance for survival.

[*Rolling Stone,* June 8, 1972]

Payola

It's in the Grooves

◼

P ayola is a word generally used to describe record companies or representatives of recording artists giving money/gifts/ favors to disc jockeys and program directors to obtain airplay of records. Actually it is a practice endemic in American business, professional and political life.

Recently I saw "Petulia," the film with George C. Scott and Julie Christie, on TV. Shot in San Francisco, it was a gas to see again, with shots of Janis Joplin and Pig Pen and other music scene people as extras.

But there was an unexpected bonus for me, in the scene where Scott, a prominent doctor at a big hospital, was opening all his Christmas presents. One of the most expensive gifts came from a clinic and was obviously designed to make the doctors think of the clinic when he next had a chance to use whatever service it was they sold.

That was payola.

So is a press junket to Fargo, North Dakota for the premiere of a film. The studio picks up the plane fare, food, drink (plenty of that) and motel accommodations in the hope that the writers will dig the film and write about it favorably. But in any case write about it, because bad publicity is better than none at all.

And when a baseball or football team, college or professional, gives a sports writer a free seat on the players' plane, that, too, is payola. It's also payola when the Pentagon flies writers to some Air Force base to write about a new piece of cosmic lunacy the heavy hardware boys are peddling.

It is payola when the ordinary American businessman takes a client to lunch, arranges a kickback or makes a gift, from a vicuna coat to a refrigerator, to a purchasing agent who buys a fleet of cars, ten fire engines, a ton of sweat socks or whatever.

It was payola when the officials of Westinghouse and General Electric in 1962 paid off everybody in sight to fix prices and obtain special privilege. This one was so bad 29 firms were involved, fines totaled $2 million and seven executives went to jail. And isn't it payola when IT&T or some other corporation, or even a city, gives hundreds of thousands of dollars to a political party? You think all that cash floating around the Committee to Re-elect the President wasn't there to buy something? And isn't it payola when a President or a Senator or a Congressman is flown somewhere in an airplane owned by a corporation?

It's payola when a company that does business with the Pentagon hires the general it did business with when he retires and it's payola when the government arranges price support for some section of business or, in another sense, when it sells guns and planes to some Arab country and gets oil.

PAYOLA AND LOBBYISTS

There is a remarkable paperback book titled "The Washington Payoff" written by a former lobbyist named Robert N. Winter-Berger (Dell). In it, among many other fascinating things, Winter-Berger tells of his relationship with Rep. Gerald Ford, minority leader of the House. Ford was personally honest, Winter-Berger insists, but "each favor Ford did for me involved a contribution by my client (to the Republican campaign fund) but nothing directly to Ford."

That, friends, is payola, too. And I thought of it the other night when I watched Sen. James Buckley, the prominent Republican conservative, piously nattering on about investigating payola and Columbia records.

Sen. Buckley's attention and energy might better be redirected to the Senate and the House. I wonder has he ever accepted a "campaign contribution" in cash or check for making a phone call to get somebody a passport, urge a contract be given a friend or any of the innumerable other red tape cutting bits of special privilege that make up the unpublicized business of the House and the Senate where, as John McCormack told Winter-Berger, the motto is "Nothing for nothing." A country where this is the common practice is in no position to make a moral issue out of a trip to Vegas for a disc jockey.

Which brings us to the whole overblown, paranoid mess that constitutes the current payola scandal.

Let's begin by understanding that the natural greed of people in a capitalist society allows them, nay, drives them to exploit every possible advantage they can get away with, to bribe and yes, to steal if they think it will make their sales pitch work.

There are people in the record business who will take money, just as there are people in Congress and elsewhere, and as long as somebody will take it, there is always somebody who will give it, because the concept of payola not only is built into the American character (you scratch my back and I'll scratch yours) but it is an absolute necessity as a concept for the salvation of the ego of many, many people in the record business. It is the only way they can explain their own bum guesses. Payola, like Catholicism, explains all things and is, in a religious sense, the opium (if I may mix this delicate metaphor) of the record people.

But the trouble with the payola thesis is that it runs counter to several natural laws of the mass record business which, when he gets down to the nitty-gritty, every professional record man knows are true.

SOUND OF MONEY

The first of these is what old Jack Kapp, the man who started Decca Records in the U.S. and successfully challenged R.C.A. and Columbia 30 years ago, said: "The hit is in the groove." In other words, you got to have the music or they won't buy.

The corollary of that, which everybody in the record business also knows, is the natural law that states: You can't buy a hit.

The third law of records is that you can make it without payola. Plenty of records do. Now let's look at what I'm saying here. You can't buy it. Payola says you must buy airplay with money and/or presents/ dope/trips, etc. but if all it took was money, R.C.A. would have all the tickets because they have more money than anybody. A company like Bell would never have had a chance.

And if buying airplay was the answer, how do you explain Grand

Funk (Railroad), which made its huge success without even being played on the air, for Christ's sake?

I'll give you an illustration of how payola does not work. Some years ago there was a single record on Columbia by a female singer who was married to a man who packaged concert tours that went across the country playing in 30 or 40 key cities.

In each city, the tour manager spent money like water on newspaper and radio ads, sometimes up to thousands of dollars with one station. Every time you made a deal to buy time, he made an unofficial deal that the station would also plug the record of the singer who was married to his boss. They never did sell any records. I don't mean they didn't sell 100,000. I mean they didn't sell 5000. Total. National. Coast-to-coast. The record was a stiff.

There are many other examples of great campaigns, all the hype that money can buy, and still no sales. There was Rod Lauren, who R.C.A. tried to make into a successor to Elvis by a $100,000 campaign when Elvis went into the Army. There was the lovely ad campaign about a song called "Chimney Sweep," I think, sung by Peggy Lee and produced for Columbia by Mitch Miller who printed an ad in Billboard, saying "I stake my professional reputation on this record." He should be grateful no one took him seriously.

The public and the straight press insist on believing that taste can be perverted—if not by payola, then by other means. The McClellan committee in its investigation of the mob, jukeboxes and records years ago showed the truth about that. Despite the fact that a certain singer's manager had successfully negotiated a deal with one of the Chicago mobsters who controlled jukeboxes to put several thousand of that singer's record on the jukeboxes, it didn't produce a hit. In short, even the mob's muscle, much less payroll, could not make a stiff into a hit.

Another myth the public cherishes is that there is no chance for a hit without payola, despite the fact that the whole history of the record industry goes to prove that all kinds of one-shot labels and oddball records make it overnight without handouts of any kind. The records people use to support these claims of payola are always those on the edge of the business, usually a used car dealer recorded some girl singer he met in a bar.

The real question is, does anybody seriously think that the Beatles were made into stars by payola? Does anyone believe that you have to bribe radio stations and/or disc jockeys to play the new Paul Simon record? That Aretha Franklin got her hits by payola? If so, why didn't she get hits on Columbia? They had more money than Atlantic.

LOTS OF AIR

There are God knows how many disc jockeys on the 1000 or so a.m. stations in the country and if your record has anything going for it at all, it will get on the air someplace. Everybody wants to break a hit. The most important place to get airplay is on the Bill Drake programmed stations, that are the biggest and the best in the largest markets. But if there is one thing everybody agrees on in the business, it is that you can't buy your way onto a Bill Drake station with money. I know, from personal experience, that being played by a Bill Drake station does not automatically make your disk a hit. Aside from Drake and a couple of competitors, the most important other contract is Bill Gavin, who writes a pop music tip sheet and nobody has ever accused Bill of bribe-ability. They accuse him of being old-fashioned and a square and all that, but you can't buy him. No way. Cal Rudman can be hired to work on the promotion of a record and he is also the publisher of a report sheet used by programmers, as well as of a column, and it would be a lot cleaner if you couldn't hire him. But even if you can, he can't make a hit no matter what you pay, and you can get a hit without his help and many have and will.

However, since the big payola scandals of the late 50s and early 60s, there has been relatively little payola in the old sense on top 40 a.m. stations. It carries a bum rap, there is pressure from the Federal Communications Commission, and, ultimately more important, the individual disc jockey, with rare exception, is subordinated to a program director method of operation that has produced very few personalities like those of the 50s. In addition, today's jock on a top 40 station has a chance to really make a lot of money by his work. He can rise from an obscure suburban station to a metropolitan station where, if he's as hot as Don Imus, he can earn a yearly salary passing six figures. He has a lot to lose if he blows it with payola.

Black stations are another matter. This is a fact and the rebuttal from black program directors that to say this is to be or act racist is a copout. The truth is that economic necessity operates here as it does everywhere else. In a state such as California, there are less than half a dozen black stations (there are less than 75 nationally), whereas there are possibly as many as 100 white stations and certainly over two dozen stations playing white music (I.E., Rock) where you can start to break a hit. A black disc jockey has fewer alternatives, as black people do in every walk of life, and as a result his employers, who are mainly white owners of black stations, pay him on the average less than his opposite number on a white station. And also he has infinitely fewer places to go. His upward and lateral mobility are both distinctly limited.

Why should it surprise anyone if a black disc jockey felt that, since he knows there's a lot of money in black music, his chance to make it is right now. He simply cannot look to a future Metropolitan top 40 job with a six-figure salary.

Also, the black society has always recognized that the true ethic of the American society is bread. There are ample sociological studies to support the fact that this recognition, which is in essence the recognition of necessity, gives a rather different orientation to a lifestyle.

The act of paying off for exploitation of music has been with us since long before the phonograph record. Arnold Passman, in his fascinating book "The D.J.s" (McMillan), points out that in Victorian England, Arthur Sullivan (of Gilbert and Sullivan) gave a portion of the future royalties of a song, "Thou Art Passing Attempts," to a leading singer of the time, Sir Charles Stanley. "When the tune was played at (Sullivan's) funeral in 1900," Passman points out, "Sir Charles was still collecting."

That pattern was followed all through the early days of pop music. Many famous singers and vaudeville performers got a piece of the song because they sang it. Later, bandleaders got their names on songs their sidemen wrote. Managers' names cropped up as co-writer on songs, and in the 50s and early 60s, when some singers were under the control of a greedy manager, you had to give the singer or the manager a piece of the song to get it recorded.

Today, radio is the channel through which most of the public gets its first taste of a song. No matter how many promotion men are clogging the hallway, a radio station absolutely has to audition material. The promo men are like salesmen; go-betweens, bringing the record to the station and hopefully getting it played. When money can be used to speed up this process (like getting a congressman to make a call to the right Bureau to have a contract considered favorably and giving him a contribution for this act), money is probably used. But what is more likely is that the promo man does everything he can, the same as any salesman, out there in the blue, riding on a smile, to ingratiate himself with the program director and the disc jockey. He adopts their lifestyle as they adopt the lifestyle of the groups who make the records. If the P.D. or the jock smokes dope, the promo man will smoke dope and bring some to the station. If the disc jockey or the P.D. digs ice hockey, the promo man will pick up on ice hockey. If they dig booze, he'll drink and bring them booze (E. F. "The Days of Wine and Roses").

So will any salesman of any American business product; it is as simple as that. Record companies send Christmas gifts to disc jockeys. Some promo man may give some jock some coke sometime, but as a friend of mine who is in a position to know says, "I know Columbia wasn't buying any dope for the disc jockeys because I didn't get any!"

On the other hand, if a record company has a group or one they believe is about to be a hit group, and that group insists on smoking dope in the studio, the record company will close its eyes to that and even hire a special guard to keep anybody who might blow the whistle out of the studio. Under some circumstances, the company might, not on the executive level but on the operational level, spend some money to buy some dope, to bring it to a session. The company man who is trying to sign a group might do the same thing and, like any other American businessman/salesman, pad his expense account to cover that expense. The same goes for girls, for God's sake, with the groupies wall-to-wall in the motel lobby, who needs to pay brokers for groups? For jocks, maybe. But that is done in many more areas than records, believe me. I once worked—years ago—for a radio network (now a TV network) where a vice president's secretary kept a card file on the habits and special requirements of station managers so she could be sure they got what they wanted when they came to New York. And they wanted more than theater tickets.

In the current brouhaha over Columbia and payola, a lot of arrant nonsense has been printed in very elite publications. In one, I read a critic who said his agent (critics have agents?) was offered $25,000 by a song publisher to have the critic write three "presentations" about the publisher's songs. I don't know what a "presentation" is, but I do know that nothing any critic can now or ever could do for a song publisher, except write a song, is worth $25,000. Either that critic misheard an offer for $2500 to write several special songbooks (a decent fee for a decent editorial task) or he has such an incredible sense of his own importance that he actually thinks his opinions can influence enough people to buy something that is worth $25,000.

I have been writing about music and records for over 20 years in *Down Beat, Stereo Review,* the *San Francisco Chronicle* (and for some years in a syndicated column for over 20 newspapers, including the *New York Post*) and for *Rolling Stone.*

In that time, nobody has ever offered me one single dollar of payola. I got a box of plastic swizzle sticks worth about $.25 from R.C.A. once. Columbia gave me a lovely felt pen and a personal friend whom I've known for 25 years and knew long before he was in the record business, once sent me six bottles of wine. A couple of times record companies have sent me cigarette lighters and things like bottle openers and crummy carving sets. But payola? Not one thin dime ever. I have been invited to numerous lunches and dinners and parties and sometimes out-of-town junkets to idiotic places to see groups I wouldn't go to see if they played across the street. And I never went. But that's my idiosyncrasy.

Still, I don't believe I am all that much of an exception. I do think if managers and others, believed they could make hits by paying off disc jockeys and critics they would try to do it. But they know it really doesn't work.

As for the standards of the music press, which have also been attacked, it should be pointed out that only the trade papers bothered to check out Tommy Falcone's initial claim he was Sly Stone's manager. The *Times* printed it and so did *New York* magazine. Of course he wasn't.

Years and years ago, when I first got to know the professional entertainment trade press, I found out very quickly that they had integrity. It was not possible to buy lunch for a *Variety* reporter in New York. You either went Dutch or traded lunches.

And Abel Green, who died a few months ago, laid down the law at *Variety* that all Christmas presents were given to charity.

I hope it's still true. I know it's true that you can't buy it. I wish I was sure you can't buy a congressman or a senator. Or a President.

[*The Real Paper*, August 8, 1973]

Law & Order & the Business of Politics

■

Politics makes strange bedfellows, which is why a truly ambitious politician is willing to go to bed with anyone.

We saw a raw example of that in the days when Hubert Humphrey was running for the nomination against McGovern. Hubert was perfectly willing to embrace Lester Maddox, the Georgia ax handle wielder who barred blacks from his restaurant and later became governor. Hubert could embrace Maddox and turn right around and embrace James Brown and talk about how he, Hubert, also had soul!

Words become meaningless when you run off at the mouth running for office.

We just saw another example of the same kind of political ploy when Senator Edward Kennedy flew down to Alabama to symbolically embrace Governor George Wallace, the same Wallace who stood on the steps of the State University barring the way to James Meredith and Bobby Kennedy's federal marshals.

To make the point, as Kennedy did, that Wallace is a brave man and has fought back heroically against the crippling bullet with great courage has nothing at all to do with it. Tyrants and despots from the beginning of time right down to Goering and Goebbels had courage.

No. What Kennedy did was make an early play for the Wallace votes in the Democratic Party and by so doing came out of the closet as a candidate and as a politician who will sleep with anybody to get votes. The lust for power is no trivial thing; it can corrode a man, and it would've been more honorable had the senator let powers seek him rather than seek it. But then, the Kennedys have always been aggressive, a fault he shares with his older brothers, not to speak ill of the dead.

I am all for reasonableness and reconciliation in the interest of saving the union and like that, but the reconciliation must come from both ends, not just from one. To date there is no indication that Gov. Wallace is any less rabid a segregationist than he was when he stood on the steps and faced the US marshals. Scratch the crippled victim of the would-be assassin and you will find a man who believes black and white must not mix. Embrace him and you embrace racism and I do not see how the senator from Massachusetts can make this out to be anything else.

Unless the conservatives like the John Birch-ites in the segregationists retreat from their extreme position, it is not possible to work with them and maintain integrity. And they show no sign of any retreat.

True, their social position (if not their economic one) is merely an extension of basic American WASP racist reality, as is being shown even in New England now by the positions taken by Senators Brooke and Kennedy in the dispute over how to control exploitation of Martha's Vineyard and other recreational areas. But that does not make it any more acceptable.

One of the reasons why lawyers such as John Mitchell were willing to subvert the Constitution and to break laws, they said, was their belief that they had to do this in order to save the Constitution and protect the law. (Do I hear that officer in Vietnam saying "we had to destroy the village in order to save it"?)

Anything, including breaking the law, was better than the possibility the other candidate (McGovern) might defeat Nixon, John Mitchell told the Ervin committee and hence the nation via TV.

This is the true meaning of Watergate: that the president holds himself above the Constitution and the law and that his aides, whom he selected and continues to endorse, are willing to break the law and subvert the Constitution in his service.

That is the truth behind the hypocritical law and order stance Nixon and his band of conspirators have maintained.

They do not now, and they never did, believe in law and order except when it suited them to. If, for instance, some government types had made the proposition in Mitchell's office to kidnap leading birch-ites and/or segregationists and take them to Mexico for the duration (even

Nazi party or KKK leaders) what would Mitchell's reaction have been? He was an officer of the court—as a lawyer you still lose—and faced with a plan to break the laws so outrageously; would he merely have dismissed those who proposed it telling them it was impractical and too expensive, or would he have blown the whistle and called the cops? That question runs through the whole situation. Turn it around, ask yourself how it would work if others had done what the Nixon/Mitchell conspiracy did.

I call it a conspiracy. Actually it was. A conspiracy is a decidedly accurate term for what went on. The objective of the conspiracy, as Anthony Lewis of the *New York Times* has noted, was to overthrow the duly constituted government of the United States and substitute for it a cabinet government by the executive staff. The conspiracy went almost to success and had it gone all the way, we would've had the criminal code rewritten as well as many other changes in the way our system works day by day.

To implement that conspiracy, to protect it from its own stupidity by compounding the stupidity, was the effort that became the Watergate cover-up. Read or listen to the testimony and see how the world appeared to those sick, paranoid conspirators locked into Nixon's embrace.

The American system is in need of change; no way over the coming years to avoid it. But the change that is needed has to come from the people and for the people and not, as the Nixon-ites tried to bring about, be thrust upon them by force, conspiracy and corruption.

When the final truth about all this is out, we will see why Vietnam, how Nixon really got his money to campaign all his life, who owns the property in San Clemente and all the rest of the mystery that is wrapped in mysteries which this devious man and his devious friends put together. And they will all connect.

Nothing Nixon has done, and he is probably worse than even I think he is, at bottom represents anything inconsistent with the American style in business. He is the American businessman carried to the ultimate and without other than oral pretense to be otherwise. This is what needs revision; the American business ethic. Until it is revised we will have more Nixons even if we are able to cast loose from this one.

That is the basic problem.

In the meantime, as always, we need to live and work and plan to legally and intelligently make over our system for the benefit of the people and not the corporations. We have to do it without killing. And that is really hard.

[*Rolling Stone*, August 16, 1973]

Acknowledgments

MY FATHER'S ASTOUNDINGLY prolific career would not have been possible without the love and constant support of his wife, my mother, Jean Gleason. She was his primary editor, his head researcher, his secretary, his partner, companion, hostess, mother of his children and the keeper of his voluminous files. She was his inspiration and his muse. Without her, he would have been far less than he was.

I would like to thank the many newspapers and magazines that published his work: *Down Beat*, the *San Francisco Chronicle*, *Rolling Stone, Ramparts, American Scholar, Lithopinion*, the *Daily Californian, Evergreen Review, Encyclopedia Britannica*, and many others too numerous to have included them all in this volume. I would also like to thank all of the record companies and recording artists for whom he wrote album liner notes: Fantasy Records/Concord Music Group, Columbia Records/Sony Music Entertainment, RCA Victor for their kind permission to include those works here.

Special thanks to my wife, Vera, for her inspiration and assistance in putting together this book. My thanks, also, to Peter Richardson, author of *No Simple Highway*, for his assistance in the book proposal process, and to my agent, Andy Ross, who made finding a publisher smooth and easy. And to my editor at Yale University Press, Steve Wasserman, an old schoolmate and a man with the patience of a saint.

I would also like to thank authors Greil Marcus and Peter Richardson and editor Paul Scanlon for their insightful suggestions, and Jann Wenner and Paul Scanlon for the wonderful foreword and introduction, respectively.

To my sisters, Bridget and Stacy, and the rest of our extended family, I hope you will be pleased with this collection. And to all my father's readers, both new and old, I hope that you will find his words as relevant and important today as they were when he wrote them.

Credits

"A Folk-Singing Social Critic" © 1964 *San Francisco Chronicle*; © Renewal 1990
Toby Gleason

"A Warm and Groovy Affair" © 1967 *San Francisco Chronicle*; © Renewal 1990
Toby Gleason

"Altamont Revisited on Film" © 1971 *Rolling Stone Magazine*; © Renewal 1998
Toby Gleason

"Another Candle Blown Out" © 1970 *Rolling Stone Magazine*; © Renewal 2000
Toby Gleason

"B. B. King—Completely Well" © 1969 Bluesway Records

"Ben Webster—Another Giant Gone" ©1973 *Rolling Stone Magazine*; © Renewal
1998 Toby Gleason

"Billie Holiday-The Golden Years, Vol. II" © 1966 Columbia Records (Sony
Music Entertainment)

"Cal Tjader—Los Ritmos Calientes" © 1973 Fantasy Records (Concord Music
Group)

"Dawn of True Sexual Hysteria" © 1969 *Rolling Stone Magazine*; © Renewal 1990
Toby Gleason

"Duke Ellington—The Pianist" © 1974 Fantasy Records (Concord Music Group)

"Farewell To The Duke" © 1974 *Rolling Stone Magazine*; © Renewal 1990 Toby
Gleason

"Fighting Fire With Fire; An End To Logic" © 1970 *Rolling Stone Magazine*;
© Renewal 1998 Toby Gleason

"Frank: Then and Now" © 1974 *Rolling Stone Magazine*; © Renewal 1998 Toby
Gleason

"God Bless Louis Armstrong" © 1971 *Rolling Stone Magazine*; © Renewal 1998
Toby Gleason

"Guaraldi & Sete—A Happy Union" © 1964 *San Francisco Chronicle*; © Renewal
1990 Toby Gleason

"Hank Williams, Roy Acuff and Then God!!" © 1969 *Rolling Stone Magazine*;
© Renewal 1999 Toby Gleason

"Jazz: Black Art/American Art" © 1965 American Scholar; © Renewal 1993 Toby
Gleason

Credits

"Jefferson Airplane—Takes Off" © 1966 RCA Records

"Jimmy Witherspoon; At the Monterey Jazz Festival" © 1959 Hi Fi Jazz Recordings; © Renewal 1990 Toby Gleason

"John Coltrane; Olé Coltrane" © 1961 Atlantic Records

"John Handy—Recorded Live at the Monterey Jazz Festival" © 1966 Columbia Records (Sony Music Entertainment)

"Jonathan Winters—Another Day, Another World" © 1962 Verve Records (Universal Music Group)

"Law & Order & the Business of Politics" © 1973 *Rolling Stone Magazine*; © Renewal 2002 Toby Gleason

"Like A Rolling Stone" © 1967 *American Scholar Journal*; © Renewal 1990 Toby Gleason

"Louis Plays the Claremont" © 1963 *San Francisco Chronicle*; © Renewal 1990 Toby Gleason

"Miles Davis—Bitches Brew" © 1970 Columbia Records (Sony Music Entertainment)

"Mingus Mail Album a Huge Success" © 1965 *San Francisco Chronicle*; © Renewal 1990 Toby Gleason

"Odetta the Incomparable" © 1963 *San Francisco Chronicle*; © Renewal 1990 Toby Gleason

"Payola; It's In The Grooves" © 1973 The Real Paper; © Renewal 2002 Toby Gleason

"Perspectives" © 1954 *Down Beat* Magazine

"Pete Seeger Is Here Tonight" © 1963 *San Francisco Chronicle*; © Renewal 1990 Toby Gleason

"San Francisco: The American Liverpool" © 1965 *Hullaballoo Magazine*; © Renewal 1990 Toby Gleason

"Satire, Reality and Dick Gregory" © 1963 *San Francisco Chronicle*; © Renewal 1990 Toby Gleason

"School Jazz Has Quality" © 1963 *San Francisco Chronicle*; © Renewal 1990 Toby Gleason

"Simon & Garfunkel—Parsley, Sage, Rosemary & Thyme" © 1966 Columbia Records (Sony Music Entertainment)

"Soul Sauce—A Hummer's Hit" © 1965 *San Francisco Chronicle*; © Renewal 1990 Toby Gleason

"Sound Is Without Color" © 1967 *Rolling Stone Magazine*; © Renewal 1998 Toby Gleason

"The Beatles' Mersey Sound" © 1964 *San Francisco Chronicle*; © Renewal 1990 Toby Gleason

"The Bill Cosby World of Youth" © 1967 *San Francisco Chronicle*; © Renewal 1998 Toby Gleason

"The Casualties of Mass Society" © 1964 *San Francisco Chronicle*; © Renewal 1990 Toby Gleason

Credits

"The Flower Children" © 1968 *Encyclopedia Britannica Yearbook*; © Renewal 1990 Toby Gleason

"The Greatness of Carmen McRae" © 1964 *San Francisco Chronicle*; © Renewal 1990 Toby Gleason

"The Limeliters—Through Children's Eyes (Little-Folk Songs For Adults)" © 1962 RCA Victor

"The Magic of Joan Baez" © 1963 *San Francisco Chronicle*; © Renewal 1990 Toby Gleason

"The Real Lenny Bruce" © 1975 Fantasy Records (Concord Music Group)

"The Rewards In Mingus' Music" © 1969 *San Francisco Chronicle*; © Renewal 1990 Toby Gleason

"The San Francisco Jazz Scene" © *Evergreen Review*; © Renewal 1990 Toby Gleason

"The Sunlight and Beauty of Johnny Hodges" © 1970 *Rolling Stone Magazine*; © Renewal 1998 Toby Gleason

"The Times They Are A Changin'" © 1965 *Ramparts Magazine*; © Renewal 1990 Toby Gleason

"The Tragedy at the Greek Theater" © 1964 *San Francisco Chronicle*; © Renewal 1998 Toby Gleason

"This Year At Monterey" © 1963 *Saturday Review of Literature*; © Renewal 1990 Toby Gleason

"Unreleased Bob Dylan Album" © 1990 Toby Gleason

"We Need An Honest President" © 1972 *Rolling Stone Magazine*; © Renewal 2001 Toby Gleason

"We've Got To Get Rid Of Nixon" © 1973 *Rolling Stone Magazine*; © Renewal 2002 Toby Gleason

"Who Really Is Bob Dylan?" © 1964 *San Francisco Chronicle*; © Renewal 1990 Toby Gleason

Index

Note: Bars, clubs, halls, and theaters that hosted musical or comedy acts are noted as "(venue)."

Index

Index

Index

1960s counterculture and, 242–43, 256; as payola, 283; Williams and, 166. *See also* marijuana

Dulles, John Foster, 42

Dunhills, 218

Dunlop, Frank, 46

Duran, Manuel, 114

Durant, Jack, 219

Durante, Jimmy, 267

Durgom, Bullets, 218

Dutrey, Honoré, 9

Dvorak, Ann, 220

Dwarf Music (publishing company), 255

Dylan, Bob, xi, xvi, xvii, 72, 161, 163, 179, 212, 213, 243, 244, 247, 249–51, 254–60; Lennon facetiously identified with, 155–56; liner notes for unreleased album of, 182–84; on the music of, 149–51, 229–32, 234–38, 267–68; Seeger on, 146

Ed Sullivan Show (television show), 11, 78, 84, 152–53, 216, 247, 252–53

Eisenhower, Dwight D., 43, 79, 201, 274

Eldridge, Roy, 35

Electric Flag, 161

Elizabeth II, Queen, 19, 153

Ellington, Edward Kennedy "Duke," xviii, 5, 9, 11, 17, 18–19, 27, 28, 55, 67, 70, 72, 74–77, 107, 109–11, 120, 125–37, 207, 225, 232; Sacred Concerts, 19, 77, 125, 127

Ellington, Mercer, 136

Elliot, Cass, 186

Elliott, Wally, 166, 168–69

Eltinge, Julian, 219

Emergency Civil Liberties Committee, 231

Encounter (magazine), 251

Eric Burdon and The Animals, 160, 185, 196

Europe: jazz in, 3–4, 6–7, 18, 20–21, 82; popularity of black American musicians in, 262–63

Europe, James Reese, 6

Everly Brothers, 163

Evers, Charles, 85

Fack's II (venue), 30, 206–8

Faithful Virtue Music (publishing company), 244, 255

Falcone, Tommy, 284

Fallen Angel (venue), 209

Family Dog (production company), xii, 244, 255, 259, 260

Family Tree, 185

The Famous Door (venue), 8

Fantasy Records (record company), xv, xviii, 31, 203–5

Farina, Mimi, 186

Farina, Richard, 236

Farrell, Glenda, 220

Faubus, Orville, 78

Federal Communications Commission, 281

Ferlinghetti, Lawrence, 31, 184, 228, 236

Fetchit, Stepin, 216

Fillmore Auditorium (venue), 173, 185–86, 196, 239, 255, 258, 261

Fillmore West (venue), 173

Fitzgerald, Barry, 220

Fitzgerald, Ella, 264

Fletcher, Andrew, 230

flower children. *See* hippies

folk music, 147–48, 150, 167, 229, 233–34, 238, 248. *See also* topical songs

Folkways Records (record company), 203

Index

Index

Hall, Adelaide, 132, 133

Hall, Minor, 9

Hall, "Ram," 9

Hamilton, Jimmy, 128

Hammond, John, xviii, 45, 47, 51, 59

Hampton, Lionel, 113

Handy, John, 22, 58–61

Handy, W. C., 5, 16

The Hangover (venue), 30

Hansen, Peter, 57

Hardin, Tim, 179

Hardman, Bill, 69

Hardy, Emmitt, 7

Harrison, George, 154, 177, 241–42

Hassapakis, Gus, 40

Hassilev, Alex, 141

Hawkins, Coleman, 8, 15, 35, 120, 132

Hawkins, Erskine, 13

Hayes, Clancy, 32

Hays, Lee, 232

Head, Roy, 253

Head Lights, 160

Heath, Percy, 19

Hefner, Hugh, 202, 209

Heider, Wally, 199

Heinlein, Robert, 247

Heller, Joseph, xviii, 226, 250–52

Hells Angels, 176, 178, 257, 259

Helms, Chet, xii, 161

Henderson, Fletcher, 12, 90–92, 120, 132, 135

Hendricks, Jon, 46

Hendrix, Jimi, 174

Henry, Pat, 31

Hentoff, Nat, xviii, 134, 155

Herman, Woody, 13, 26–27, 35, 199, 254

Heymer, Warren, 220

Hibbler, Al, 28, 67

Hilliard, David, 267

Hines, Earl "Fatha," 21, 30, 34–36, 91, 107, 113

hippies, xvii, 239–45, 253, 255

Hirt, Al, 63

history, questioning of traditional content of, 237

Hitler, Adolf, 201, 202, 252, 260, 270, 274

Hodges, Johnny, 74–77, 128

Hoffman, Abbie, 267

Holiday, Billie, xvii, 14, 43, 46, 48–53, 102, 106, 121, 174

Hollywood, 102

Homes, Clellan, 14

Honey Bucket (venue), 30

Hooker, John Lee, 18

"Hootenanny" (television show), 145, 234

Hoover, J. Edgar, 214

Hopkins, Sam "Lightning," 17

Hoppe, Willie, 110

Horne, Lena, 100

Hot Five, 90, 91

Hot Seven, 90, 91

Howard, Darnell, 45

Howlin' Wolf. See Burnett, Chester "Howlin' Wolf"

Hudson Theater (venue), 93

Hug-A-Mug (venue), 30

Human Be-In, 258, 259, 261n

Humphrey, Hubert, 134, 275, 286

hungry i (venue), 191, 193, 207, 209, 218

Hunter, Alberta, 103

Hunter, Ivory Joe, 263

Huntley, Chet, 247

Imperial (record company), 248

Imus, Don, 281

Indians. See American Indians

The Interlude (venue), 207

Israel, 270

Jack's (venue), 60

Jackson, Mahalia, 55, 147

Index

Index

Index

Index